STUCK?
Diagrams Help.

Words & Diagrams by
Abby Covert

Literature Review by Jenny Benevento
Developed with Caren Litherland
Edited by Alja Kooistra

© 2022 Abby Covert
All Rights Reserved
www.abbycovert.com/STUCK

ISBN 979-8-218-02041-5

For Jamie Bug,
I wrote this while you were small
with hopes that the world might be a little less stuck
by the time you are big.

Blueprints
Charts
Concept Maps
Data Visualizations
Descriptive Geometry
Diagrams
Flow Charts
Frameworks
Graphs
Infographics
Maps
Schemas
Schematics
Statistical Graphics
Visual Language

Diagram (n.)
A visual representation that helps someone*

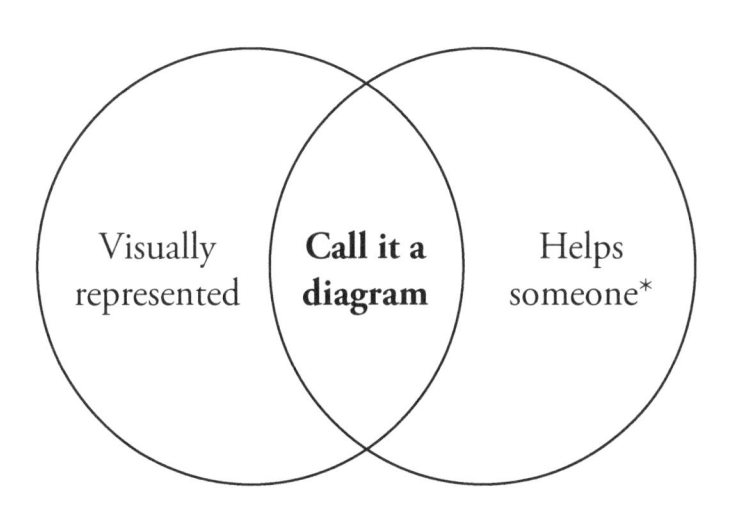

Visually represented | **Call it a diagram** | Helps someone*

You are someone

Contents

	Introduction	9
1.	**Purpose**	15
	Volatility and Uncertainty and Complexity and Ambiguity, Oh My!	20
	What Is and Is Not a Diagram?	34
	Common Elements of a Diagram	39
	Common Types of Diagrams	42
2.	**Process**	55
	Step 1: Set an Intention	60
	Step 2: Research Your Audience	68
	Step 3: Choose Your Scope	84
	Step 4: Determine Scale	92
	Step 5: Set Shapes	98
	Step 6: Add Lines	122
	Step 7: Refine Labels	132
	Step 8: Add a Key	136
3.	**Craft**	145
	What Makes a Diagram Good?	148
	Accessible	150
	Content Driven	174
	Visually Supported	186
	Diagram Critique BINGO	210

4.	**Recipes**	213
	Which Recipe Should I Try *First*?	214
	Block	220
	Concept	222
	Continuum	224
	Flow	226
	Gantt	228
	Hierarchy	230
	Journey	232
	Quadrant	234
	Schematic	236
	Sign	238
	Swim Lane	240
	Venn	242
	Don't Let Templates Constrain You	244
5.	**Collaboration**	247
	Wren: Changing the Center	249
	Oli: Agreeing on Definitions	254
	Randi: Addressing Collective Anxiety	258
	Kris: Expanding the Assignment	262
	Ilhan: Struck by a Vision	268
	Lee: Provoking Conversation	274
	Dani: Asking Obvious Questions	280
	Cyd: Changing the Metaphor	286
	How to Diagram with Other People	292

Resources	297
Literature Review	299
Indexed Lexicon	329
Bibliography	340
Recommended Reading	346
About the Authors	348
Acknowledgments	349

Introduction

When was the last time you felt stuck? Maybe it was because of a decision you were struggling to make, a complex topic you were trying to understand, or a project with so many moving parts that you felt somehow both motion*less* and emotion*ful*.

There are obvious tools for when we are physically stuck: jaws of life, life rings, tug boats, and tow trucks, just to name a few. But what tool do we turn to when we feel this kind of *emotionally* stuck?

Diagrams are visual representations that help. Especially when we feel stuck. Like emotional tow trucks, diagrams have been helping people for hundreds of years across industries, fields, and cultures when they feel this kind of stuck.

Diagrams are everywhere if you are paying attention. Designers, engineers, project managers, teachers, analysts, technical writers, architects, salespeople, and product managers are just some of those who are making good use of diagrams on the job. Museums, parks, post offices, and grocery stores are a few of the everyday places where you might encounter a diagram—or five. Their labels are as diverse as the contexts they serve: *charts, infographics, schemas, models, workflows, information visualizations, canvases, maps, figures, etc.*

The doodle on the whiteboard to illustrate a point in a meeting? *Diagram.* The simple map used to highlight where the birthday party will be next weekend? *Diagram.* The instruction manual used to put together that new bookcase? *Diagram.* The visual your team used to get to that big goal?

That's right, *diagram.*

Whom Is This Book For?

If diagrams relate to so many paths and goals, when are we actually taught how to use this tool that has proven so good at helping when we feel stuck? And are we ever taught what makes a diagram *good*?

For too many people the answers are *never* and *no*. But everyone feels stuck sometimes and diagrams help.

If you have never made a diagram in your life or feel under-skilled in this area, know that I wrote this book primarily for you. We will dissect diagrams into their basic elements while working to build your confidence both in the process and with the outcomes to expect from diagramming. And if you are a true novice, in the first few pages, we will learn *just* enough to make your very first diagram.

If you already make (or dare I say even *enjoy* making) diagrams but are not sure if your diagrams are as effective as they could be, I wrote this book for you as well.

Many experienced diagrammers came to diagramming through a fairly narrow entry point, with a specific method or template that does not allow a diverse exposure to diagrams in other contexts.

This book begins to fix that.

About This Book

In the first two chapters on purpose and process, we will learn a controlled vocabulary for the common elements and process of diagramming across contexts. Then chapter 3 on craft will teach us what it takes for a diagram to be good. Chapter 4 contains twelve of my favorite and most trusted diagrammatic recipes. And chapter 5 presents stories and strategies for collaboration.

At the end of the book are resources that you might find useful over your diagrammatic lifetime, including a literature review in which a librarian, Jenny Benevento, dives into how much there there is when it comes to diagrams.

There is an indexed lexicon provided in the back, and throughout the book, bold in-line text is used to call your attention to the first use of any new lexicon term.

Over one hundred sensemakers helped to bring this book to life by testing the content as it was written. For a list of names to thank, make sure to read the acknowledgments.

The diagrams in this book were made by me and typeset in a combination of Abby Covert New Regular, Adobe Garamond, and Atkinson Hyperlegible.

Choose Your Own Adventure, Dear Reader

This book was created to be useful across your diagrammatic lifetime, so there are a few paths that you might take through its pages, based on where you are *currently*. And yes, of course I made a diagram.

If you are a beginner, I suggest you start at the beginning and read the first four chapters and practice making some diagrams on your own. If there are other people involved with or impacted by your diagrams, keep going because the stories in chapter 5 are going to be invaluable to using this skill with and for other people.

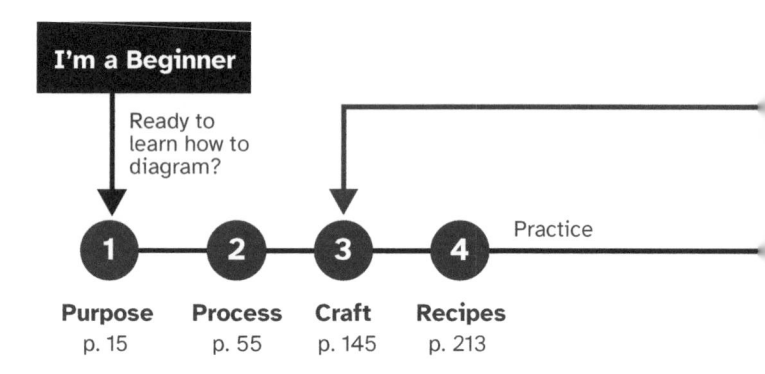

I'm a Beginner

Ready to learn how to diagram?

1. **Purpose** p. 15
2. **Process** p. 55
3. **Craft** p. 145
4. **Recipes** p. 213

Practice

If/once you are a diagrammer, chapter 3 was designed for whenever you need a diagram critique. See how your latest diagram fares against my nine principles and 25 common diagram violations. Also, isn't it tempting that the literature review and resource lists in the back are seemingly all that stand between the you of today and the diagram nerd inside you waiting to shine?

If you are a diagram nerd, welcome like-minded friend. I don't know if what I have to teach in the first few chapters of this book will be all that impactful to your diagram practice, and yet I have to believe you might pick up something valuable for your practice, based solely on how much I learned about diagramming in writing this book. One thing that I know for certain is that the perspective on diagrams that Jenny Benevento takes in the literature review is one that hasn't been taken in other places when it comes to the largesse of diagrammatic thought and historical gravitas. Also, the resources lists are fire.

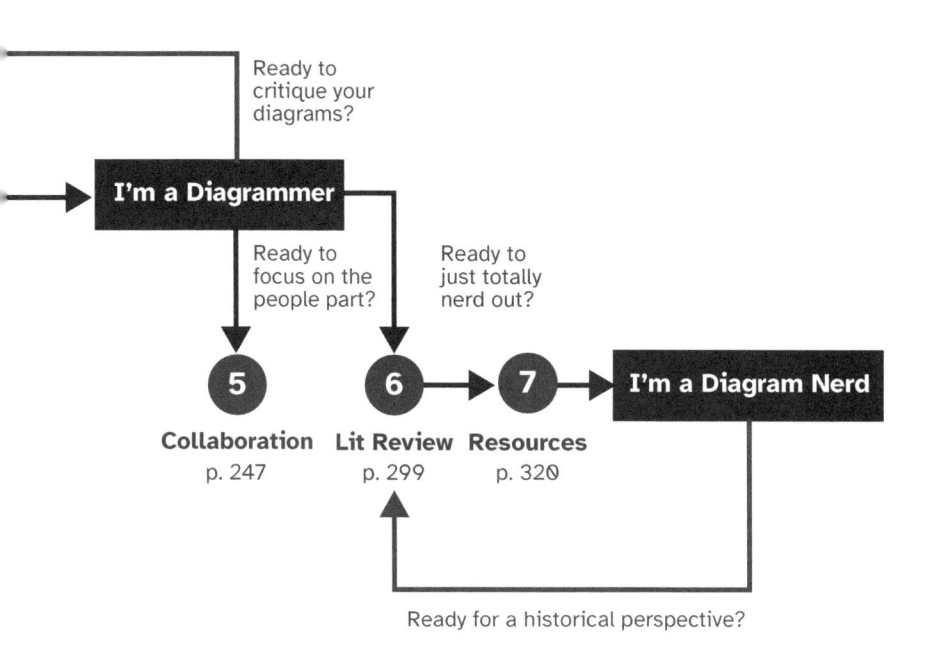

Ready to critique your diagrams?

I'm a Diagrammer

Ready to focus on the people part?

Ready to just totally nerd out?

5 **6** → **7** → **I'm a Diagram Nerd**

Collaboration Lit Review Resources
p. 247   p. 299   p. 320

Ready for a historical perspective?

Introduction | 13

1

Purpose

I was recently helping a family member as they recovered from major surgery. At discharge time, the hospital gave them what emotionally felt like a metric ton of prescriptions, instructions, and glossy handouts. On the way home, we picked up another pile of equipment, medical supplies, and pill bottles from the pharmacy.

When we got back to the house, the patient took a much-needed nap, and I was left with a kitchen counter covered in everything I had just carried in from the car.

I *supposedly* had everything that I needed to care for my family member who was unable to care for themselves. And yet I had no clue how to tackle what was ahead of us. I felt so volatile. I was uncertain about what needed the most immediate attention, and it all felt so complex. Many of the papers used words and concepts that were totally new to me. The next few hours, and then the days and weeks thereafter, felt so ambiguous.

Once I calmed myself enough to recenter, I remembered that as an information architect I was well prepared to tackle this kind of mess. "All we need is some useful categorization to organize this pile," I said to myself.

I got to work sorting through the pile based on *what* we needed to pay attention to *when*. I asked one simple question of every piece of paper and medical supply that I encountered in the pile:

When does this start to matter in this recovery process?

1. If it mattered for that day, I put it into one pile.
2. If it didn't matter for that day but we needed it in the next two-week recovery period, I put it in the second pile.
3. If it was about longer-term recovery, past the next hospital check-in, it made it into the third pile.
4. And if it was simply trying to sell us something or did not have any pertinent information I could glean for recovery, then I put it in a fourth pile. *Note: I was tempted to throw this pile into the trash but didn't out of pure fear.*

Once there were piles, things felt less overwhelming, but it was still not clear what my family member's recovery was going to look like. I still felt incredibly volatile as a caretaker, not sure what was coming or how to plan or react. The uncertainty of what was ahead had lessened a bit, but the ambiguity and complexity abounded.

The problem was that it still felt like a million tiny things in these piles were ready to be lost but needing to be remembered. It was *just* a pile of papers, equipment, supplies, and pill bottles, even if it was better organized now.

It was not something I could expect someone going through a life-altering event to use to take care of themselves or in planning to get help from others.

In an effort to visualize what I had in front of me, I drew a line to represent a day. Then I went through the piles and marked when each piece of information was important during the course of what I was starting to understand as a typical recovery day.

What emerged in the next 10 minutes would change the next two weeks. It was a diagram to help us understand how a "recovery day" would be demarcated by certain medications, visits from care team members, and equipment care tasks that we now needed to keep up with daily. It was the first clear picture of what life would look like for the next two weeks in recovery.

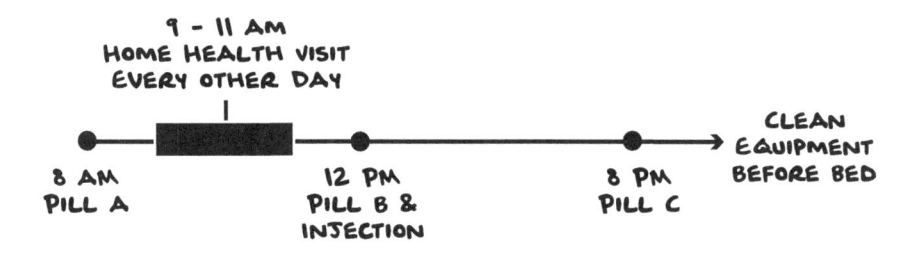

```
        9 - 11 AM
    HOME HEALTH VISIT
    EVERY OTHER DAY
           |                                              CLEAN
   ●─────[████]────────●─────────────────●──────────→   EQUIPMENT
  8 AM              12 PM              8 PM              BEFORE BED
  PILL A            PILL B &           PILL C
                    INJECTION
```

The next day, another family member arrived to help out. Using that same simple timeline, I was able to explain to them in a passing moment what it had taken me all afternoon to figure out the day before. They never even saw the pile that created the need for the diagram. The pile had informed the diagram and wasn't needed now that the diagram was in charge.

While it's certainly not the most complex or beautifully articulated diagram I have ever made (in fact, I don't even have a real picture of it because it didn't even occur to me to catch it as a stellar example of a diagram until hindsight kicked in), it will go down in my memory as one of the most helpful diagrams I have made.

With just that one diagram, I went from totally overwhelmed to ready to educate. And that changed pretty much everything about the coming days.

Chapter 1: **Purpose** | 17

18 | STUCK? Diagrams Help.

I think about how things would have been different that day had I not had the prior life experience that led me to diagramming.

I think about the reality of hospitals sending patients and their families home with nondescript piles of paper and medical supplies, without an information architect on staff.

What if patients were sent home with a diagram mapping out what the days of their recoveries should look like instead of the post-op paper pile I fear that too many face?

I posit that simply telling you this story has already influenced how you might approach such a moment in your own life, whatever your path or purpose.

I can only hope that a hospital staff member reads this and has a think about how diagrams might be the preventer of many frantic phone calls in those confusing and emotional post-op days.

When we talk about the purpose of diagramming, the topic of *anxiety* warrants deeper discussion.

Anxiety is a feeling of tension or worry about the future. Most of us experience some level of anxiety as part of everyday life.

Diagrams are particularly helpful in grounding us when we feel anxious because we can use diagrams to fly through time and space and consume a fuller picture.

We can zoom out on problems and see different solutions. We can find secure footing in an unsure environment. The freedom and expression that diagrams can provide are an answer to many types of everyday anxiety about our life and work.

Volatility and **U**ncertainty and **C**omplexity and **A**mbiguity, Oh My!

Diagramming is a skill we can learn to lean on when there is a swell of volatility, uncertainty, complexity, and/or ambiguity (VUCA).

VUCA is a set of situational concerns based on the leadership theories of Warren Bennis and Burt Nanus as developed in the 1980s by the US Army War College. This set was first brought to my attention by information architect Jorge Arango.

In my experience, for each concern that makes up VUCA, diagrams boast a tailor-made superpower. Diagrams wrangle volatility, uncertainty, complexity, and ambiguity by creating a sense of stability, transparency, understanding, and clarity.

When life hands us ...	Diagrams can provide ...
Volatility	**Stability**
Uncertainty	**Transparency**
Complexity	**Understanding**
Ambiguity	**Clarity**

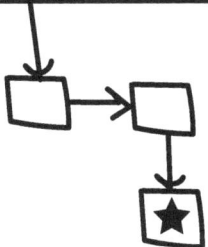

Before Reorganization

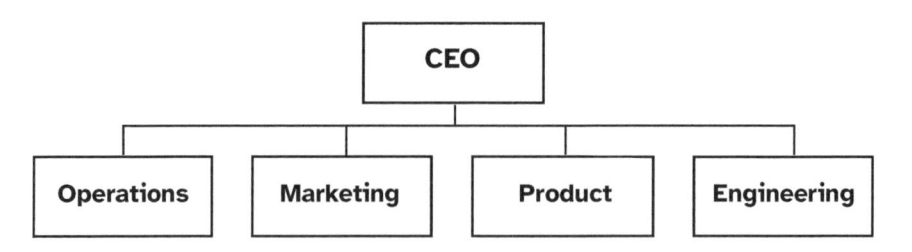

```
            ┌─────┐
            │ CEO │
            └──┬──┘
    ┌──────────┼──────────┬──────────┐
┌───────────┐ ┌─────────┐ ┌────────┐ ┌────────────┐
│ Operations│ │Marketing│ │Product │ │ Engineering│
└───────────┘ └─────────┘ └────────┘ └────────────┘
```

After Reorganization

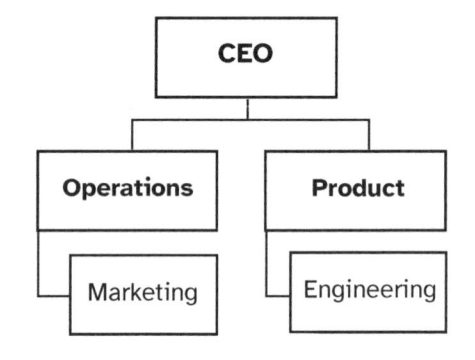

```
            ┌─────┐
            │ CEO │
            └──┬──┘
         ┌────┴────┐
    ┌─────────┐ ┌────────┐
    │Operations│ │Product │
    │ ┌───────┐│ │┌──────────┐
    │ │Marketing││ ││Engineering│
    │ └───────┘│ │└──────────┘
    └─────────┘ └────────┘
```

22 | STUCK? Diagrams Help.

Diagramming
for Stability

The uneasiness that we experience during times of change or the potential for change is called **volatility**. It's what we find at the emotional depths of life's big shifts and existential changes.

In times of volatility, we seek **stability**.

Diagrams are good at helping make known what *is* and *is not* changing and at what cadence. Diagrams can be a stable thing to point to when everything else is moving. When communicating big changes, diagrams can meet the anticipated volatility that the change brings with it by proactively addressing concerns.

When organizations perform a "reorg," there is often an accompanying diagram representing the changes to the corporate reporting structure. This helps everyone feel a little less volatile because it shows exactly where everyone's job is "going" in this new order.

Diagrams spurred by a volatile situation and seeking stability for their audience are often not just powerful in communicating what will be changing. These diagrams can also serve as active canvases, providing a stable place for *making* decisions about *what* changes.

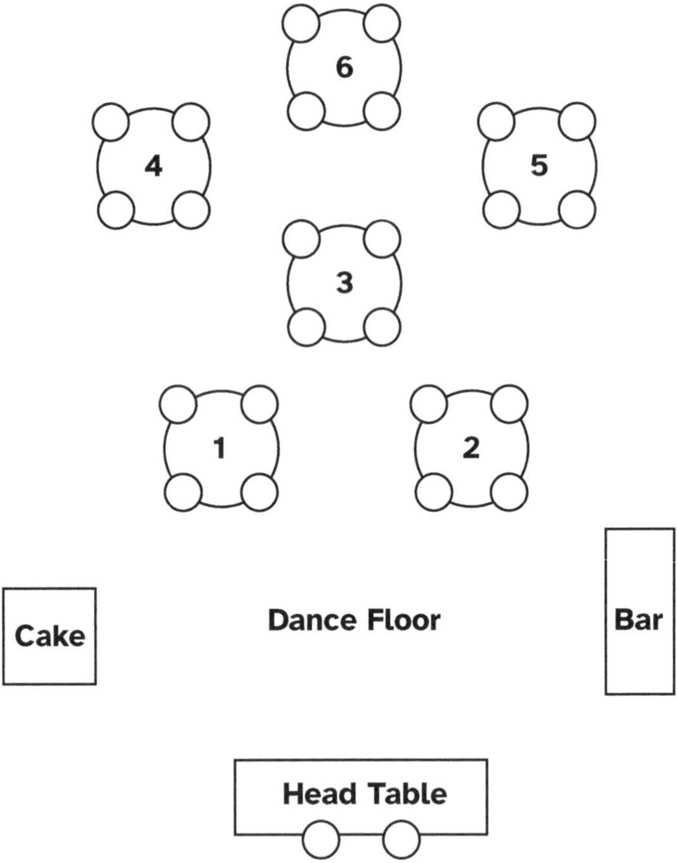
6
4
5
3
1
2
Cake
Dance Floor
Bar
Head Table

Diagramming
for Transparency

When we face a period of unpredictability or decision-making ahead, **uncertainty** is the mounting sense of doubt that often develops about the future. When times are uncertain, **transparency** helps tremendously. We can face uncertainty as long as we know we have all the information available—and, even more importantly, all the same information as everyone else.

Whether you are making a map to lead an upcoming trip or putting together a project plan, having a diagram outlining the paths, events, and decisions ahead can provide needed transparency when wading into the unfamiliar and uncertain, especially with other people.

We have all felt the anxiety of being stuck in a strange place without a clear sense of direction, or map. The transparency that diagrams provide can be mundane, like finding the pick-up window at a new restaurant you're trying, or making sure your wedding day goes off without a hitch (welp, without any unplanned hitches, that is). But diagrams can also be life altering or even lifesaving.

For example, the earliest organizational chart was actually visualized to provide needed transparency of a railway line across geographic regions in an attempt to lessen the potential for collisions when schedules became misaligned.[1]

Diagrams spurred by uncertainty to create transparency are places where we can "go" to see what's up ahead or decide what to do or where to go next.

---

[1] Liz Stinson, "The First Org Chart Ever Made Is a Masterpiece of Data Design," *Wired*, March 18, 2014, https://www.wired.com/2014/03/stunningly-complex-organization-chart-19th-century.

Diagramming
for Understanding

Complexity is an inescapable reality of everyday life. Everything around you is complex if you look hard enough. This complexity stems from the fact that everything is connected to everything else. If you are struggling to see how complexity and anxiety might relate to each other, stop and think about my last assertion for just a second longer: *Everything is connected to everything else.*

I mean ... how overwhelming is that?! If that's true, then everything we are making in this world is connected to every other thing being made and that has ever been made, or that ever will be made. [*Stops typing to huff into a paper bag.*]

At this point in my life, I have learned one thing that I am more certain of than anything else: We can't understand the complexity of *everything*, and if we try to do so, we will much more likely fail to understand *anything*.

Simply put, complexity will always win, and we need boundaries to survive it. We can use diagrams to draw boundaries for the purpose of understanding parts of this complex web of people, places, and things in which we all operate every day. In tightly bounded places within this chaos, sparks of contained **understanding** can be gleaned, and diagrams are often there to help with the gleaning.

If, for example, I wanted to better understand the political system in the United States, I could read about how it all works. But keeping all the connections in my head would prove a challenge.

So, I made a diagram of the flow of approval and appointment within the US federal government to try to understand the complex rules and relationships that drives the system's decision-making.

US Federal Government

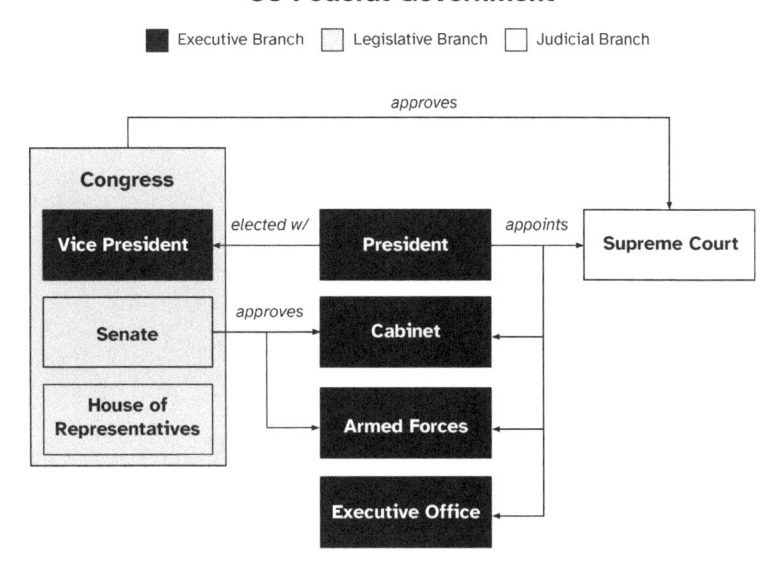

■ Executive Branch ☐ Legislative Branch ☐ Judicial Branch

If I want to explore deeper topics, such as how voters are or aren't represented, where disenfranchisement is bred, or how forces outside the federal government influence it, having this basic understanding of the system "as designed" is invaluable.

My point is that diagramming is not just for the purpose of *simplifying* the complex, although it can be used to do just that.

There are times when the complexity cannot be simplified.[2] It still needs to be understood so life can move forward.

When the complexity you face can't be simplified, try giving it a diagrammatic form. Complexity can feel easier to approach and relate to when we see it and can point to its parts.

---

[2] Larry Tesler's law of conservation of complexity states that complexity can't be removed; it can only be dealt with through user interaction or product development. See Dan Saffer, *Designing for Interaction: Creating Innovative Applications and Devices* (Berkeley, CA: New Riders, 2010), 136.

Chapter 1: **Purpose** | 27

Cases in Brevard County Florida

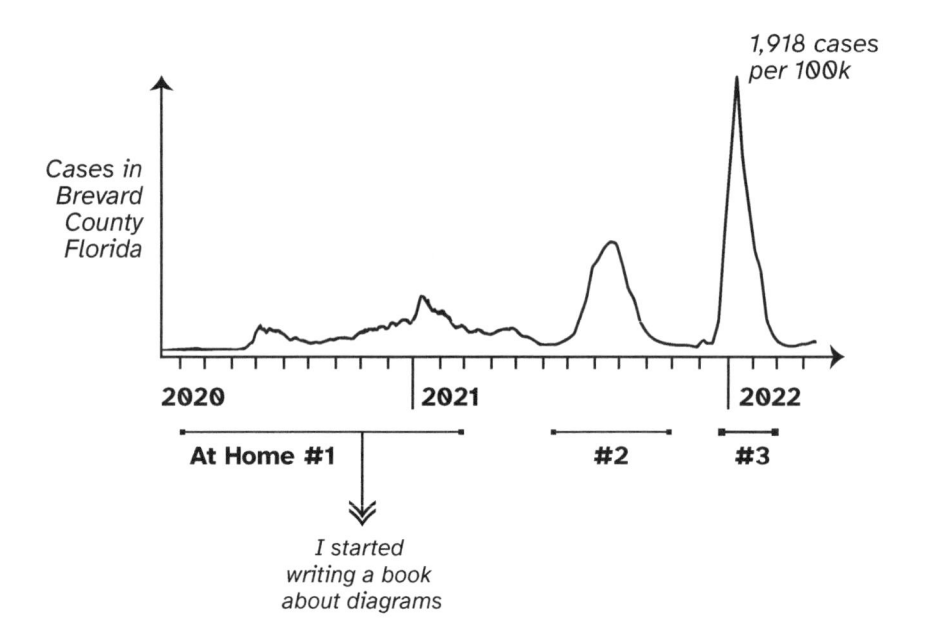

```
2020          2021              2022
     |——————————————|    |————|  |——|
       At Home #1          #2    #3
              ⇓
         I started
       writing a book
       about diagrams
```

1,918 cases per 100k

28 | STUCK? Diagrams Help.

Diagramming
for Clarity

Ambiguity occurs when something is open to interpretation and we aren't sure if our interpretation is what it ought to be. When ambiguity is on the rise, we go hunting for **clarity** wherever we can find it.

Think about the last thing you put together that came with an instruction manual. There were likely times when you knew where something went and other times when it was more *ambiguous* and you were less clear about what to do.

The clarity of diagrams is not just needed when making sure bookcases are assembled correctly or navigating other consumer goods drama. Sometimes the ambiguity is more weighty, even a matter of life and death.

I would be remiss to write about ambiguity without mentioning what it has been like living through a global pandemic relying on diagrams to make decisions about where to go and whom to see. The diagrams used to report on COVID-19 infection rates alleviated some of the ambiguity that came with the pandemic. These diagrams told us how much of an ambiguous fire was raging near us or our point of current interest. Truly a life or death moment for diagrams.

Diagrams are great messengers. Even if the news is not good, more clarity is almost always helpful in ambiguous situations.

Diagramming
for Kindness

When I started to write about VUCA in terms of highlighting the tailor-made superpowers of diagrams, I didn't think too much about the acronym, STUC, that might fall out as a result. Given the title of this book, you can probably anticipate how important a conceptual turn we are about to take, dear reader.

It turned out to be an accidental acronym with a gift for the author, the teacher, and the completionist in me. It gave me a clear invitation to add the K for STUCK and write about the kindness that diagrams can provide to those experiencing VUCA. But it also reminded me that sometimes diagrams still leave people deep in the VUCA, while a kindness can still have been paid.

Whether you are going through a big change, making a big decision, recovering from a life-altering event, or taking on a big project, VUCA enters your real life at some point or another.

When we face this kind of anxiety, the tool that works the best and the fastest every time is kindness.

We can better face VUCA when we are kind to ourselves, when we are kind to others, and when others are kind to us. In my experience, diagrams are both a kindness we can pay to ourselves and a kindness we can give to others.

Diagrams allow us to take our time while remaining focused on the bigger picture. Diagrams also provide needed rest. We can walk away from a diagram knowing we can return to it, like a jigsaw puzzle.

We can emotionally hit pause when things get deep or weird or scary.

We can take a bathroom break or a walk or get a tea. And it will all still be there for us when we return ready to trudge ever further.

The impact of this kindness becomes even more helpful when we are digging deep with others. We know we can pause or slow things down at any point while always maintaining our ability to jump right back to where we were.

In my opening story, I initially made the diagram to be kind to myself. I was tired, and there was a lot going on that day. I knew the piles would start to lose meaning quickly if I didn't capture what I had learned from sorting through everything.

I was kind to myself by drawing a little line on a scrap of paper to catch my thoughts as I dropped them onto that overcrowded kitchen counter.

That same diagram went on to be a kindness to others as well. It was a kindness to my family member in recovery when they awoke from a nap and were informed they didn't have to face that pile from the car for two weeks (or until they felt more up to it) because I had put everything they needed to know into something easy to understand in their current doped-up state.

It then went on to pay a kindness to other family members and friends as they helped throughout those early days of recovery and to the first home health nurse who came to visit and could quickly confirm that we understood what we had to do.

We were able to use the diagram to answer important questions, including "What time should we have meals based on your medications?" and "What's a good time of day for visitors?" and "How many of each supply do we need for these two weeks to keep everything sterile and clean?"

What a *kindness* that little tattered piece of paper turned out to be.

32 | STUCK? Diagrams Help.

Diagram When
You Feel Stuck

Whether we are caught in a gale-force VUCA storm or just in the early drizzle of an imminent squall of daily anxiety, we can use diagrams to create a sense of stability, transparency, understanding, clarity, and kindness for ourselves and for others.

What is something that you have faced that was volatile, uncertain, complex, or ambiguous enough that it was hard to keep up with in your head alone?

As we dig into learning how to diagram, I want you to meet me in that moment when you are stuck in your head and need a bit more space to do something about whatever it is. With diagrams we can get further than when we are only in our heads.

For generations, diagrams have been essential to how we help people who are stuck. There is even empirical evidence of a phenomenon called **conjoint retention** or **dual coding**, meaning the combination of verbal and non-verbal representations to facilitate increased retention of information.[3]

Most people encounter diagrams in their daily life. Whatever it is that you are stuck on, a diagram might just help.

---

[3] Dual coding is a theory hypothesized by Allan Paivio that cognition simultaneously processes verbal and non-verbal objects and events. See Allan Paivio, *Imagery and Verbal Processes* (New York: Holt, Rinehart and Winston, 1971).

What Is and
Is Not a Diagram?

When I talk about diagrams, a common question is, What counts as a diagram? Diagrams are a large concept. So large a concept that I hired a librarian to help me make sense of it (see the literature review at the end of the book).

In defining the word *diagram* for this book, I used a simple pair of criteria for knowing if something we are making is a diagram *yet*.

Diagram (n.) A visual representation that helps someone.

1. Does it help someone? *Even if that person is you?*
2. Is it visually represented?

If yes to both, welcome to Diagram Town.

This is not a diagram of a pipe.

STUCK? Diagrams Help.

This also means that if it is visually represented but doesn't help someone, it isn't really a diagram.

Even if it looks like one.

For example, this book doesn't show a diagram of a pipe. It shows a badly rendered visual representation of a pipe that doesn't help anyone. To make matters worse, it was made without even citing the famous artwork that it makes reference to. Because if it did, it might help you get this stuffy art nerd joke—therefore making it a kind of diagram after all.

If we allow visual representations that aren't helpful to *anyone* to be called diagrams, then diagrams definitionally eat the world.

And every Magritte painting (that's a clue to the example) is suddenly a diagram. And if everything visually represented is a diagram, well then I fear we lack a way to talk about diagrams deeply enough to learn how to make them better.

There are so many *truly terrible* visual representations parading around as diagrams because we aren't teaching people about the role an audience has in our diagrammatic success or failure. The helpfulness of a diagram is always in the eye of the beholder. The trick is knowing it isn't always found in the eye of the maker.

As a teacher, I find a needed clarity in being finicky about the boundaries of what we call a diagram. And when I am making diagrams, that same finickiness reminds me when I am diagrammatically done vs. agonizing on visuals long after the diagram is helpful to its audience.

Learning to Diagram *Like How I Learned to Cook*

When I graduated from college and started working as an information architect in a nine-to-five, entry-level job, I learned a lot of on-the-job skills. But as that was happening, I was also learning a few important, non-job life skills. One of the most important being how to cook.

When I started writing this book, my experience learning to cook came back as a strong memory. Like diagramming, I had picked up some cooking basics out of necessity, but it was not until I had an increased need for this skill that I really looked into learning it.

Some of you might be coming to this book with a similar relationship to diagramming as I had to cooking back then. Perhaps you have made some diagrams, like I had made some scrambled eggs and knew some basics, such as how to boil pasta or peel potatoes.

You might even know how to put shapes and lines on a screen or page and label and arrange them in some tried-and-true ways you have been taught or created for yourself. You also likely know a few forms diagrams can take, having experienced them often in daily life. Similarly, I was familiar with lots of types of foods without having a clue how to go about cooking any of them myself.

When it comes to diagramming, what you might be lacking is broader knowledge of technique and confidence in expressing yourself through this skill that is much more art than science.

Like me in those early days of cooking, you can diagram to get by but maybe you aren't thrilled with the idea of sharing the results of your diagramming with others just yet. No diagrammatic dinner parties on your schedule at the moment, perhaps just diagrams for one. Or maybe you, brave soul, are hosting what is akin to a diagrammatic dinner party (hello, I want an invitation!), and you are turning to this book for some just-in-time learning.

Either way, I've got you.

When I first learned to cook, I would use a recipe for everything, and I would go line by line. My cookbooks from back then are covered in saucy fingerprints and smudges of who knows what. Now, almost two decades of cooking later, I prefer to look at several recipes, usually following a quick web search, and then decide on a way I want to proceed.

It is quite rare that I rely on another cook to guide me line by line with a recipe anymore. And in the cases where that happens, it's because I am attempting a complicated technique or working with an ingredient that is new to me. I turn to recipes only when I lack confidence or need inspiration.

This is because I was taught to cook *between* the recipes. To know what to do with certain ingredients or under certain pressures. I learned to pick, clean, and prepare ingredients before I learned to make a stew with them. The beginners cooking class I took started by teaching us about ingredients and how to prepare them. Next, we talked about how different ingredients relate to the basic process of cooking. Very much *lastly*, we started making actual dishes.

I want this book to teach you to diagram in the same way that I learned to cook. I had to learn a lot before we covered specific recipes in depth, and, sure, some simple recipes were thrown into the mix. But those were there to teach us technique. And mostly they went into the bin, not our mouths, for the first class or two.

Focusing on ingredients and techniques before recipes allowed us to better understand and practice what we learned generally and then apply that knowledge to whatever recipe we were presented with throughout our lives as cooks.

In this book, I propose a set of common diagrammatic elements and process steps along with some life- and work-tested diagrammatic recipes, *not* because I believe it to be exhaustive but because I believe there are commonalities that help when you are on your own, off recipe, in your own unique context, where the majority of diagramming is done.

As you learn about my way of diagramming and try out my recipes, I hope you will gain enough confidence to discard my direction altogether in favor of your own curiosity or experience.

Diagramming, like cooking, is more about what the cook does than what the recipe says. I can teach you about the elements and the steps to the process, I can even hand you a recipe, but you, dear

reader, you do the diagramming.

Tools for Diagramming

Diagramming is totally free. You can make a diagram with pretty much anything that allows you to draw lines, make shapes, and add text. I make a majority of my diagrams in the free tools provided in Google Drive. If you are comfortable with using presentation software such as PowerPoint or Keynote, they provide easy-to-use diagramming tools as part of their basic tool set.

If you want to get more specialized, there are a ton of diagramming tools out there, many of which are aimed at collaborative whiteboarding.

And if all other tools feel like too much, there is always good old paper and pencil!

Common Elements
of a Diagram

There are two sets of elements that are common to all diagrams:

1. **Visual elements:** What the audience *sees* as the diagram
2. **In-visual elements:** The decisions *behind* the diagram

I draw a distinction between these two sets of elements to point out that there is more to a diagram than just what meets the eye, literally. A series of decisions lead up to your ability to *actually* make a visual representation that is helpful to someone.

In my experience, there are often unlabeled and unspoken parts of a diagram that the viewers can't see, but they can absolutely feel them. I am calling this set of elements *in-visual* because they are encoded *in* the visual elements but are not visualized as elements themselves.

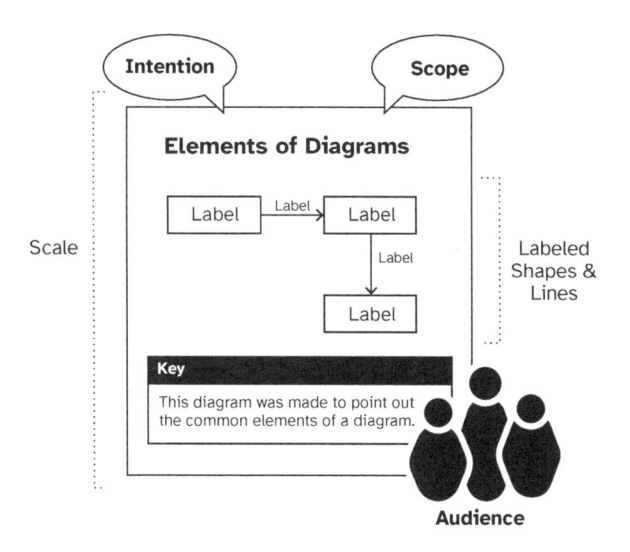

Chapter 1: **Purpose** | 39

Diagramming is about making a series of decisions about *how* to visualize something. But it is the combination of the visual and in-visual elements that determine a diagram's success or failure.

> **Visual Elements**
>
> Regardless of the context or type, all diagrams share a set of visual elements that constitute what we see as a diagram.
>
> The five common visual elements *seen* in diagrams are:
>
> - **Scale:** How big or small and active or passive is the space you have to get the diagram to its audience?
>
> - **Shapes:** What are the objects you need to represent in the diagram?
>
> - **Lines:** What are the relationships between the objects that you need to represent in the diagram?
>
> - **Labels:** What are the visual and verbal markers you provide for viewers to interpret the diagram?
>
> - **Key:** What are the hints you leave for viewers in case they get confused about what something means?

In-Visual Elements

When diagrams are made only with the visual elements in mind, there are three critical decisions that end up left to chance.

The three in-visual elements *behind* every diagram are:

- **Intention:** What is the service you wish the diagram to deliver to the audience? What is the action or change you hope for in making the diagram?

- **Audience:** Whom are you making the diagram for? What do you know about them, and what do they know about the subject of the diagram?

- **Scope:** What are the boundaries of the content you are representing? What did you decide *not* to show the audience?

Common Types
of Diagrams

From pointing out the animals living in certain areas of the zoo to working through a series of lightning-fast costume changes backstage at a theatrical production, I have seen so many powerful ways that diagrams are helpful to people. And in order to serve such a broad range of needs, diagrams come in lots of forms.

If you were to visit the Wikipedia page for diagrams, *which I hope you will*, prepare yourself for the fire hose of diagram types! There are hundreds, and they are in alphabetical order! And alphabetical order might as well be random order if we don't know the names of things already, so they also provide a useful set of types of diagrams based on the dataset that's behind them.

- Logical/conceptual
- Quantitative
- Schematic

While this is a useful way to think about dividing types when *looking* at diagrams, I want to introduce an alternative that I hope is useful when actually diagramming.

Determining the kind of data sources available isn't where I see people get stuck when diagramming. More often I find people get stuck because they lack the right frame of reference for what they are *doing* with the data that they have. Knowing you are making a diagram from a quantitative or conceptual source isn't all that useful when determining what kind of diagram you are making. In fact, it can be unintentionally limiting.

I have, for example, found times when I used a diagram type that would have been classified by this set as *conceptual* but introduced *quantitative* datasets in interesting ways, and vice versa.

In my experience, answering the question of diagrammatic form requires us to think about the part of the dataset we want to center on rather than just the source of the data.

Centering is a term used in areas as far afield as pottery, meditation, architecture, and psychology, just to name a few. In all cases, it roughly means to concentrate or position on a central point. In diagrams, it figuratively means, What's your point? And literally means, What do you want to point to?

I want to introduce three common centers that diagrams tend to have. Like various types of cuisine or courses, each of these has a slightly different interpretation of how to use the common visual and in-visual elements to center something about the data, and each can serve as a good starting place.

- Diagram types centering **time**
- Diagram types centering **arrangement**
- Diagram types centering **context**

Flow

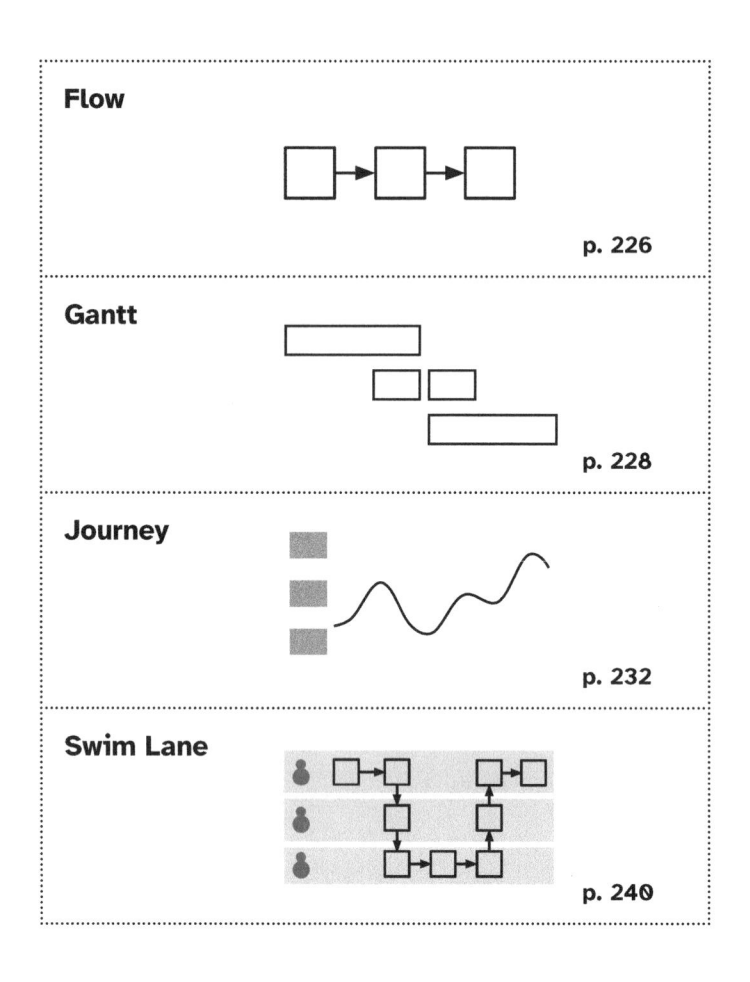

p. 226

Gantt

p. 228

Journey

p. 232

Swim Lane

p. 240

Centering
Time

Whether it be to form empathy for our users or to dig into the efficiency, quality, or equity in a system, we can use diagrams to explore how time impacts things.

If you are stuck on questions that start with "when" or "how," then centering time might be the best place for you to diagrammatically start.

- When is _____ happening?
- When will _____ need _____?
- How long is between _____ and _____?
- How does _____ hand off _____ to _____?
- How is _____ impacted by _____?

By centering time, common diagrams such as flows, Gantts, journeys, and swim lanes can zoom out of a process or event far enough so that the abstraction can provide a new perspective on how an intention is being met or hindered by the (often unintended) results of the whole.

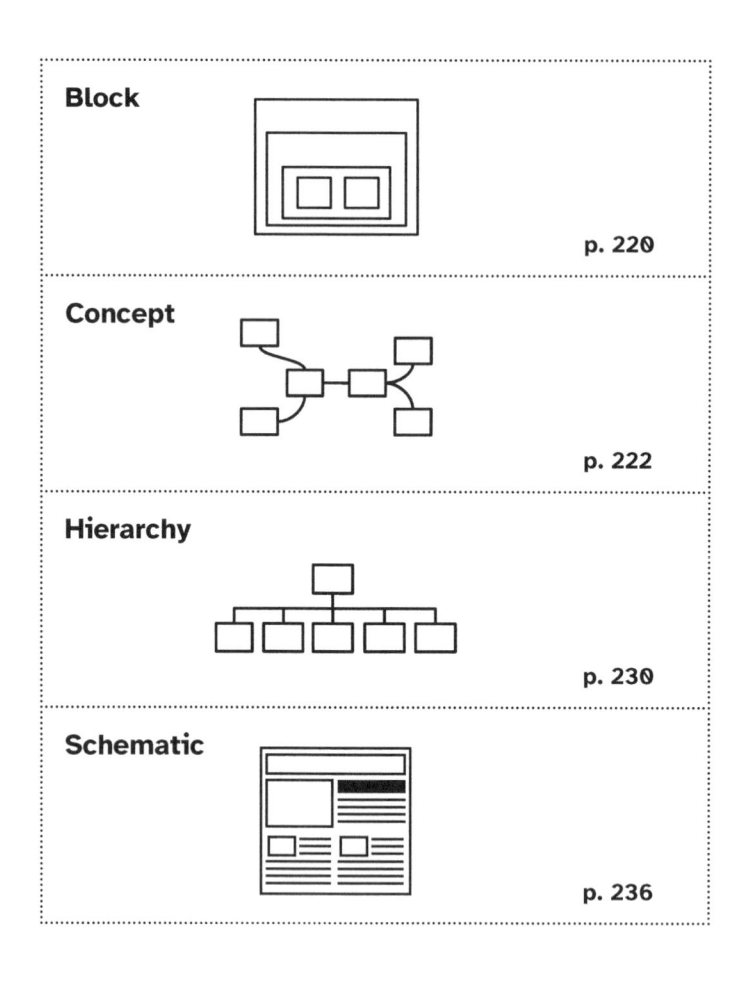

Block

p. 220

Concept

p. 222

Hierarchy

p. 230

Schematic

p. 236

Centering
Arrangement

Whether it is the arrangement in our own mind or the one dictated by an interface, concrete wall, or database, we can use diagrams to see arrangements that are hard to grasp otherwise.

If you are stuck on questions that start with "what" or "where," then centering arrangement might be the best place for you to diagrammatically start.

- What will _____ look like?
- What are the pieces or parts of _____?
- What belongs to _____?
- Where does _____ connect to _____?
- Where is _____?

By centering arrangement, common diagrams such as blocks, concepts, hierarchies, and schematics show what's there and how things relate at a glance. These kinds of diagrams are commonly used to save time and money by making it possible to make better decisions in lower-cost materials than concrete, pixels, and code.

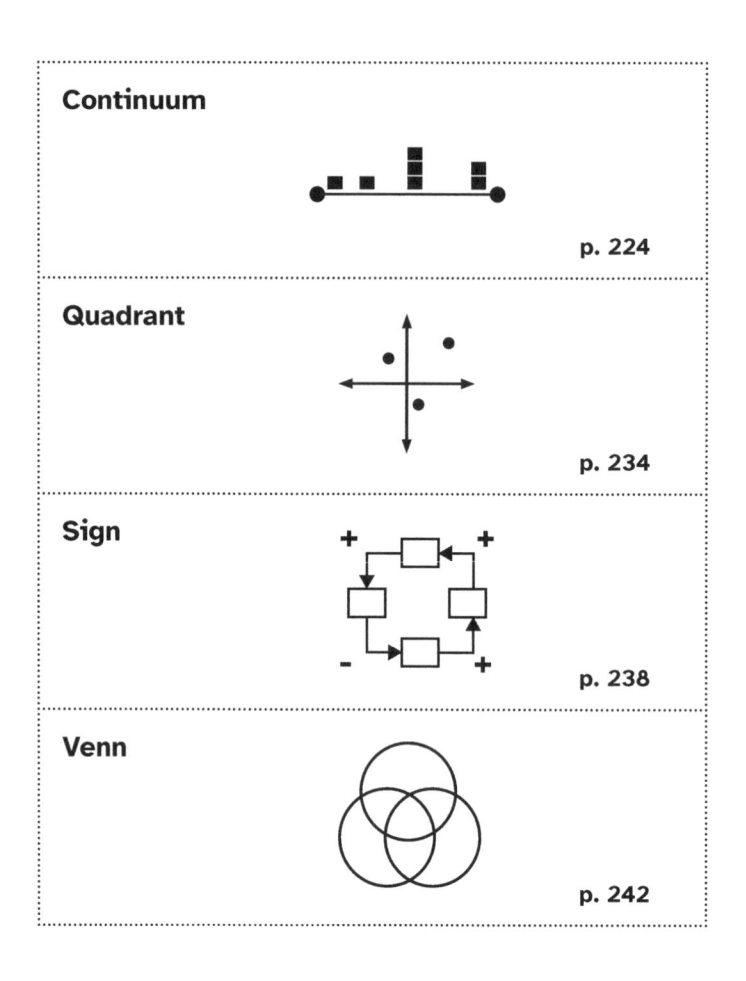

Continuum

p. 224

Quadrant

p. 234

Sign

p. 238

Venn

p. 242

Centering
Context

Whether comparing multiple options or directions, or revealing potential gaps in alignment, we can use diagrams to understand the subtle nuance of context.

If you are stuck on questions that start with "which" or "why," then centering context might be the best place for you to diagrammatically start.

- Which _____ is better?
- Which way should we direct our energy?
- Which overlaps matter and which are meaningless?
- Why might we focus on _____ over _____?
- Why is this more _____ than that?

By centering context, common diagrams such as continuums, quadrants, sign diagrams, and Venns can provide a shared experience with other people so that deeper discussions might be had or decisions might be made.

These Are All *Just* Shapes and Lines

In each of these common types of diagrams, the shapes and lines are arranged in different ways to achieve different outcomes.

As we get into the process of diagramming, I want you to keep the common centers that diagrams have in mind, but try to not be limited by them.

Diagrams are, to the naked eye, just shapes and lines. There is a freedom in that for many people as they learn this skill. But for some, an overwhelming desire to find a starting place or a tried-and-true recipe can become an impossible quest.

Stop looking for directions to a diagram that no one has ever seen before.[4] There is a diagram called Venn because some dude named John Venn decided that his labeled, overlapping circle diagram was the first of its kind and that it might be helpful to others. Maybe your unique arrangement of shapes and lines will help you and then go on to bear your name and help others forever! Who knows?

Regardless of the forms your diagrams take, there are a lot of steps before we get there. In the next chapter, we explore how each element of a visual representation is born and what it takes to raise it into a diagram.

But before that, let's make your first diagram (and maybe a snack?) under my tutelage.

---

[4] This is an allusion to Glennon Doyle, *Untamed* (New York: Dial Press, 2020), 60: "I have stopped asking people for directions to places they've never been."

Chapter 1: **Purpose** | 51

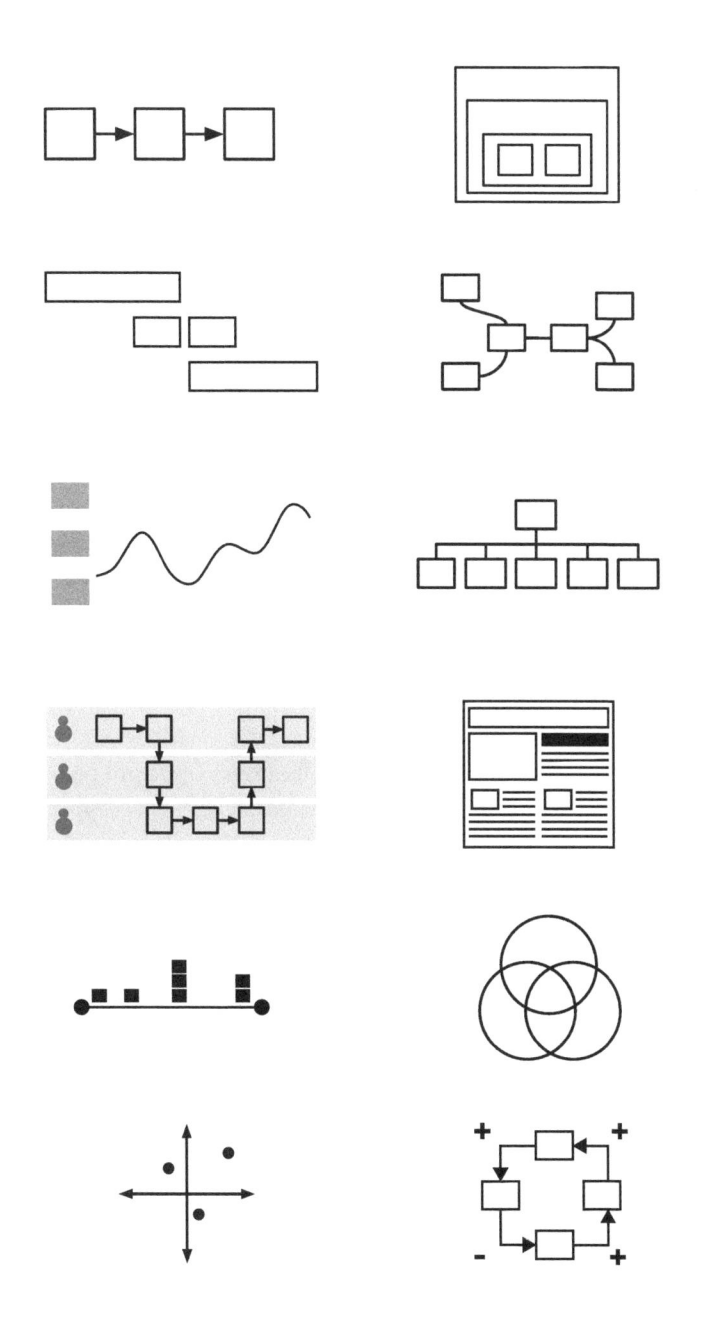

Let's Break
Some Eggs

In my very first cooking class, we made omelettes. And the teacher's omelette looked and tasted *scrumptious*. Mine, not so much. But I learned more every class and got better and better.

Then one day, I could make a basic omelette in my sleep (or more likely on little sleep).

When learning a new skill, sometimes making something just to experience the parts of it, even when the result is likely to be not so good, makes a lot of sense. So let's gather some ingredients and get started making our first bad omelette, er ... diagram.

Here is a recipe for a basic omelette:

1. In a medium bowl, beat 2–3 eggs until no whites remain, then season with salt, pepper.
2. In a medium skillet over medium heat, melt a pat of butter.
3. Pour egg mixture in a thin layer fully covering the skillet.
4. Once the bottom is set (but the top is not), add the desired fillings on one half of the omelette.
5. Fold over and flip to cook both sides evenly.
6. Serve immediately.

Exercise 1:

Make a diagram to help someone who is new to cooking understand how to tackle this recipe.

- Is it best to center time, arrangement, or context?
- How would you teach them about the ingredients and the equipment they need?
- How would you visualize the process?
- Which parts of the recipe will need words to be clear? What can be more visually driven?

Advice for Beginners

Tackle this *eggxercise* in a tool you are comfortable with. Take out a sheet of paper and some markers. Or open PowerPoint or whatever digital tool you have familiarity with making basic shapes, lines, and words.

Have fun; use clip art or pictures you steal from the internet. This is just for you. Go wild!

As a bonus assignment, test the diagram on an unsuspecting person. And if you are super confident, ask them to cook using the diagram.

… and once you try it on your own, check out mine: https://bit.ly/eggxample.

Chapter 1: **Purpose** | 53

2

Process

In chapter 1, we talked about the purpose of diagramming, and I introduced a set of common elements, visual and in-visual, that make up every diagram. In this chapter, I want to more fully explore each of those elements as nouns while covering the word *diagram* as a verb.

So many skill sets, walks of life, career paths, and processes rely on diagrams. For zookeepers, theater techs, nonprofit administrators, and many others in between, diagrams and diagramming are a part of daily life. But given the general application of the concept of diagrams, little attention has been paid to documenting a process of diagramming for the purpose of teaching it as a basic life skill.

After deeply researching other people's approaches to diagramming and making what I estimate to be over a thousand diagrams in my lifetime so far, I want to break down a common process of diagramming for you.

I have come to understand that it is in the verb form that all diagrammatic decisions are made. While we are making visual representations we hope to coax into diagrams by the end of our process, we are diagramming that whole time. We are using diagrammatic approaches, weighing diagrammatic considerations, and, most importantly, we are thinking diagrammatically.

In this chapter, we will cover the *ing* part of the diagram step by step to see how the diagrammatic sausage is made.

As we get into my process for diagramming, I want to make it clear that—as is the case with most things—there is no one right way to diagram. The following is my way.

In this process, I have slowed us down to form explicit steps where implicit thought might already be happening if you are currently making diagrams. Take a breath and my invitation to go through this slower than you expected to. I slow us down not to force you into one right and proper way to practice diagramming, but to point out how the elements of a diagram come together practically over time.

As you become better versed in diagramming, you will likely come up with your own ways to diagram, some of which might even be contrary to the advice I lay out here. I want to encourage that kind of expansion on this critical skill.

Think about my process *less like* a standard to follow and *more like* a set of training wheels to rely on while exploring your bravery around this new skill you are acquiring in your own unique context.

We are never just mechanical operators dealing in objective nouns connected by straight lines. An **emotional process** of what we are feeling along the way runs in parallel with the **mechanical process** of diagramming. Both equally contribute to whether or not we end this process as stuck as we started it.

The mechanical process, with its nouns set in their tight little boxes, might even make this all seem easy, when the truth is that it barely ever is.

As we navigate the diagrammatic process, I will call out practical mechanical advice as well as the emotional dips and loops to expect along the way.

Emotional Process *of* **Diagramming**

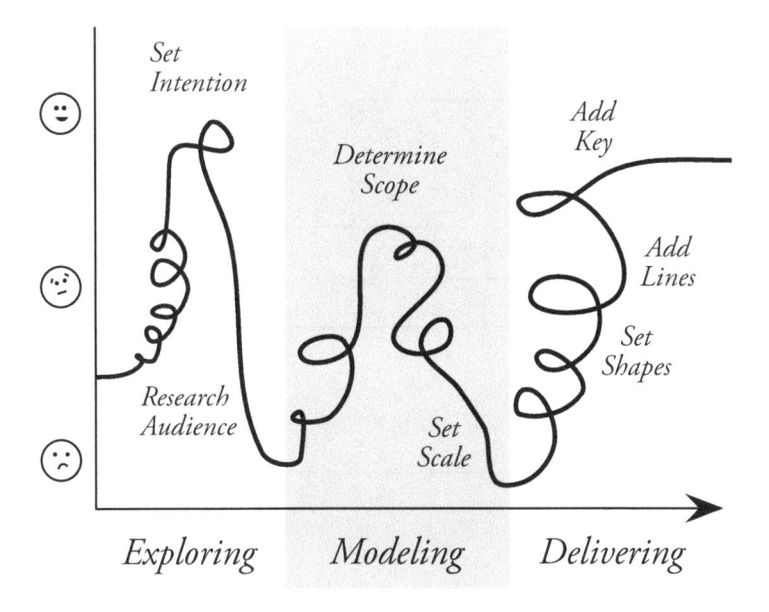

Exploring | Modeling | Delivering

Set Intention · Research Audience · Determine Scope · Set Scale · Add Key · Add Lines · Set Shapes

I have identified three distinct *ings* that serve as phases we move through while diagramming: explor*ing*, model*ing*, and deliver*ing*.

- **Exploring:** When we hike the rugged terrain of emotions while researching an audience and setting an intention

- **Modeling:** When we climb the mountain of feelings involved in deciding on the scope and scale of the diagram

- **Delivering:** When we finally reach the emotional peak of actually making the diagram

I chose to write about emotions while diagramming, however dramatic it might read, because I fear that too many people abandon the act of diagramming the second it gets too hard emotionally. When put together it's a bit of a steep trek. But fear not, dear reader, this is why we have a mechanical process to follow.

How to Diagram Anything

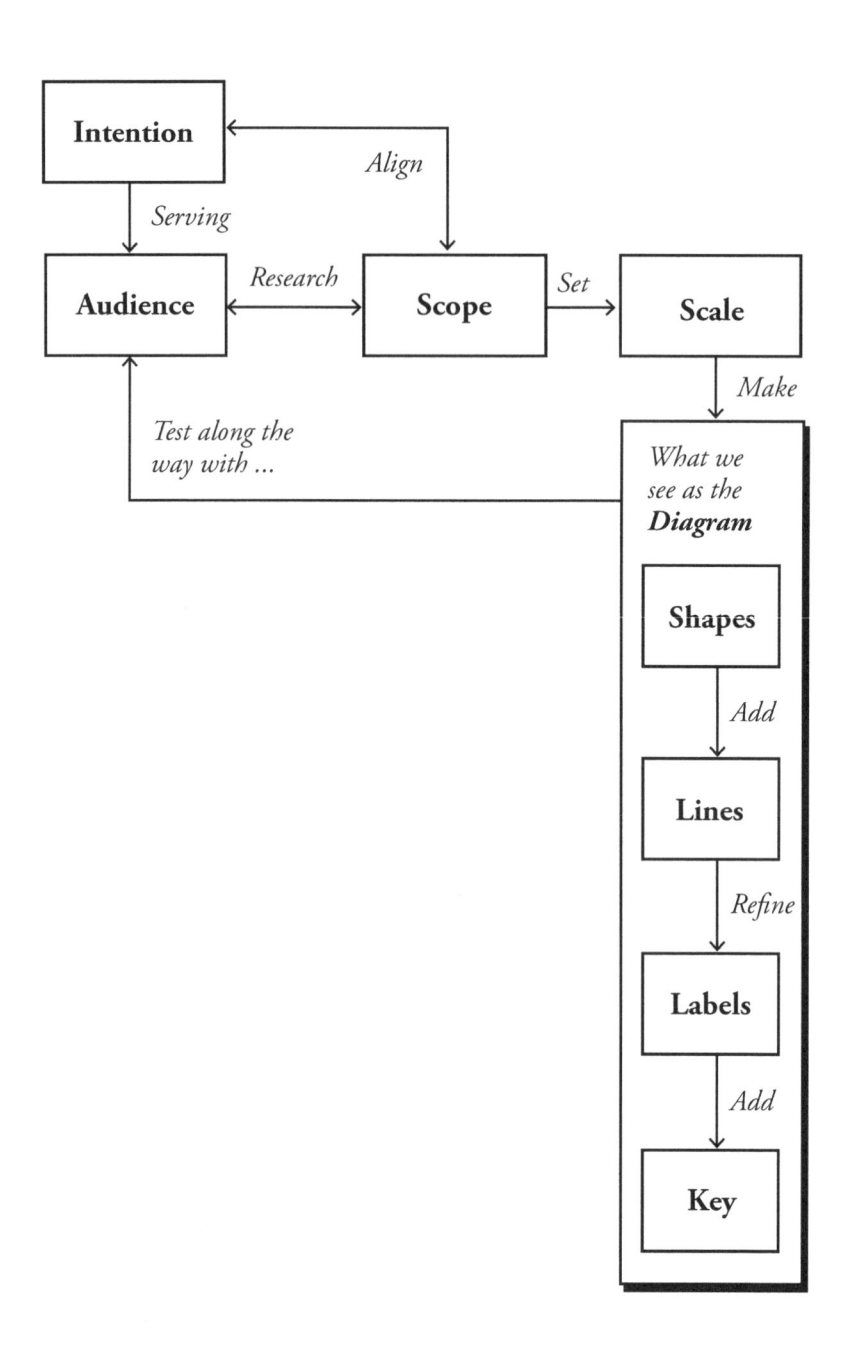

```
Intention
   │ Serving        ← Align
   ▼
Audience ──Research──▶ Scope ──Set──▶ Scale
   ▲                                    │ Make
   │ Test along the                     ▼
   │ way with ...           What we see as the Diagram
   │                              ┌──────────┐
   │                              │  Shapes  │
   │                              └────┬─────┘
   │                                   │ Add
   │                                   ▼
   │                              ┌──────────┐
   │                              │  Lines   │
   │                              └────┬─────┘
   │                                   │ Refine
   │                                   ▼
   │                              ┌──────────┐
   │                              │  Labels  │
   │                              └────┬─────┘
   │                                   │ Add
   │                                   ▼
   │                              ┌──────────┐
   └──────────────────────────────│   Key    │
                                  └──────────┘
```

When the emotional process feels too chaotic, or like too much incline to keep going, the mechanical process reminds us how far we have come and what's objectively left to do.

When I diagram, I start by setting a diagrammatic *intention*. This provides focus as I research the *audience* I seek to serve and set the diagrammatic *scope* that best aligns to those decisions at the diagrammatic *scale* I am working at.

After I am more clear on those in-visual decisions, I start to play with the visual elements that make up what other people see as the diagram: the *shapes*, *lines*, *labels*, and *key*.

This chapter guides you step by step through a process I believe can be used to diagram anything.

Step 1: Set an Intention

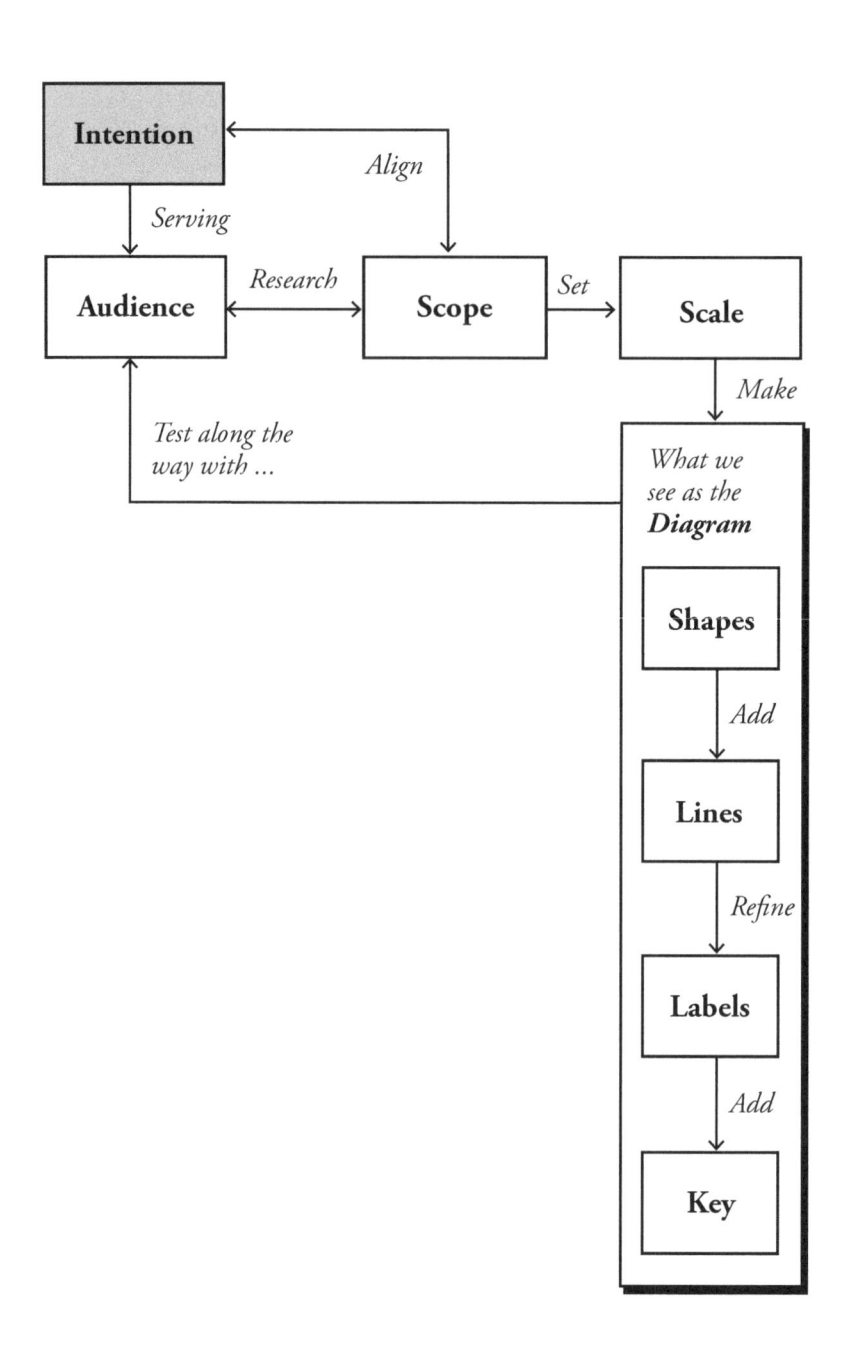

Intention → *Serving* → **Audience** ← *Research* → **Scope** → *Set* → **Scale**

Align (Scope → Intention)

Scale → *Make* → **What we see as the Diagram**

Shapes → *Add* → **Lines** → *Refine* → **Labels** → *Add* → **Key**

Test along the way with ... (Diagram → Audience)

When we are diagramming, it is for a specific reason (or we would not be doing it, right?). Our diagrammatic **intention** is our unique reason for diagramming in a specific moment.

Diagrams (like anything else) are never made without intention, even if we disagree on the merits or morals of certain intentions. For example, I can assure you that plenty of diagrams are made with the intention to make something complex look pretty or to scare people away from understanding it.

Intention is not something we get to choose our way out of. This is an important point that I think a lot of folks miss. For example, when we think we got away with never deciding on our intention, we actually just fulfilled an intention of not knowing what we are making and why.

Should you *actually* complete a diagram with that kind of lukewarm, unsure intention, you won't be surprised when the reception from your audience is equally lukewarm and unsure. Before we get too far into the act of diagramming, we need to spend some time thinking about what it is we are seeking to accomplish with the diagram we are making.

This early in the process, we need to feel out what the right way forward is, and if we have no diagrammatic intention to align our actions to, we might end up nothing but diagrammatically confused.

A good way to look at your diagrammatic intention is to identify the mindset or action that you want from the audience's engagement with the diagram.

If we set an intention early in the diagrammatic process, before deciding what we are actually diagramming at all, we have a litmus test built in from the beginning. At every step after this, we can ask, *Will this help or hinder my intention?*

Our intention might keep us from putting in too much detail, not including enough detail, getting too cute, being too vague, or any number of other mistakes we can make if we let the diagram evolve its own intention as we go.

Diagramming Is Not an Intention in Itself

Something I see folks get wrong is viewing diagramming (or visualizing, depicting, mapping, etc.) as the intention that they are pursuing with their diagrammatic efforts. We can trick ourselves into believing that the act of diagramming is what we are *doing*.

The following questions keep me from making this critical mistake I see many a sensemaker make when setting their intention:

Is your intention something a diagram *could* actually do?	This question ensures you aren't turning diagramming into magic (or a scapegoat) by making sure you can actually achieve the thing you are setting out to achieve.
Is your intention achievable with something *other* than a diagram?	This question makes sure you aren't being too prescriptive about the form the diagram will take and that you aren't diagramming for diagramming's sake.

For example, we might frame our intention in one of the following ways:

Intention A

"*Identify* contributing factors to climate change."

This is something a diagram *could* actually do, but you could also imagine *many ways* to get at that same intention.

In this example, the word *identify* becomes the critical verb by which all diagrammatic decisions can be made. Does this piece of content help us to *identify*? If not … bye.

Intention B

"*Visualize* contributing factors to climate change."

While a diagram *could* do this, this intention relies too heavily on the visualization part to serve as a strong intention for your diagram.

When the going gets tough and decisions need to be made, you don't want to be left with a weak litmus test such as "is it visualized?"

Five Common Diagrammatic Intentions

Intention	Example
Reflecting Diagrams that point to a problem	A diagram reflecting on the impact of climate change on the coasts of Florida
Considering Diagrams that show something as it could be	A diagram for citizens to consider how they might help end hate crimes
Instructing Diagrams that teach a skill or task	A diagram instructing corporations to change their daily habits to better serve a green future
Identifying Diagrams that break down complexity	A diagram identifying the systemic issues that oppress Black, Brown, and Indigenous people in the United States
Planning Diagrams that illustrate future actions or goals	A diagram planning the steps towards an economic system that serves all people more equitably

Exercise 2:

Write five intention statements for diagrams you might make serving yourself as an audience.

I could make a diagram to ...

Verb	Subject
UNDERSTAND	SELF-CARE HABITS INCREASING MY ANXIETY
1.	
2.	
3.	
4.	
5.	

Then test the strength of each intention by asking:

- Is your intention something a diagram *could* actually do?
- Is it achievable with something *other* than a diagram?

Heads up, *expected emotional dip ahead!*

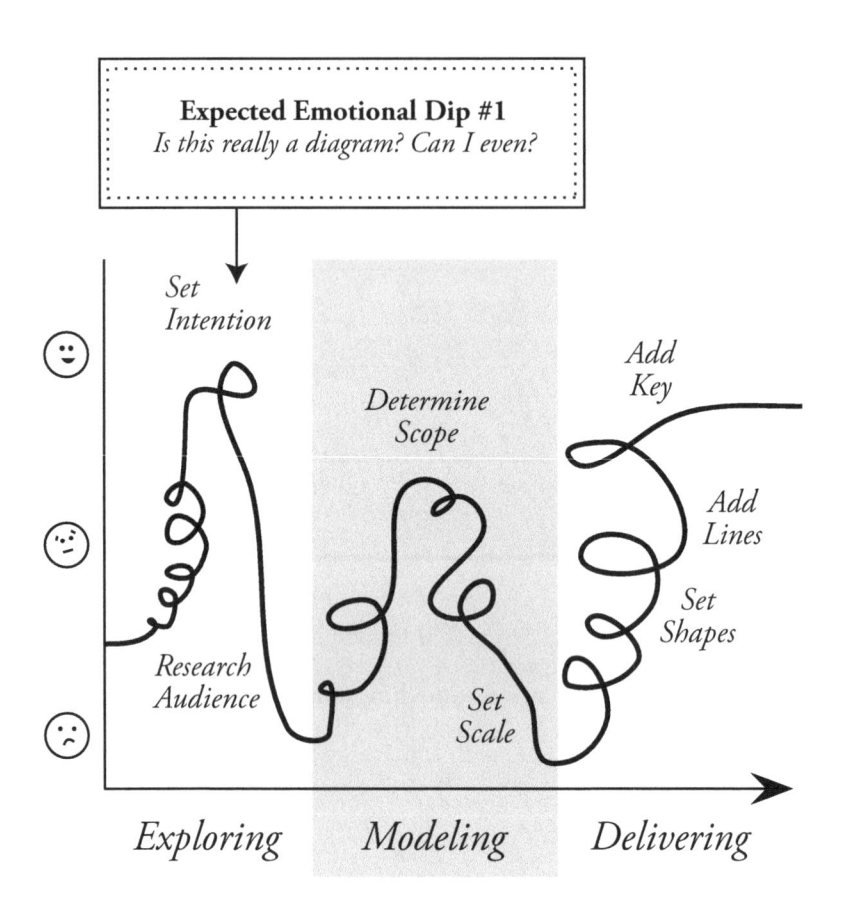

Expected Emotional Dip #1
Is this really a diagram? Can I even?

Set Intention

Determine Scope

Add Key

Add Lines

Set Shapes

Research Audience

Set Scale

Exploring — *Modeling* — *Delivering*

66 | STUCK? Diagrams Help.

Depending on the task at hand and the level of stuck you find yourself at, you might be making a diagram that could better be a conversation or a workshop, a one-pager or a white paper. Maybe that diagram could have been an email? Or maybe that diagram would be better as a book about diagrams. (Oh hey, it's me!)

By stepping back and thinking about our intention, we give ourselves the grace and space to determine if diagramming is even the right next thing to do. This is a moment in the process that is ripe for an emotional dip.

Here are some common places to find yourself in should you experience this first emotional dip as you work to determine your diagrammatic intention:

A. *"I need to do a lot more research before I can pursue this intention."*

B. *"I need to talk to more people before I can pursue this intention."*

C. *"I need to <insert hard and time-consuming thing> before I can pursue this intention."*

D. All of the above

Sigh. While your emotional self might be slowly recovering from the new knowledge of not being *quite* ready to diagram just yet, I can share that finding a home on this list of thoughts is to be expected at this point in our mechanical process.

In my experience, the intention setting step of diagramming is always helpful, even when we are not yet ready to proceed further into the process as a result of the work we did this time around. This step is to make sure we don't waste time thinking we can diagram our way out of something we need different tools or more time to work through.

Step 2: Research Your Audience

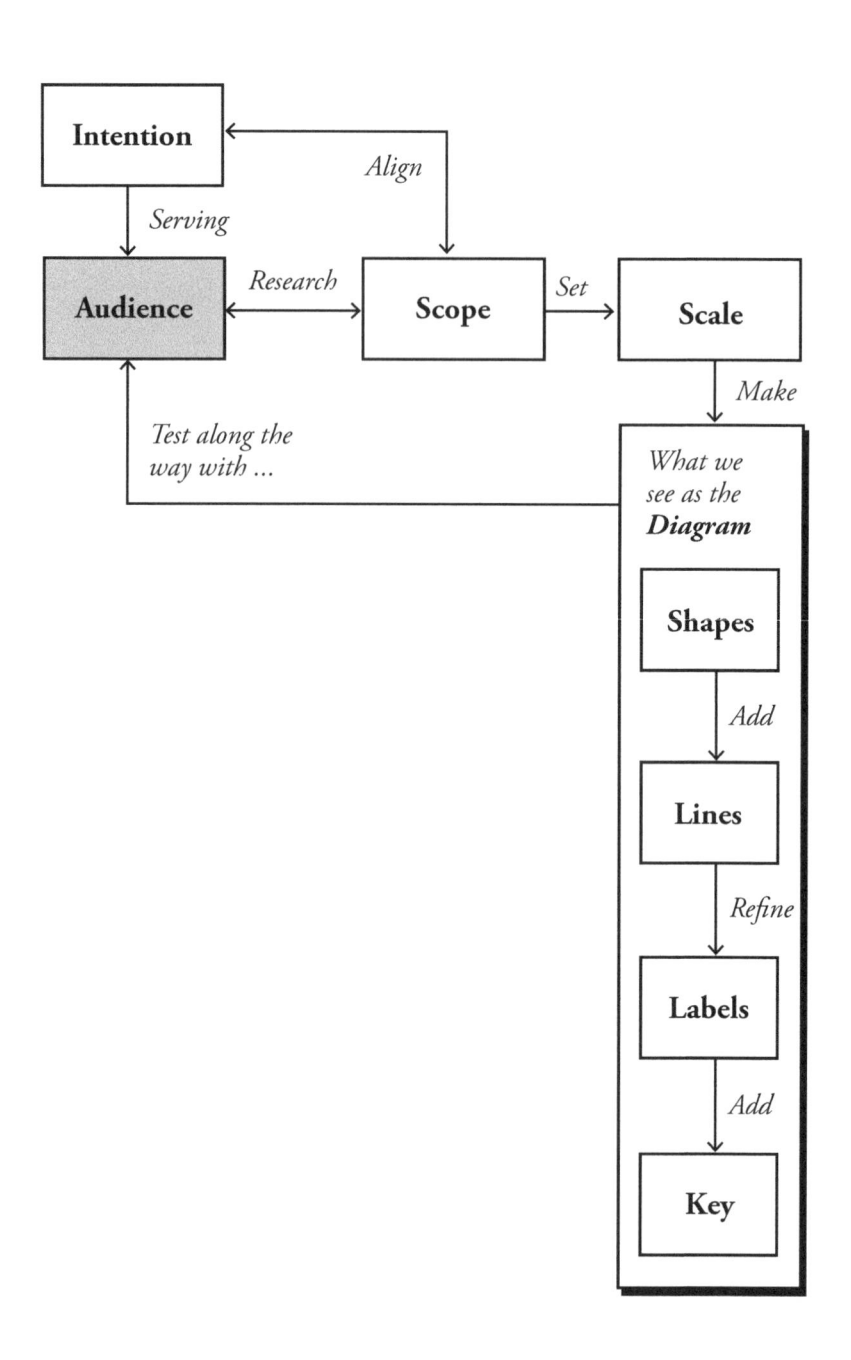

Intention → *Serving* → **Audience** ← *Research* → **Scope** → *Set* → **Scale** → *Make*

Align (Scope → Intention)

Test along the way with ... (from Diagram back to Audience)

What we see as the Diagram

- **Shapes**
  - *Add*
- **Lines**
  - *Refine*
- **Labels**
  - *Add*
- **Key**

Something hard for folks to get comfortable with is that a diagram is only *good* in the eye of the beholder. In other words, if a diagram does what you intend for your intended audience, you are doing a *good* job. Otherwise, well … you're *not*.

This also means that there is no such thing as a *bad* diagram; there are just diagrams that won't help you meet your intention.

Now, to me, this is where things get interesting. The *subjective reality* of diagrammatic quality reveals two important lessons to keep in mind as we make diagrams.

- A diagram can make sense to someone and be nonsense to someone else.

- There is no such thing as a diagram that can serve all audiences equally.

So, once we have a good handle on our intention, at least for the time being, we can think deeply about our audience and what they uniquely need from the diagram to help us reach our intention.

And when we make decisions with our diagrammatic intention in mind, we have to understand the audience that we seek to serve with our intention.

If my intention is to "*Identify contributing factors to climate change*," an obvious next question is for whom am I identifying them. If I am making the diagram for adults, my decisions will be different than if I am making the diagram for kindergarten students. Although one diagram might be able to serve both audiences, there are decisions I would need to make in order to make that work.

Have you ever seen the dashboard that pilots use in the cockpit of a plane? Or the playbooks that football teams reference? It might seem like an overwhelming gibberish pile to someone unfamiliar, but to a pilot and their crew or the coach and their team, it's ordered and meaningful visual information provided in a format that is helpful for them to do their jobs.

How Do I Decide Who My Audience Is?

This seemingly simple question can get quite complex in more contexts than you might expect. Let's say we are designing a hierarchy diagram of the navigation structure for a website. Who is the audience for the diagram? There are two options:

- **Users:** People navigating the website
- **Stakeholders:** People helping you to build the website

In this case, we are making a diagram of the structure of something *users* will or do navigate. It might be easy to assume that the website's users are therefore the audience for our diagram of the navigation structure. But if you think about the diagram as the object being made, instead of the website the diagram is depicting, the intention of the diagram is actually to serve *stakeholders* and will likely never be seen by users.

Now, where I think people can get confused is that in a case like this, part of the diagram's job is to allow the stakeholders to understand the users' experiences. So, while the diagram has to make sense to these stakeholders, we can't make the mistake of thinking the diagram *is* the website.

We have to think about what the use of the diagram is. If the use of the diagram is to get to agreement on the final labels for the navigation that users will use, we must be careful that we don't perfect the diagram but spoil the experience by making decisions that while making sense to stakeholders and ourselves in the diagram, don't make sense to users in the experience.

Diagrams that serve stakeholders who ultimately serve a user are often work zones and not the final intended output of those stakeholders. Construction crews often use diagrams to work out changes to plans before they set foot on worksites. But it is the building that they are concerned with; the diagram is secondary and often only for their eyes.

Similarly, product teams often rely on whiteboard spaces to share diagrams illustrating processes or goals. They are making a product together; the diagram is just for their use. Diagrams like these are places where decisions are made, so we must have both audiences in mind at once.

Getting the audience right can be tricky, but it's valuable work to prioritize up front. Sometimes it's cut and dried, such as when you are with a person or small group and need to make a visual to help someone who is stuck. In a moment like this, your existing understanding of your audience matters greatly in your ability to get through to your audience the message you intend. In other diagrammatic circumstances, there is a lot of background research and time spent outside the diagram part of diagramming.

For example, one of the most complex diagrams that I ever made took me nine months to complete. It represented a 96-week timeline that Nike used to take a product from idea to delivery. Before I made that diagram, no one had ever seen how the process worked as a whole. Each team or function had their own experience, their own tool, and their own hook into the process. But it wasn't until some smart people at Nike started wanting to know something about this volatile, uncertain, complex, and ambiguous pile of disconnected processes as a system that they needed a picture.

Maybe the most poignant and common use of diagrams is to help someone understand something that impacts their own intentions.

When the team at Nike needed to understand this process, it was to build a platform to connect all these disparate processes together.

To make a diagram of a process no one had ever seen in its entirety before, I had to make a lot of tiny diagrams of the process from many different vantage points. And in order to do that, I had to spend a lot of time with the people who had this process stuck in their heads and, in many cases, their heads alone.

As I met people serving in different roles in the process, I had to form both empathy and curiosity for their part in the system in order to capture its nuance and detail. They were salespeople, merchandisers, and assortment planners who would ultimately be the end users for the system being built. I needed to talk to them to tell the designers, engineers, and product teams what their users needed the tool being designed to do.

So while I was researching the most with the users of this system, my audience through this whole process was markedly different from whom the team working on designing and building the tools to support the system saw as *their* audience.

My audience was the product team doing the work. In order to deliver a diagram that worked for my intention, it had to make sense to those people. But in order to be useful to that team, it also had to be representative and truthful from the standpoint of their audience, the users of the system.

If we look at how a diagram fits into the system of making decisions, it becomes clear how connected everything really is.

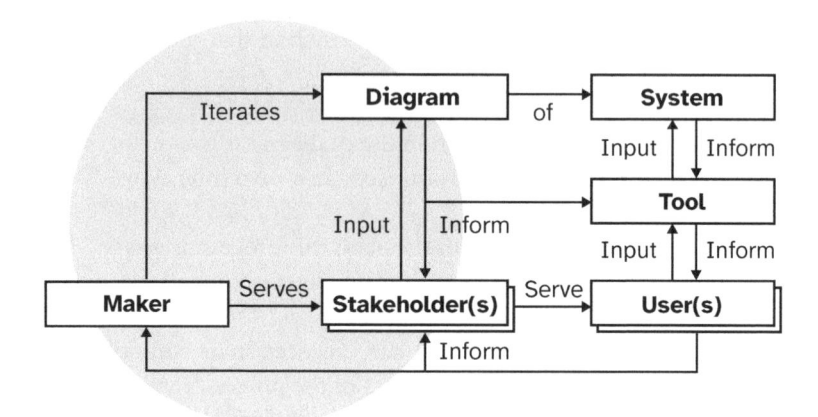

72 | STUCK? Diagrams Help.

What If I Am the Someone Who Is Stuck?

Sometimes the someone stuck is us. When this is the case, diagrams can help us in a way I haven't seen other tools be able to. When we make diagrams for ourselves to gain a sense of stability, transparency, understanding, or clarity, we are almost always doing ourselves a kindness.

For years I have given phone, video, and email advice that basically all boils down to this: *Do you have a diagram of it yet?* People write to me and ask for my advice on any number of agonizingly volatile, uncertain, complex, and ambiguous things. And often it is the case that those people are sitting smack dab in the middle of all that VUCA with no map. When we feel a VUCA storm a-brewing, getting the problem out of our heads and onto a page always helps. And when the to-do lists, long scroll docs, and spreadsheets start to give off their own VUCA-like energy, it's often time to lean on the superpowers of diagrams.

Introspection is the act of looking within one's own mind. I heard an NPR reporter recently call introspection *mesearch*. Yuck, but yeah. When we come to diagramming, we bring with us our own experiences, skills, and biases. Whether we are making a diagram for ourselves or for others, there is a level of introspection that goes into diagramming well.

In the time I spent with people talking about their experience diagramming, many of them told tales of diagrams that started as something helpful to them, not something they intended for other people. Many went on to make versions of their diagrams or different diagrams entirely for the purpose of sharing with others the insights they gained from that introspection.

Sometimes we have to make an agonizingly complex diagram for ourselves to help us gain some stability and transparency before we can start to work on simple diagrams meant to create understanding and clarity for others.

Phased Activities
of Diagrammatic Research

Draw & Share

Ask members of your intended audience to draw something (a concept, a problem space, a process, etc.) based on a prompt and then share what they drew with a group.

Qualitative Interviewing

Speak one-on-one with members of your intended audience to ask about the subject you are diagramming.

Collaborative Diagramming

Observe members of your intended audience diagram with one another around a prompt using a diagrammatic template like a canvas.

While we are doing a lot of foundational research up front about our audience, it is important to note that the research that goes into a diagram is less a step on its own and more a thread we ideally weave through the whole journey. Here are some of the research activities I find useful while diagramming.

Observational Usability

Have your intended audience look at your diagram and show you how they would use (or not use) it.

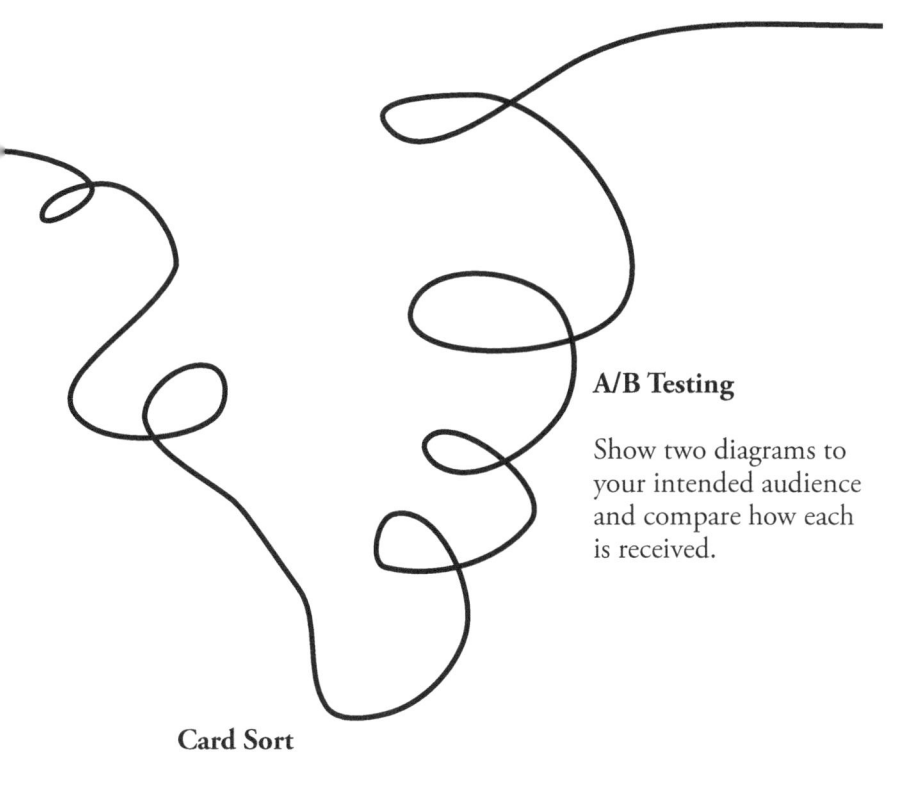

A/B Testing

Show two diagrams to your intended audience and compare how each is received.

Card Sort

Provide members of your intended audience with a set of cards, each representing a concept, process, object, etc., and ask them to organize the cards into groups based on some context around a task or environment.

Qualitative Interviewing

If you don't feel like you really understand what your audience might need from the diagram you are making, or you are still just exploring the possibilities, start with interviewing them.

There is no better activity to start pretty much any project (in my humble opinion) than qualitative interviewing. By sitting down one-on-one with a specific and unique member of your intended audience to ask about the subject you are diagramming, you put yourself in the best possible position to explore how a diagram might help them.

You do not need to tell the audience member you are interviewing them because you are making a diagram. In fact, *don't* tell them that unless you need to for some reason this early in the process. In my experience, it is better to instead tell them about your intention.

For example, if we are conducting interviews with the intention of making "*a diagram for citizens to consider how they might help end hate crimes,*" we would do better to focus on each person's experience and point of view on the subject at hand than to talk about their diagrammatic preferences.

I like to think about qualitative interviewing as a job interview for the diagram that I am making. I am interviewing this person to determine, Is this the right job for this diagram? Or for *any* diagram for that matter?

Draw & Share

I like to do an exercise with small groups at this early stage of exploring that I refer to as Draw & Share. This activity can be added to any interview or workshop, and it exists by many other names and iterations.

It's *very* simple. I ask everyone to draw something (a concept, a problem space, a process, etc.) based on a prompt and then share what they drew. See, I told you it was simple.

I find this activity helps when working through diagrams that have mental tangles that are hard to communicate verbally about but stand squarely in the way of understanding. Sometimes we can use shapes or stick figures or arrows to express things we struggle to keep up with in our heads alone.

For example, if we are diagramming to "*instruct corporations to change their daily habits to better serve a green future,*" we might recruit people from our intended audience to draw pictures to explain their current understanding of what a green future for their organization would look like.

By having them each draw and then share with the larger group, we would likely spur interesting discussions about everything from places of misunderstanding to times when terminology is predictably fraught in this problem space.

Collaborative Diagramming

As you move past the *exploring* phase and start to think about the modeling behind how the diagram might come together, one of the most effective research methods I have used is to collaboratively diagram with others—or even better, observe members of your intended audience collaboratively diagram with one another.

Now, I want to be super clear here, if you go into this assuming that this activity is a collaboration and iteration towards a final diagram—or diagram by committee—then you may end up lost in a world of hurt and disappointment. Instead of thinking you're going to shepherd all these people towards a single diagram they can all agree on, I find collaborative diagramming is a wonderful method for researching how people in your intended audience model for themselves.

This method is powerful because, when modeling for others, it helps to watch members of your audience make decisions together. Unlike Draw & Share, this exercise forces them to synthesize what is unique to them vs. a common experience of others like them.

Where your audience finds commonalities and differentiations will be fascinating for you, the diagrammer, to observe and learn from.

For example, if we are diagramming to "*identify the systemic issues that oppress Black, Brown, and Indigenous people in the United States,*" we might use collaborative diagramming to bring together people of diverse backgrounds to synthesize and learn from one another's stories.

Card Sorts

Card sorting is a tried-and-true method for figuring out how people model things in their minds without getting too mired in the specific visual presentation layer with your audience. When card sorting, you provide your audience with a set of cards and ask them to organize the cards into groups based on some context around a task or environment.[5]

- Open sort: Users make their own categories
- Closed sort: A set of categories is provided

While the participants are sorting, you are listening to them unpack why they think certain pieces are related to others and what labels make sense to relate each to for the task at hand.

When modeling a problem space in a diagram, there are all sorts of implicit and explicit structures that you can uncover using a card sort.

For example, if we are diagramming to "*teach people how to cook*," we might put together a closed card sort containing cards with different cooking techniques. Then we could ask our intended audience to sort them into groups such as "Tried & Failed!" or "What is this?" or "I can already do this!"

---

[5] The best beginners resource I can recommend for learning to card sort is Donna Spencer's book *Card Sorting: Designing Usable Categories* (Brooklyn, NY: Rosenfeld Media, 2009).

Observational Usability Testing

At the end of the day, the only way to know if a diagram makes sense to your audience is to ask them to explain it to you. The best research you can get diagrammatically is to have someone in your intended audience look at your diagram and tell you what they see and how they would *use* (or *not use*) it.

The question you are asking is not whether they liked it or not. Instead, you want to know, *Can they use the diagram as you intended it?*

A method to lean on here is observational usability testing. If we see a diagram as an object that an audience uses, we can apply the same methods of usability testing that we use for other objects, such as digital interfaces and physical products.

When setting things up, tell the participant what you are showing them, without explaining it. Don't explain the diagram to the person viewing it. Let the diagram project its own intention.

Spoiler alert: if it can't project its own intention, no amount of explaining it will help.

This	Not That
I am testing some content about whom our economic system serves. Please take a few minutes to look this over in detail and then let me know when you are ready for me to ask some specific questions about what you saw.	I am testing a diagram to plan the steps towards an economic system that serves all people more equitably, and I am asking people like you what you think about it. What do you think of this diagram I just handed you? [Thirty seconds later] Oh, should I explain it ...?

Start by stating your intention for the session, not your intention for the diagram. If you tell the participant what you want the diagram to be when it grows up, they may or may not have the heart to tell you how not good a job you did. Instead, focus on communicating the intent of the *research*.

As you go through each test, you don't have to fix the diagram in front of the participant—even verbally. It can feel like you should take critique from a user like a punch list of changes, but these tests are really about helping you weigh a lot of decisions that are left to make about how the diagram comes together.

One of my favorite prompts for observational usability of diagrams is to let someone give me a tour of the diagram. By observing how well they are able to give that tour, we know what they understand and what is confusing in the diagram. This is a great way to get the participant talking about their experience without feeling like it is an express judgment, which many people struggle with delivering to other people.

There is going to be some feedback you don't want to, or can't, implement. That's to be expected. When in a test with a participant, try to not react in real time with solutions. Instead, focus on understanding what the participant would change about the diagram and why.

And don't be surprised when, like many usability studies, a participant has a notably hard time understanding your diagram, gives a ton of insight into things that could be improved, but then decides to tell you to not change a thing at the end. *Classic.*

A/B Testing

This final method is best reserved for times when you are stuck between two opposing directions for how to diagram something.

In A/B testing, you show two diagrams to members of your ideal audience and see how each is received. Below are two versions of this activity for different contexts.

If you are testing for preference	If you are testing for effectiveness
Show two versions to the same people.	**Show one version per test group.**
Showing both options to the same people can be a good method if you know that both meet your intention and it's really a matter of taste or preference.	When we aren't sure how effective either diagram is, it is better to test them each separately using the same setup, test flow and recruitment criteria, process, and incentive.
If you are showing both diagrams to the entire audience, consider alternating which you show first as you go to avoid introducing any bias.	Then randomize which diagram is shown to which person and compare them as groups to determine which approach made the most sense.

The Research Is Different Each Time

To close this section on research activities as applied to the diagrammatic process, I want to point out two realities that make research so much damn fun.

- First, the order these methods are presented in is not some magical superset you must always aim for in diagramming. Not every diagram needs six methods of research to get it right. But many do. The trick is to rightsize the research for the diagram you are making.

- Second, the methods presented here are a *drop in the ocean* of research techniques that might be useful to apply to your next diagrammatic adventure.

I hope you are leaving with a few new research methods to look into, or maybe a new diagrammatic lens on an old favorite.

Step 3: Choose Your Scope

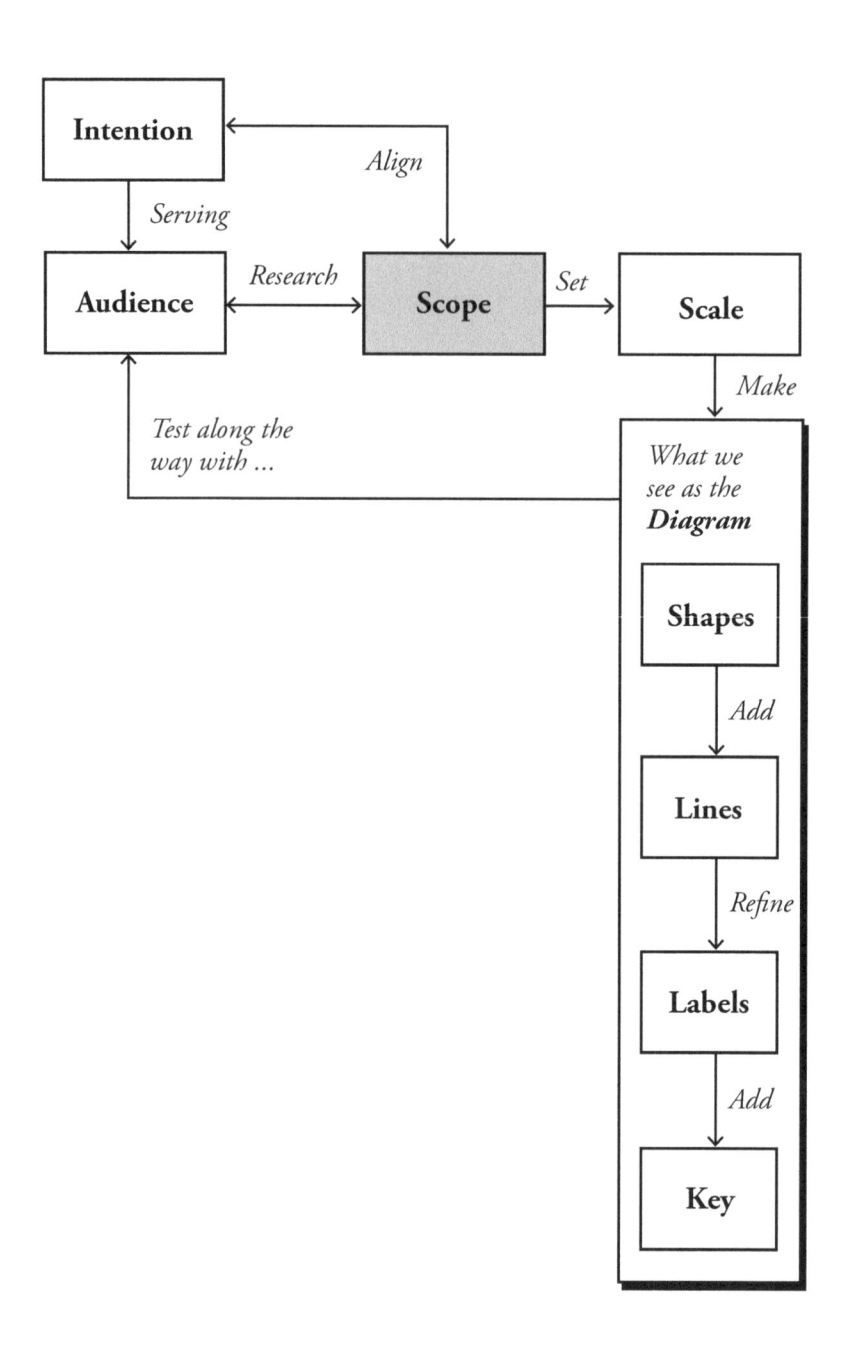

At this point in the process of diagramming, we have worked to identify our intention and research an audience we want to reach.

We are deep into the *in-visual* work of diagramming, and before we get into choosing our scope, I want to give you a heads-up: This next step is the messy middle, before any actual diagramming takes place, where I see too many diagrams fail.

After we do the hard work of setting our own intention and researching the needs of the audience we seek to serve, we still must get mired in the muck of what to include or not include in the diagram. What is in or out of diagrammatic **scope** for this intention and audience of ours?

We need boundaries on our assignment so we don't try to accidentally boil the diagrammatic ocean.

In terms of scope, diagrams suffer from the same information dilemmas as do all other information architectures:

- Too much information
- Too little information
- Not the right information

Too Much Information

When we include information that our audience doesn't *need* to know, we are adding unnecessary cognitive load to the diagram that we are making.

Cognitive load is a concept from the world of cognitive psychology.[6] Simply put, it is the amount of mental effort that someone has to put in when learning something.

By adding unnecessary elements or information to our diagram, and thereby adding cognitive load, we are making it more difficult for our audience to understand what we intended.

I see a lot of people who add too much information to their diagrams for all the right reasons: they are excited about sharing the data they have, the insights that prepared them to diagram, what they might teach the audience, and how complete the picture they are creating feels.

If you fear that you might have too much information, harshly interrogate every part of your diagram. Ask yourself if every element is needed to reach the core intention of the diagram. And then listen to your gut.

Even if the diagram feels sparse after removing the excess information, diagrams need to breathe too.

---

[6] The first experiments conducted around "cognitive load" but not by that name were written about in George A. Miller, "The Magical Number Seven, Plus or Minus Two: Some Limits on Our Capacity for Processing Information," *Psychological Review* 63, no. 2 (1956): 81–97, https://doi.org/10.1037/h0043158. Cognitive load theory as such was first developed in John Sweller, "Cognitive Load during Problem Solving: Effects on Learning," *Cognitive Science* 12, no. 2 (April 1988): 257–285, https://doi.org/10.1207/s15516709cog1202_4.

Too Little Information

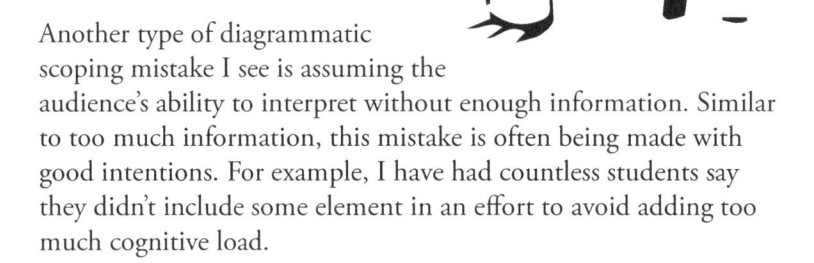

Another type of diagrammatic scoping mistake I see is assuming the audience's ability to interpret without enough information. Similar to too much information, this mistake is often being made with good intentions. For example, I have had countless students say they didn't include some element in an effort to avoid adding too much cognitive load.

Understanding the ideal scope of what your audience needs vs. doesn't need is critical for making the determination if something is not *quite* enough. The two mistakes I see that end in too little information are:

- **Forgetting** sources, citations, time frames, and/or methodological details
- **Assuming** icons, color codes, code names, and/or acronyms don't need further textual explanation

To avoid these two mistakes, make a list of questions that your audience will likely come to your diagram with. Use that list of questions to make sure they're all accounted for in what you include in your diagrammatic scope.

When making calls about what to include or not to include, insights drawn from your audience are not all you should be paying attention to. Your gut has to have a say sometimes too.

And in the rare times when I have had to decide between my audience and my gut, I can always turn to my intention (*which we learned the importance of setting in step 1*) as the tiebreaker.

Not the Right Information

Lastly, we have diagrams that just don't have the *right* information. The Goldilocks of diagrams. Maybe the audience is more linguistically savvy than your diagram assumes, or perhaps they aren't familiar with the vocabulary choices you made.

Whatever the version of *not the right information* it is, there are times when diagrams we intend to make for other people just don't quite have the right scope to get us there.

This dilemma occurs when the hard work and research that goes into setting an intention and understanding how to serve an audience has not been done or at least not done to a degree where understanding has been reached.

And at this point, say it with me: "The only way to know is to test the diagram with your audience."

STUCK? Diagrams Help.

Heads up, *expected emotional dip ahead!*

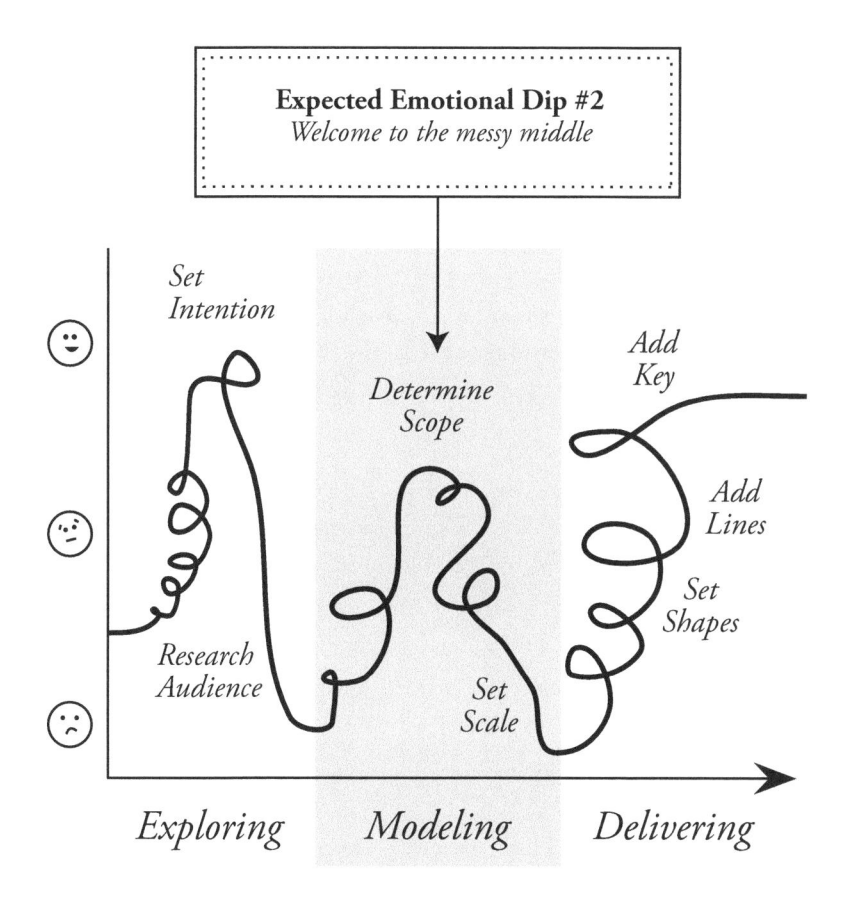

Expected Emotional Dip #2
Welcome to the messy middle

Set Intention

Research Audience

Determine Scope

Set Scale

Add Key

Add Lines

Set Shapes

Exploring — *Modeling* — *Delivering*

Welcome to the Messy Middle

As we approach the midpoint in the process of diagramming, your visual representation might feel like or actually resemble the motel walls surrounding one of those reclusive detectives in a cerebral drama. If you get to this point and feel a little overwhelmed, underwhelmed, or just plain dead wrong with your planned scope for your diagram, know that this is an expected and oft-experienced emotional dip for many who have traveled this way before you.

If we don't pay attention to the impact that this dip can have on us, we can get stuck at the very end of this in-visual on-ramp, with the vague idea for a diagram but not a clear enough sense of scope to get it out of our head and onto the page.

In my experience on this road, it is only those who push through this messy middle part who make it all the way to Diagram Town.

Exercise 3:

Complete a Mad Lib to make sure you take the in-visual on-ramp to Diagram Town.

I am diagramming to help

_____ **to** _____
intended audience   *diagrammatic intention*

To best meet my intention, the diagram will cover

_____

scope you have set

and will not cover

_____

boundary you have set

Step 4: Determine Scale

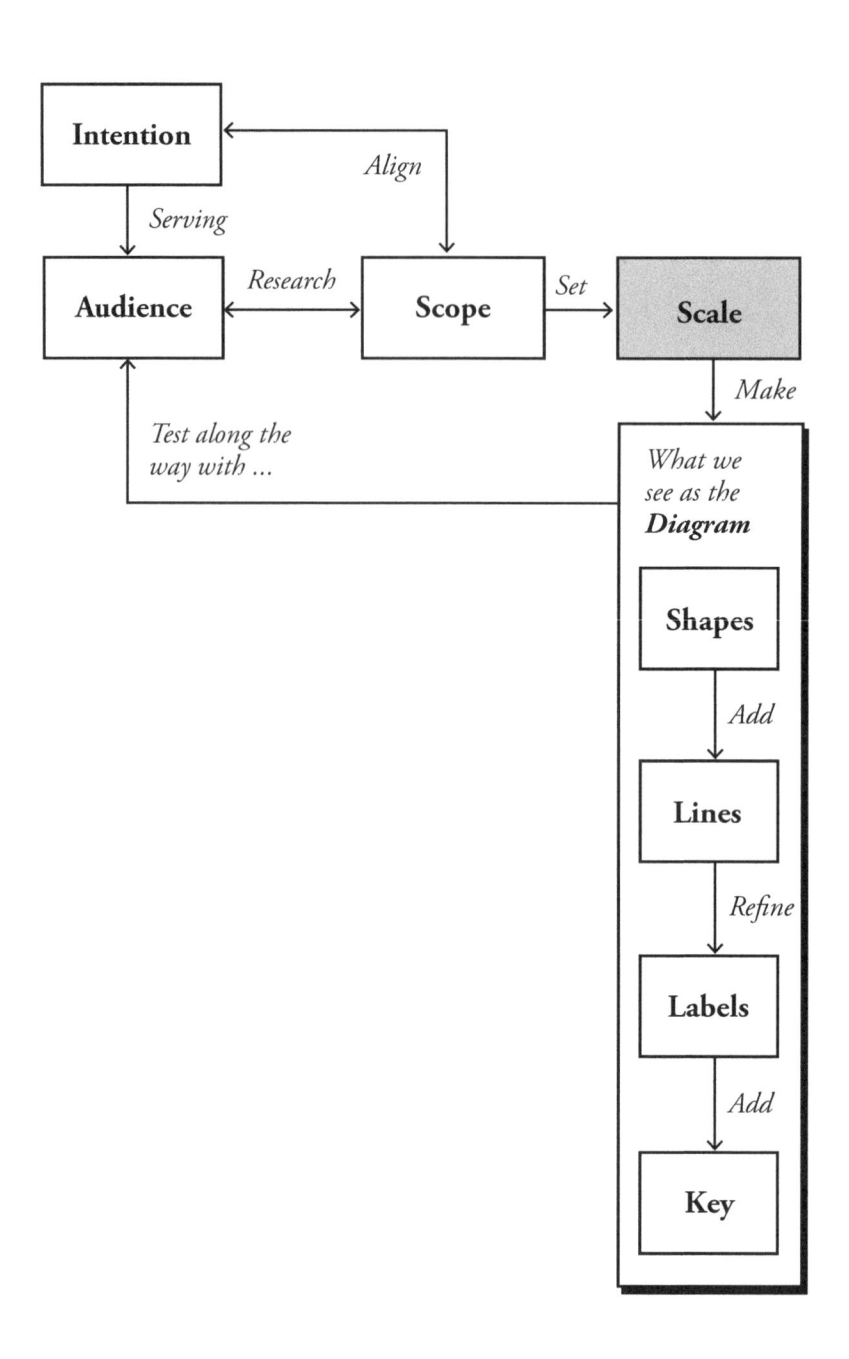

Intention —*Serving*→ Audience ←*Research*→ Scope —*Set*→ **Scale**

Scope —*Align*→ Intention

Scale —*Make*→ What we see as the **Diagram**

Shapes —*Add*→ **Lines** —*Refine*→ **Labels** —*Add*→ **Key**

Test along the way with ... → Audience

As we make the leap from the in-visual stage of diagramming to the visual stage, we have all our in-visual elements established and identified. But this doesn't mean we are set in the diagram we are making just yet. First, we have to determine the appropriate **scale** for our diagram.

The mechanical process diagram I have been referencing throughout this chapter was made for this book. The scale of it was determined by that medium. It has to be readable in a book, printed small enough to fit but set large enough to read.

With your scope now clearly in mind, you need to set a scale so that you can start to make final decisions and accommodations for the content you will and won't be including.

Sometimes our scale is obvious from the medium it is being executed in. Other times there is more flexibility. Say, for example, you had the ability to choose the channel in which you are delivering your diagram. Instead of making a presentation deck, perhaps you print it out at a larger scale, as handouts or as a poster. You can imagine how this might change the diagrammatic decisions you make as you get into the visual process.

Determining the right diagrammatic scale can also change how many diagrams you are making and how many mediums you are working in.

For example, an infographic may include any number of individual diagrams, but if we were to present it to an audience via a projector or on a large screen in a theater, it might make sense to break the larger graphic down into smaller pieces to walk through as a buildup to the full infographic.

From billboards to business cards, for diagrams to do their best work, they need to be considerate of the scale that is ideal for the audience and intention at hand.

In my experience, diagrammatic scale is a combination of size and interaction mode. The **interaction mode** is the relationship our audience has with our diagrammatic efforts.

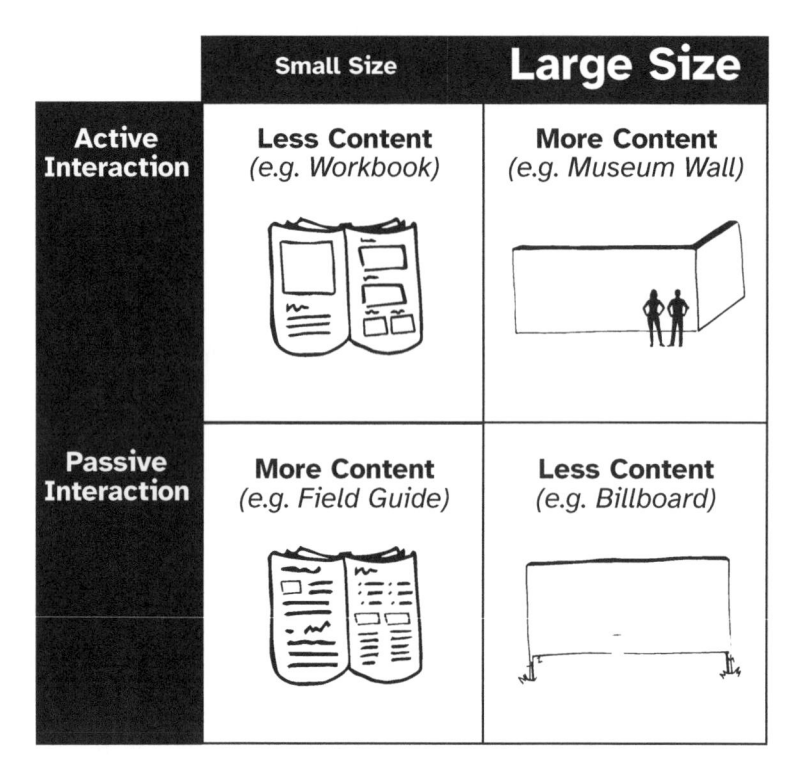

	Small Size	**Large Size**
Active Interaction	**Less Content** *(e.g. Workbook)*	**More Content** *(e.g. Museum Wall)*
Passive Interaction	**More Content** *(e.g. Field Guide)*	**Less Content** *(e.g. Billboard)*

Scale is best considered at the intersection of size and interaction mode.

To think about scale, it is important to think not only about the relative size of the diagram but also about the interaction mode you intend for the diagram.

A diagram that is made for a billboard and a diagram made for a poster will each have to serve a different interaction mode.

This inherently changes what the *size* means for your diagrammatic work. It is not *quite* right to think about it as "the more space you have, the more you can include." But it is also equally not *quite* right to think that the bigger something is, the more brief and bold we should be.

There are times when the interaction mode of the space we are given or plan for our diagram changes what the size means for the content we can include.

If, for example, we are designing a museum wall, we might have space equal to that of a billboard, but our audience's relationship to that space has changed based on their expected interaction mode with the space.

- Museum walls are meant to be approached and therefore warrant a *large-active scale*. Billboards are meant to be driven past and therefore warrant a *large-passive scale*.

- A small workbook that someone can write in warrants a *small-active scale*. A field guide that is meant to be merely referred to warrants a *small-passive scale*.

Heads up, *expected emotional dip ahead!*

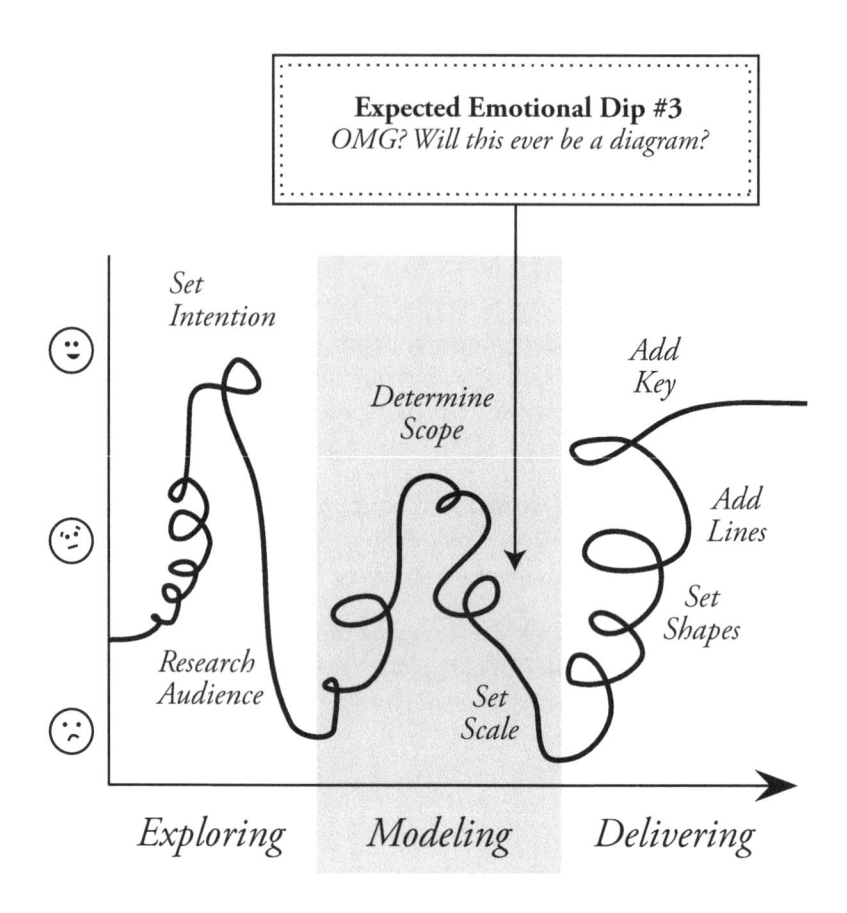

> **Expected Emotional Dip #3**
> *OMG? Will this ever be a diagram?*

Set Intention

Research Audience

Determine Scope

Set Scale

Add Key

Add Lines

Set Shapes

Exploring | *Modeling* | *Delivering*

96 | STUCK? Diagrams Help.

If you have been following this process, you are coming up for air from *a lot* of hard brain work. And this is probably hard work that hasn't even yielded anything that even resembles a diagram yet. Which I know is perhaps frustrating, but it's also *truthy*.

I feel the need to interrupt our process flow again after just doing so on the last step to talk about the deeper depths that often get plunged between when you decide what diagram you are *ideally* making and when you *actually* start to make the darn diagram.

And it's usually around the time of thinking about diagrammatic scale that we start to get into the brass tacks of diagramming and feel the deepest emotions yet as a result.

So, if you just decided the diagrammatic scale of your diagram and now looking back at your intention, audience, and planned scope has you feeling a bit stuck again, keep going.

It is in these emotional depths where the messy shape piles and crazy ideas for arrangements start to happen. There is a drive in this final emotional push, an anguish, a sense that this needs to be figured out to make things right, to get us out of the valley we feel stuck in.

If you get frustrated by how much work you have ahead or how hard it is to make your point with so little space or time, know the emotions that come along with those moments are an expected part of the journey—and perhaps even a needed one to know you are doing the work to make the diagram the best it can be made.

Step 5: Set Shapes

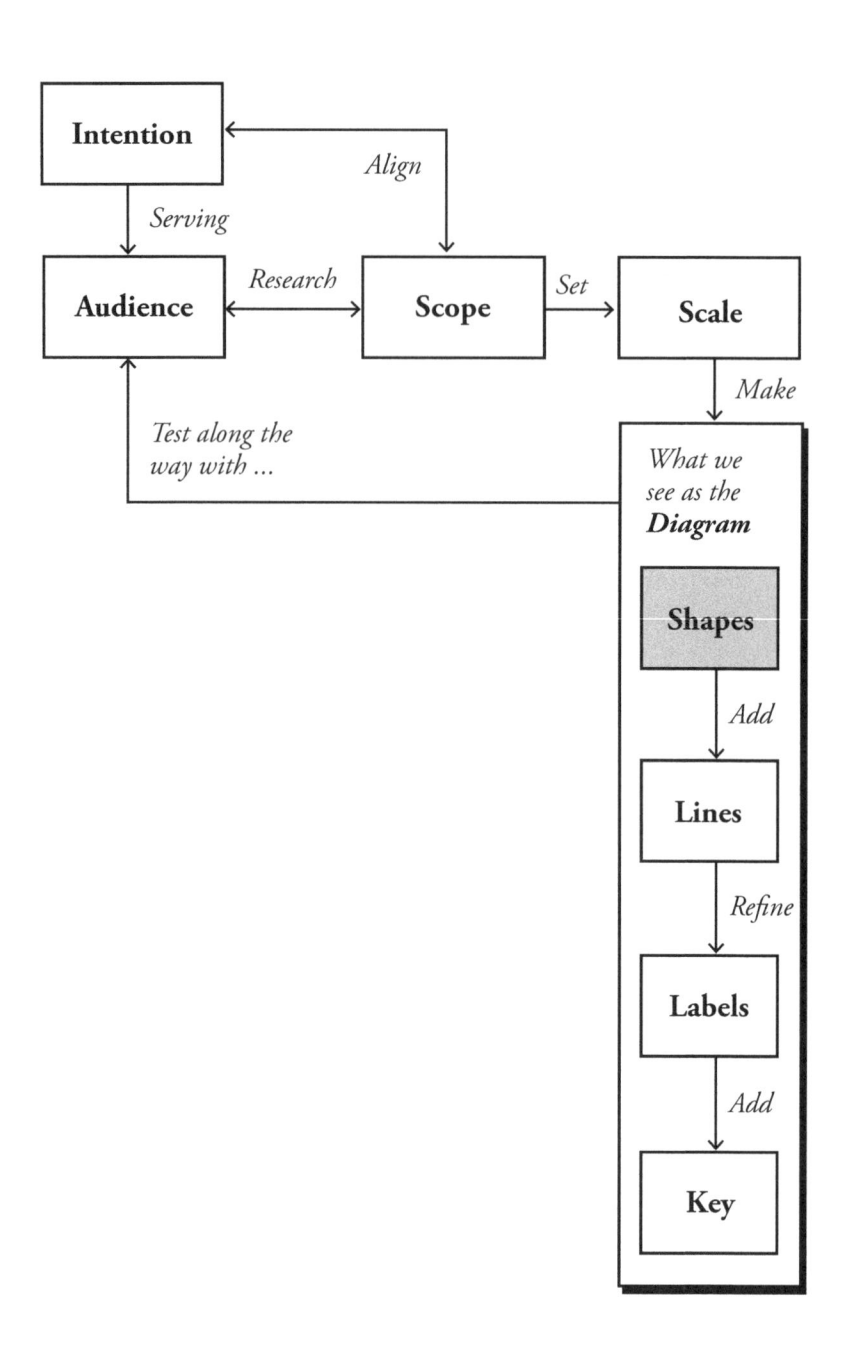

```
Intention
   │ Serving          ↑ Align
   ↓         Research        Set
Audience ←──────────→ Scope ──────→ Scale
   ↑                                 │ Make
   │                                 ↓
   │  Test along the      ┌─────────────────────┐
   │  way with ...        │ What we             │
   └──────────────────────│ see as the          │
                          │ Diagram             │
                          │                     │
                          │    ┌─────────┐      │
                          │    │ Shapes  │      │
                          │    └─────────┘      │
                          │         │ Add       │
                          │         ↓           │
                          │    ┌─────────┐      │
                          │    │  Lines  │      │
                          │    └─────────┘      │
                          │         │ Refine    │
                          │         ↓           │
                          │    ┌─────────┐      │
                          │    │ Labels  │      │
                          │    └─────────┘      │
                          │         │ Add       │
                          │         ↓           │
                          │    ┌─────────┐      │
                          │    │   Key   │      │
                          │    └─────────┘      │
                          └─────────────────────┘
```

Now that we have an understanding of our intention, audience, scope, and scale, it's time to finally make what the audience sees as the diagram. Start with setting the shapes.

Remember that diagrams are made of shapes and lines:

- **Shapes:** Elements representing objects
- **Lines:** Elements representing relationships between objects

Setting shapes and adding lines are a two-step we do over and over until things feel right.

So while this part of the process is extruded into a sort of false sense of linearity for the purpose of talking about shapes and lines theoretically, I assure you that these two are far more entwined in reality.

There is a lot of wiggle between them if you are dancing right.

> ### What Are You Making Shapes to Represent?
>
> In order to know the shapes you need, we have to determine the people, places, and things that make up whatever diagrammatic scope we have established for ourselves:
>
> - **People:** The people involved in the thing you are diagramming. Do actual people or only types of people need to be represented?
> - **Places:** The contexts, both physical and digital, in the thing you are diagramming. What are the channels being used to communicate? What are the venues for interacting?
> - **Things:** The objective or subjective things that make up the larger thing that you are diagramming. What are the systems, goods, processes, tools, decisions, objects, and concepts surrounding the thing you are diagramming? What are the pieces that make up the whole you are representing?

Exercise 4:

Make a list of people, places, and things related to your in-visual decisions from exercise 3.

Example: if we are making a diagram critiquing the local policing system, it might start with a list like this:

People	PRIVATE CITIZENS POLICE ATTORNEYS JUDGES PRISON STAFF PRISONERS ACTIVISTS
Places	PARKS & PUBLIC SPACES PRIVATE LOCATIONS POLICE STATION JAIL PRISON COURTHOUSE
Things	BODY CAM FOOTAGE RADIO CALLS EVIDENCE POLICE PAPERWORK COURT FILINGS TOWN COUNCIL MEETINGS 911 CALLS INCIDENTS

I am making shapes to represent:

People	
Places	
Things	

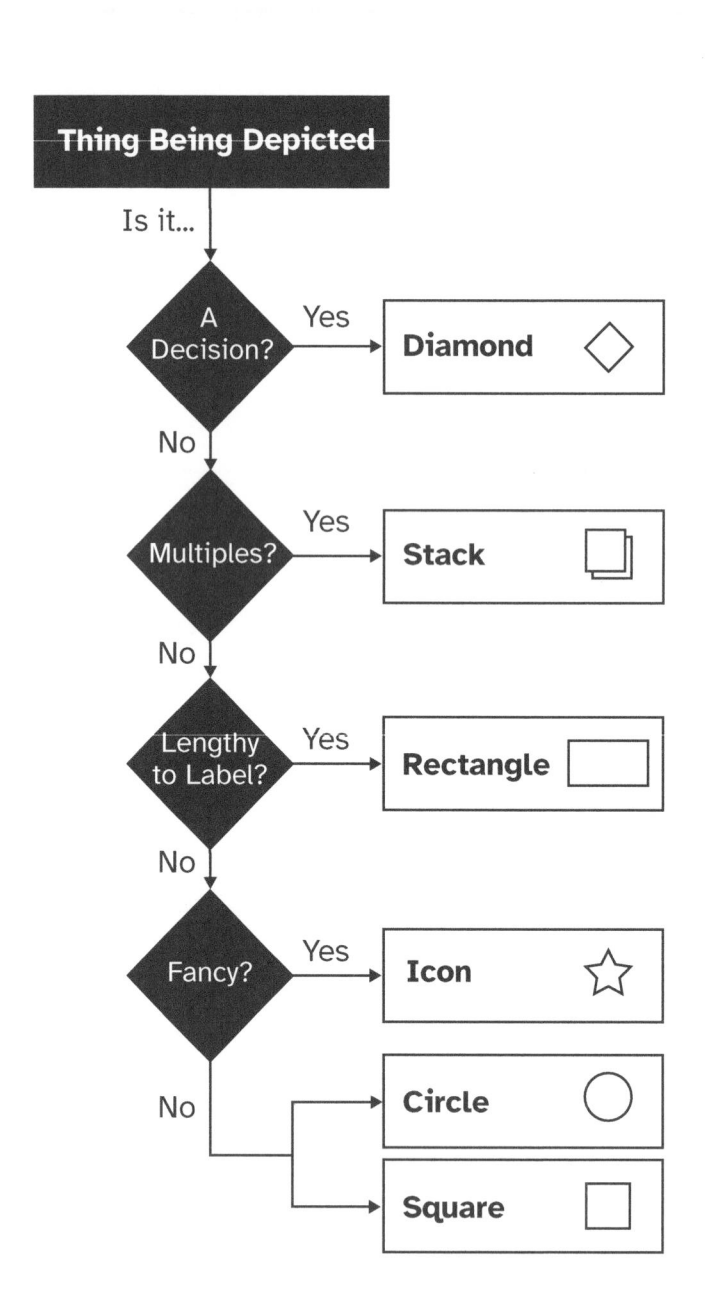

```
                    ┌─────────────────────────┐
                    │  Thing Being Depicted   │
                    └───────────┬─────────────┘
                          Is it...
                                ▼
                           ◆ A Decision? ◆  ──Yes──▶   Diamond    ◇
                                │
                                No
                                ▼
                           ◆ Multiples? ◆   ──Yes──▶   Stack      ▭
                                │
                                No
                                ▼
                        ◆ Lengthy to Label? ◆ ──Yes──▶ Rectangle  ▭
                                │
                                No
                                ▼
                           ◆ Fancy? ◆       ──Yes──▶   Icon       ☆
                                │
                                No ──┬──▶   Circle     ○
                                     └──▶   Square     □
```

What Shapes to Use?

I have watched people make diagrams for a good long time. Here are three things that I know to be true:

1. There are only so many shapes one can make.

2. The newer you are to diagramming, the fewer advanced moves the better.

3. There is no one right way.

If this all sounds like a vague pile of not answering the question proposed by the headline, don't worry. I made myself a promise when I wrote this book to never leave you with an "it depends" answer, to always try to formulate something more, some framework or advice for when you have diagrammatic decisions to make.

Choosing shapes to set in your diagram is one of those "it depends, because reasons" answers, BUT I took a swing at what I hope to be helpful when choosing the right shapes for your next diagram. This swing, or framework, asks a series of four questions that will lead you to a good enough recommendation about which shape to start with. The order of the decisions matters greatly to the lesson. I designed this flow to introduce each shape in context to its ideal usage.

If what is being visualized is a decision, diamonds are the most useful. If representing multiples, consider a stacked shape. If you are labeling something lengthy, rectangles are best. And if you are getting fancy, you can play with fancier shapes such as stars or maybe icons or images.

Otherwise, there are really just circles and squares left, both of which are perfectly fine, albeit plain, choices for your everyday diagrammatic needs.

Decisions Diamonds

When you are diagramming, you will have times when you are asking the diagram to take on a variety of *if* statements.

- *If* this happens, then XYZ happens.
- Something only exists *if* these other things happen or exist first.

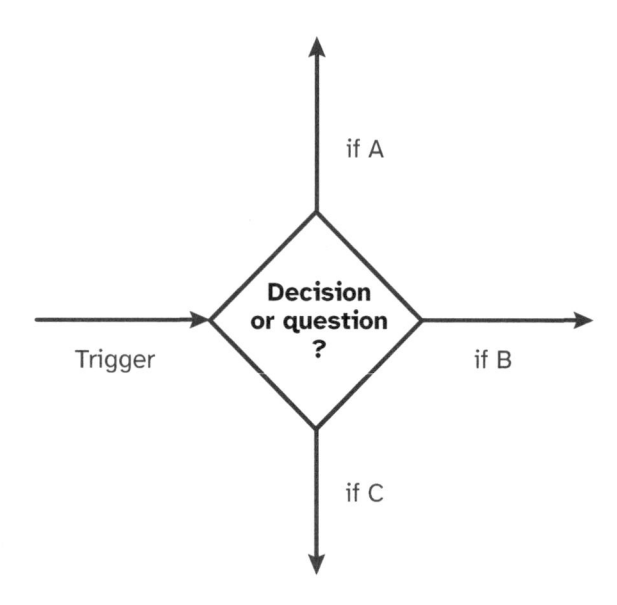

```
                    ↑
                   if A
                    
                  ╱   ╲
                 ╱     ╲
    ─────→    ╱ Decision ╲    ─────→
             ╲ or question ╱
   Trigger    ╲    ?    ╱      if B
                ╲     ╱
                  ╲ ╱
                   
                  if C
                    ↓
```

The reason a **diamond** is a good shape to use for decisions is that it quite literally has **decision points** built into the visual.[7] Each corner provides a perfect junction for a straight line to an option or condition.

---

[7] This shape is the standard used in entity relationship diagrams. It was first documented by Peter Pin-Shan Chen, "The Entity-Relationship Model—toward a Unified View of Data," *ACM Transactions on Database Systems* 1, no. 1 (March 1976): 9–36, https://doi.org/10.1145/320434.320440.

Stacks

Next let's talk about stacks.

Stacks are an essential pattern for the eventual need to represent an object that has many affinities, instances, or equivalents.

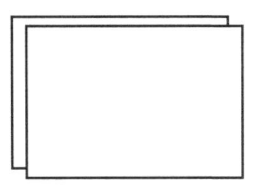

- **Affinities** are stated contextual similarities within a group. For example, if we were sorting customer feedback from a grocery store, we might place a complaint about long lines in the same stack as slow checkout processing. They aren't the same but share an affinity because they speak to the same root issue.

- **Instances** are things of the same type that exist under a higher-level label, such as *books* in a library, *products* on an e-commerce website, or *files* on a server. For example, this book is simply one of many instances of the concept of *book*. In fact, the copy you are reading right now is only one of many instances of this book.

- **Equivalents** are the multiple labels such as abbreviations, colloquialisms, acronyms, or nicknames for a single object. For example, when my family members use the label "Ab" or my college friends use the label "Abba Zabba" to describe me, they are not referring to a part of me. These labels are equivalents.

Rather than create a shape in the diagram for each book, product, nickname, or file, we can create a **collapsed stack** to show that a number of affinities, instances, or equivalents can be thought about under a single label.[8] In each of these cases, we can use a **spread stack** to show that multiple labels relate to a single concept or object.

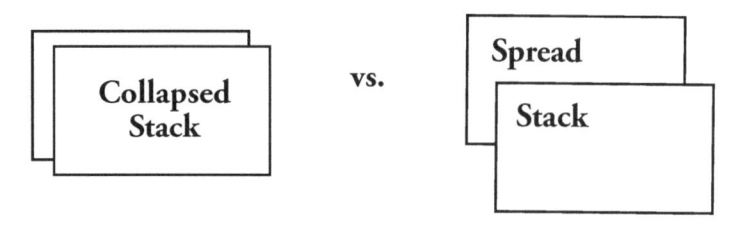

```
   Collapsed          vs.         Spread
     Stack                         Stack
```

Collapsed stacks are an especially powerful visual technique when the content you are diagramming feels like too much for the scale you are using.

Look back at your list of people, places, and things. How many of them did you default to write in the plural? For each one, ask yourself: Do the specific *instances* of this person, place, or thing have to be included, or is there a higher-level grouping that would suffice for making my point? Or, are there any *affinities, instances,* or *equivalents* I would need to spread out in the stack?

Let's use the example of making a diagram to represent that there are many *types* of diagrams. When writing my list, I might start exhaustively trying to give each type of diagram their own shape.

---

[8] As a young IA, I was first introduced to this idea by Jesse James Garrett's Visual Vocabulary, in which he introduced the concepts of pagestacks and filestacks. There are examples of this visual device in icon design throughout tech history starting back in Xerox PARC, as well as numerous examples of this graphical style in diagrams predating the digital era used to mean "equivalent" or to collapse instances of a concept. See Jesse James Garrett, "A Visual Vocabulary for Describing Information Architecture and Interaction Design," jjg.net, version 1.1b, last modified March 6, 2002, http://www.jjg.net/ia/visvocab.

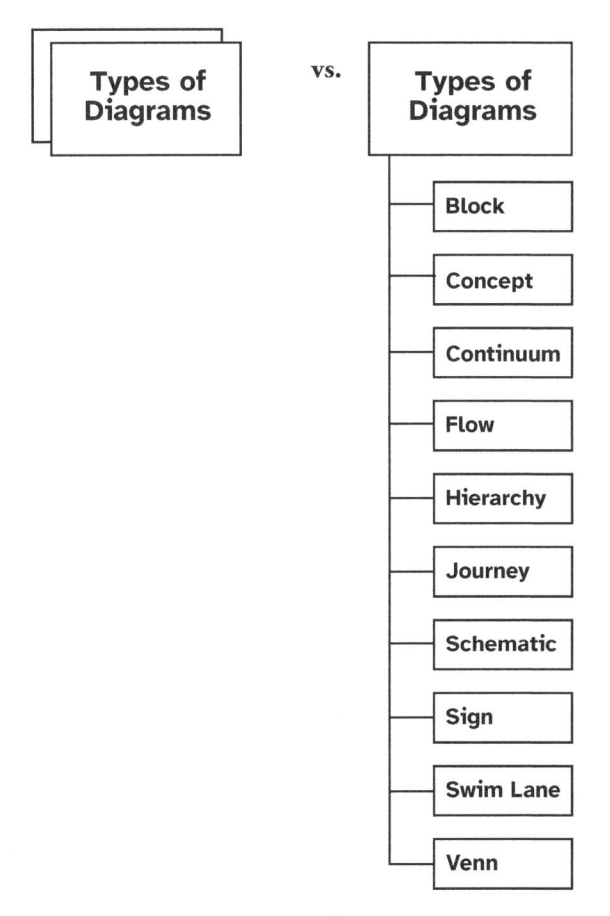

```
                                Types of
   Types of          vs.        Diagrams
   Diagrams
                                    ├── Block
                                    ├── Concept
                                    ├── Continuum
                                    ├── Flow
                                    ├── Hierarchy
                                    ├── Journey
                                    ├── Schematic
                                    ├── Sign
                                    ├── Swim Lane
                                    └── Venn
```

If I wanted to represent this in a smaller or more passive scale, I could reduce the list down to a stack called "Types of Diagrams."

Which level of specificity is more useful for your intention?

1. A stack representing that there are many
2. A list that attempts to be exhaustive of how many

There is no right way. There is only the way you decide is better to reach your intention.

Chapter 2: **Process** | 107

Rectangles & Squares

Rectangles and squares are the easiest shapes to diagram with, hands down. This is because they are the most forgiving of the shapes for labels of any real length. When you get into using circles and fancier shapes, you can end up in a finicky typography place quickly.

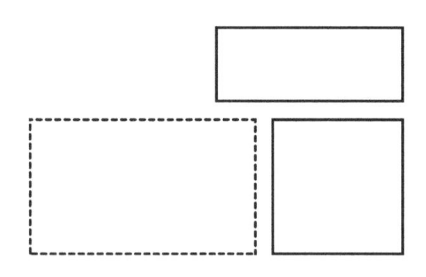

If you are new to diagramming or design skills are far from your skill set, I suggest you start by just using diamonds, stacks, rectangles, and squares. There is no shame in that game, friend.

As an experienced diagrammer, I always default to rectangles for my list-making step. I find rectangles to be the most useful shape to start to imagine things in because of their forgiving nature.

Circles & Ovals

I most often use circles and ovals when I need a shape that is representing something *very* different from what I have already used a rectangle or square for.

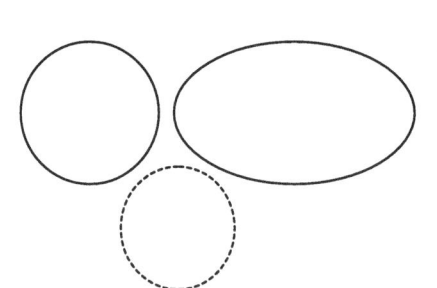

Circles are less forgiving in their ability to host lengthy labels, so this is a shape to use carefully. But they are a lovely, soft diagrammatic shape.

Fancy Schmancy Shapes: Stars, Weird-Shaped Containers, Icons & Illustrations, Oh My!

A common diagrammatic technique is to visually spice up the diagram by adding other fancier shapes that ideally reinforce the nature of the people, places, and things you are representing.

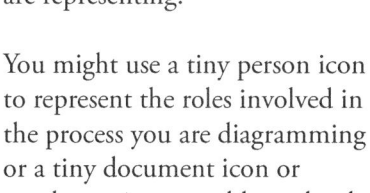

You might use a tiny person icon to represent the roles involved in the process you are diagramming or a tiny document icon or a webpage icon to add another layer of visual information to your diagram. While this might be common, it comes with great diagrammatic responsibility.

If you have access to really thoughtful illustrations or have the skill to make them yourself, then adding fancy shapes to your diagram might be really fun, cool, or nifty. But you'll want to make sure you test your visuals to ensure the intended audience understands the visual cues you chose.

If, however, icon design and illustration is not in your budget or skill set for your diagram, please try to refrain from any feelings of missing out. Those same fancy shapes can add confusion and misunderstanding if they aren't thoughtfully considered. They can become decoration, not information.

While I include fancy shapes here because they are common, I speak to them last in my shape consideration set because they are not my recommended path for those new to diagramming.

Can You Make Diagrams with Implied Shapes?

What about when the shapes are implied by the way the type is set? Is this as effective?

After giving it some thought and playing with some diagrams using what I now refer to as **implied shapes**, I have concluded that while you can make a diagram without the use of **bounded shapes**, it is not a move for the faint of heart or weak of typography.

When the type is set in such a way that a clear shape can be implied around the object, I think this can work. Especially for very brief diagrams, this might be an effective visual decision to make. But for beginners, I wouldn't start here.

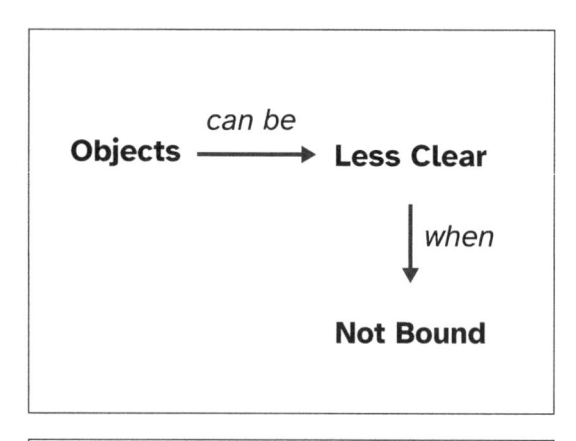

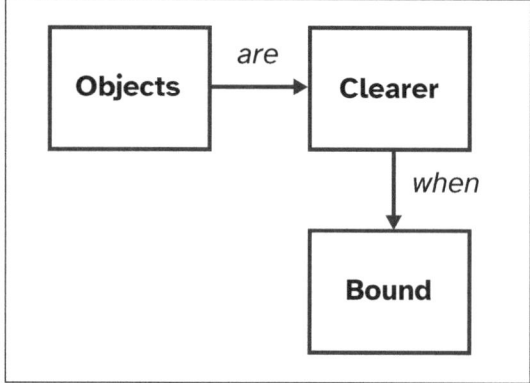

How We Set Shapes Has Meaning

If we set three boxes in a horizontal row, readers of left-to-right languages will tend to read left to right, even without lines.

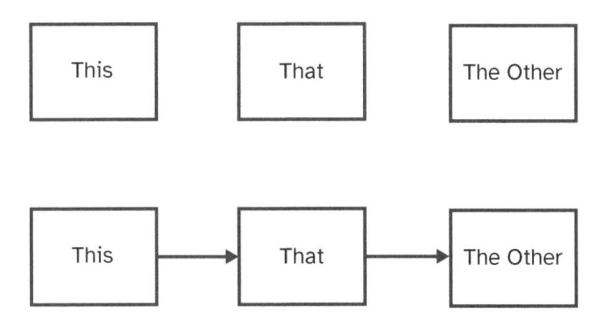

| This | That | The Other |

This → That → The Other

When I indent a shape's alignment under another shape, it starts to resemble a hierarchical relationship, but I would need a bracketed line to further reinforce the relationship.

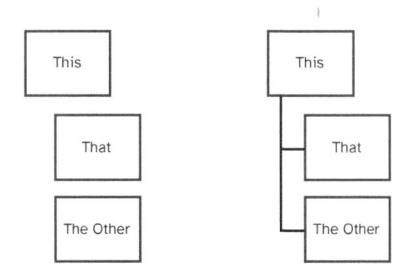

By setting our shapes, we are deciding two things at once:

- **In what order do we expect the diagram to be consumed?** This is the reading order of the diagram.

- **What are the relationships between these objects that we want a viewer to understand as a result of consuming this diagram?** This is communicated both in the spatial and labeled relationships that the objects have to one another.

Our audience will be simultaneously trying to figure out the order we want them to read those shapes in and what relationships they are supposed to glean from these specific arrangements. It's tough cognitive work if you think about it.

Once I have my list of shapes, I like to start by moving the shapes around into different arrangements. I use my imagination to draw the lines as I move things around. If you do that part right, the lines almost draw themselves at the end.

Here is the shape decision diagram without any lines. See how the arrangement of the shapes sets up where the lines go?

I don't need to add lines until I am more sure of the structure I am making.

This simple trick helps because adding lines when in a place of uncertainty about the form the shapes will end up taking is a surefire way to do a whole lot of work that ends up being redone later.

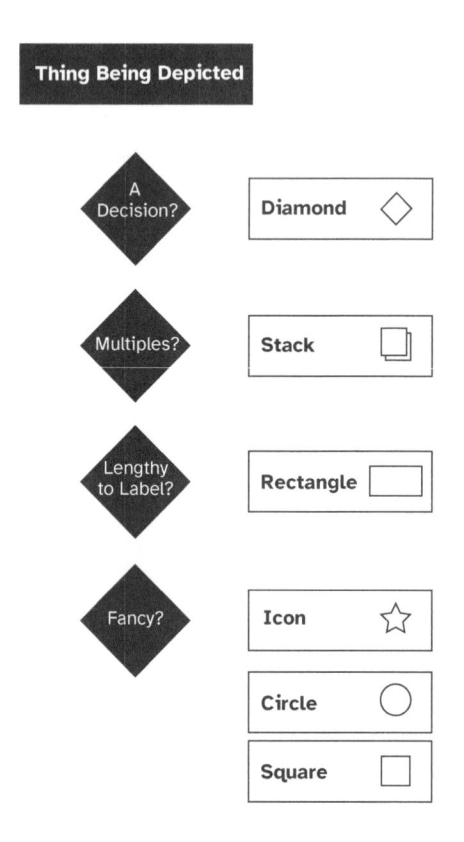

Thing Being Depicted

- A Decision? → Diamond
- Multiples? → Stack
- Lengthy to Label? → Rectangle
- Fancy? → Icon
- Circle
- Square

112 | STUCK? Diagrams Help.

Five Common Arrangements
of This and That

To better prepare you for the thoughtful placement of shapes in your diagram, this section introduces you to five common visual arrangements of people, places, and things.

Now, each of these arrangements can be found in any number of fields of origin, study, and practice. Library science, interaction design, visual literacy, and cognitive psychology to name a few.

All of the following can be found under contextually bounded and albeit more fancy naming than what is proposed below.

Rather than get bogged down in brand-new vocabulary to learn when all we really want is to wield shapes and lines more effectively, I present to you *the five relationships of this and that*:

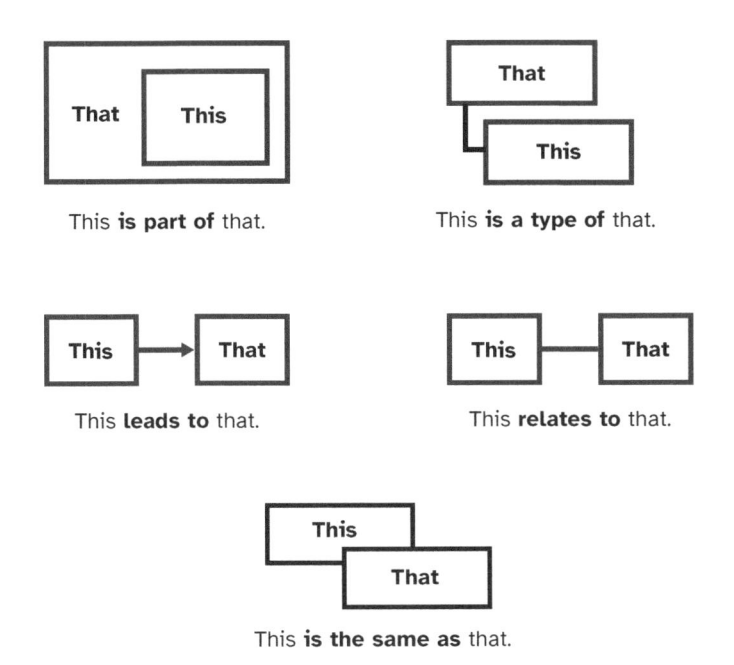

This **is part of** that.

This **is a type of** that.

This **leads to** that.

This **relates to** that.

This **is the same as** that.

This Is Part of That

You will come upon times when you want to make it clear that something is a *smaller* part, facet, or aspect of something else.

For example, if we wanted to represent the parts of a book, we might create a container labeled "book" and visualize each piece of the book as smaller shapes within it.

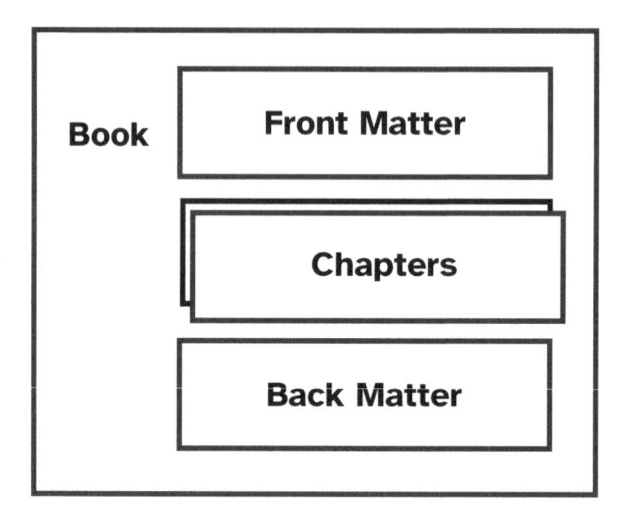

When **this is part of that**, a visual arrangement that works is setting the smaller shapes within a larger shape representing the whole.

Pop Quiz

Why did I use a stack to represent "chapters" in that last example? Did I use a collapsed or spread stack?

Answer:

If we are making a diagram to represent the concept of a book and not a specific book, we don't know how many chapters the book has. I used a collapsed stack to show that there are many chapters without being specific as to how many.

If this sounds like martian, revisit the lesson about stacks earlier in this chapter.

This Is a Type of That

There are times when you will need to visualize groups of like items. Let's say you have a simple website to visualize.

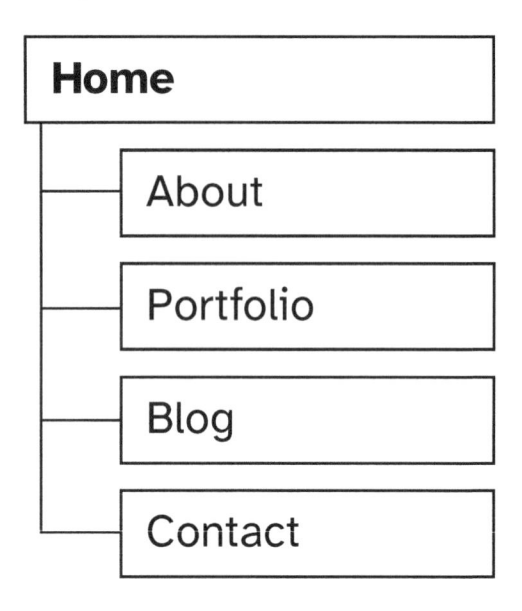

```
┌─────────────┐
│ **Home**    │
└──┬──────────┘
   │  ┌─────────────┐
   ├──│ About       │
   │  └─────────────┘
   │  ┌─────────────┐
   ├──│ Portfolio   │
   │  └─────────────┘
   │  ┌─────────────┐
   ├──│ Blog        │
   │  └─────────────┘
   │  ┌─────────────┐
   └──│ Contact     │
      └─────────────┘
```

When **this is a type of that**, the visual arrangement used most frequently is to indent each member of the group, or child, beneath a label unifying them and then connect these children to their parent with brackets.

This Leads to That

When something comes before or after something else, we use arrows to connect them.

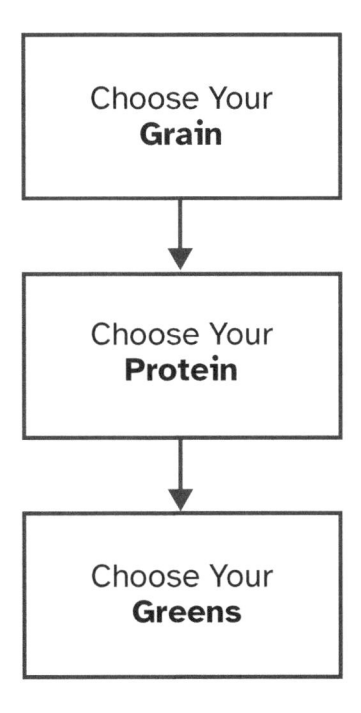

```
┌─────────────────┐
│  Choose Your    │
│     Grain       │
└────────┬────────┘
         │
         ▼
┌─────────────────┐
│  Choose Your    │
│    Protein      │
└────────┬────────┘
         │
         ▼
┌─────────────────┐
│  Choose Your    │
│    Greens       │
└─────────────────┘
```

Consider a local lunch place with a three-step process for ordering. If we are to visualize this process, we might use arrows to indicate that there is one direction that this process flows.

In this example, we are pushing the diner through a specific order to best support the assembly line of the restaurant concept.

When **this leads to that**, one-way and two-way arrows help show that there are directions that are available and therefore also directions that are not available.

This Relates to That

This arrangement is for when something has something to do with something else. If that sounds vague, it is. These relationships run the gamut, and more often than the other arrangements, they need to be labeled to make good sense.

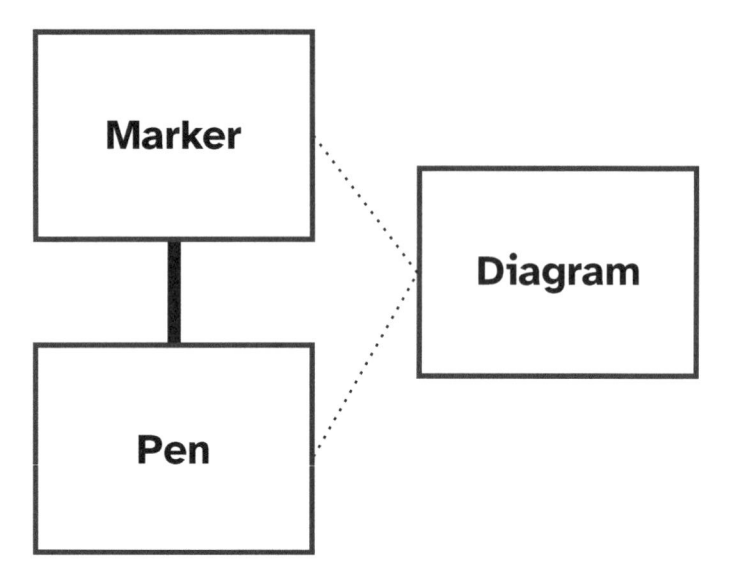

```
┌─────────────┐
│             │
│   Marker    │──────┐
│             │      ╲
└──────┬──────┘       ╲   ┌──────────────┐
       │                ╲ │              │
       │                  │   Diagram    │
       │                ╱ │              │
┌──────┴──────┐       ╱   └──────────────┘
│             │──────┘
│    Pen      │
│             │
└─────────────┘
```

For example, we might relate diagrams with markers. We make diagrams with markers, but neither is a type of the other. And they aren't a part of each other. But they have something to do with each other.

When **this relates to that**, we can use a non-directional line. We can also play with the visual weight and style of that line to communicate the strength of the connection. In this example, I used a strong line to connect "Marker" and "Pen" to each other since they are categorically similar but a dotted line to connect them to "Diagram" as if to say, "Well, they are related but not as related." It is worth mentioning that without further labeling the lines, these kinds of relationships can lead to confusion or misunderstanding.

This Is the Same as That

The final pattern revisits one from the discussion on stacks.

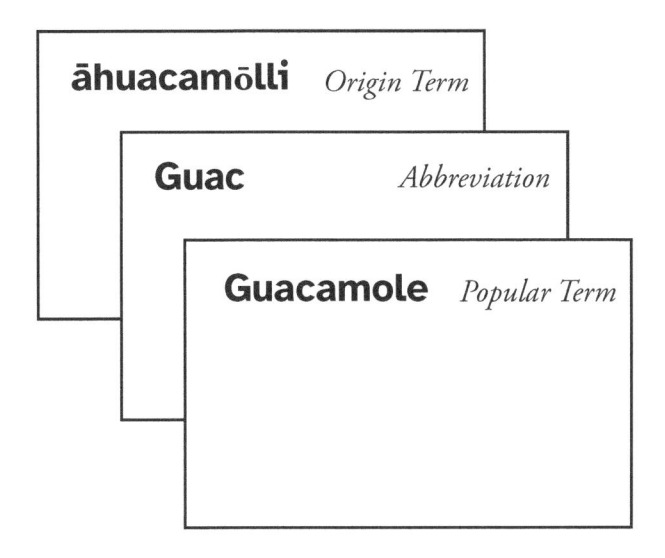

> āhuacamōlli — *Origin Term*
> Guac — *Abbreviation*
> Guacamole — *Popular Term*

When **this is the same as that**, the visual arrangement that helps is a slight or extreme overlap. This is what I consider to be one of the most essential visual arrangements for working with other people.

Other people might use terms or have ideas that are the same in intention or meaning as the terms we have in mind. Collecting and visualizing these terms can be an eye-opening exercise for teams.

When people place their thoughts, ideas, and contributions into these stacks with like-minded thoughts, ideas, and contributions of other people, it helps build a sense of community during the development of a shared intention.

Heads up, *expected loops ahead!*

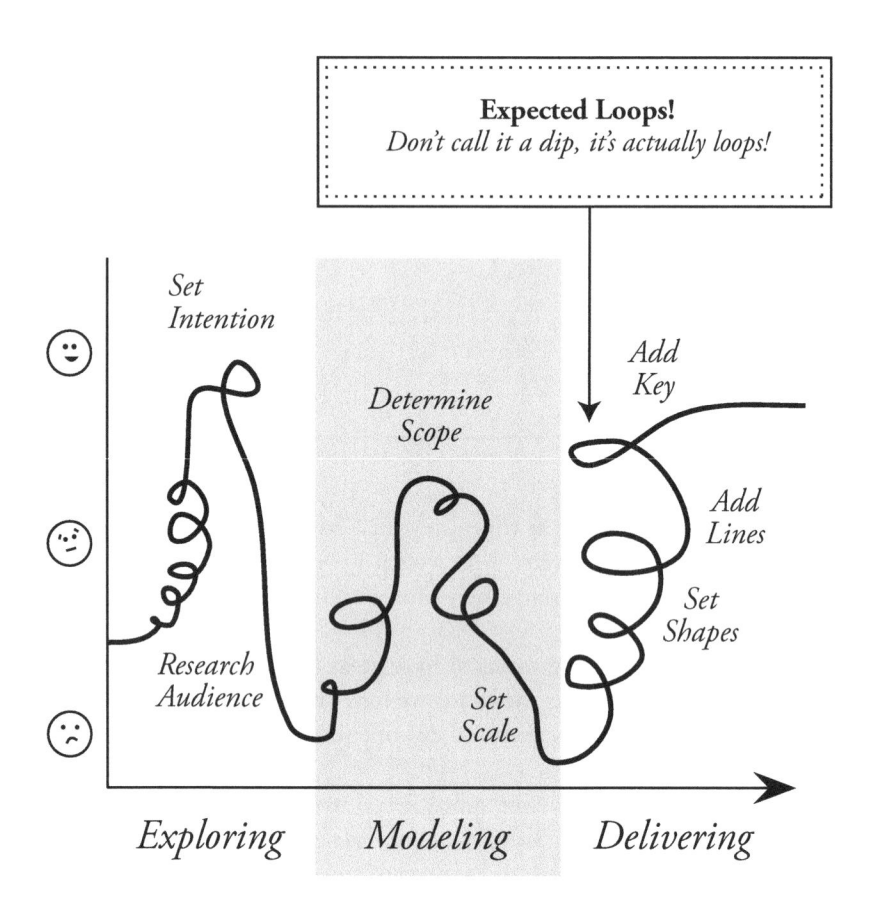

Expected Loops!
Don't call it a dip, it's actually loops!

Set Intention

Add Key

Determine Scope

Add Lines

Set Shapes

Research Audience

Set Scale

Exploring   *Modeling*   *Delivering*

As we mechanically move through the consideration of what form our diagram is about to take and how the shapes and lines will come together at the scale we have set, we should expect to go through some loops emotionally.

There is no right way (meaning there is no wrong way) and there are a million and a half fun and perfectly good ways to diagram something.

There can be agony in that thought, and many get stuck in the emotional looping of it all. If you feel yourself looking a little *too* hard for the right recipe, instead of making some messy shape piles and digging in, go off recipe.

You're ready. It's just shapes and lines, friend.

Step 6: Add Lines

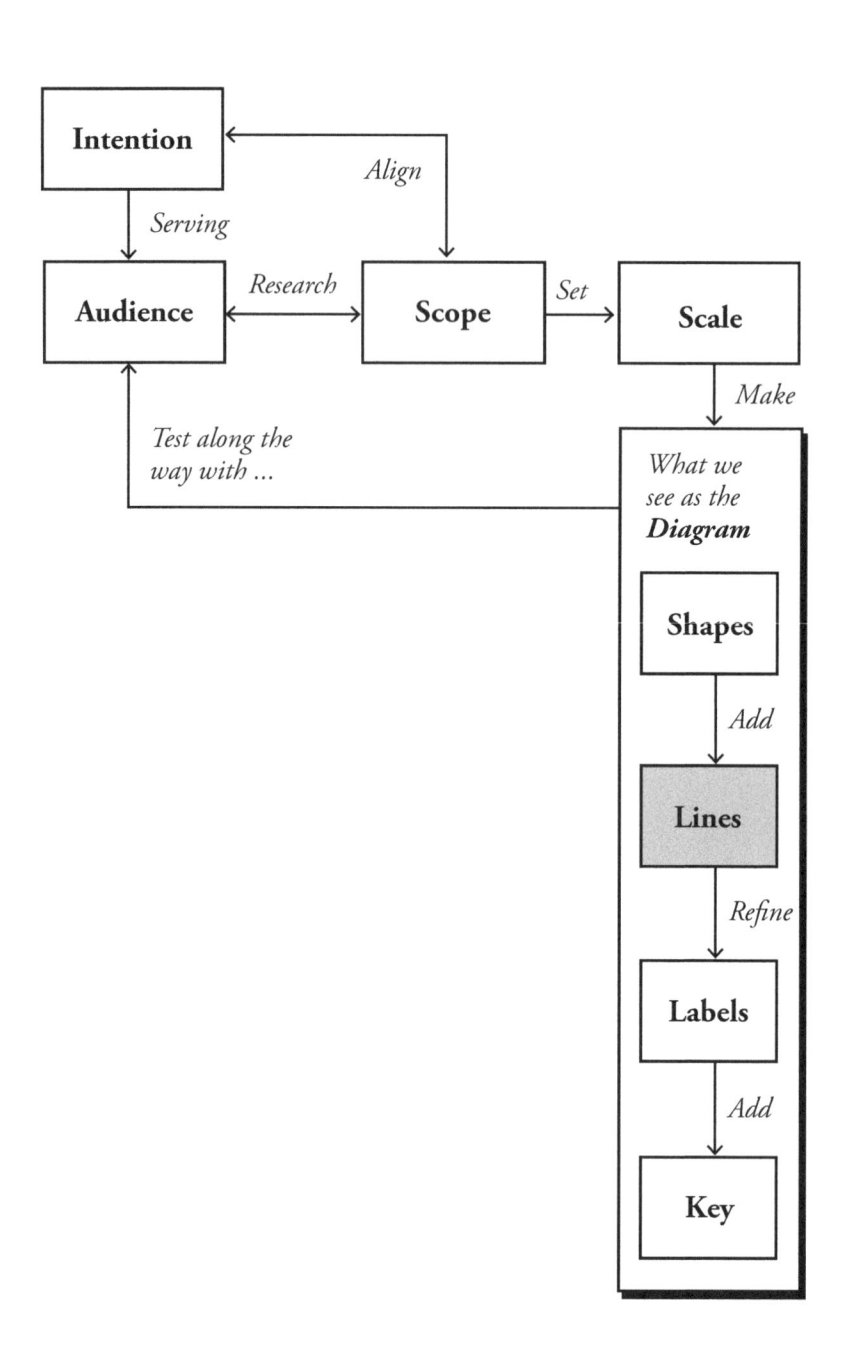

You might have noticed that we slipped in some lines when we started to get into some of the arrangements of shapes. That's how the lines part tends to work, slowly slipping their way into the diagram as they are needed to portray meaning.

When we are adding lines, we are focused on visualizing the relationships between the objects. Each of the visual arrangements of shapes we just walked through alludes to a common type of relationship that lines can help reinforce.

Some common line patterns we see in daily diagramming life are, in my experience, as follows:

- **Non-directional lines** for *associations* ▬
- **One-way lines** for *sequences* ➡
- **Two-way lines** for *reciprocation* ⬌
- **Brackets** for *hierarchy* ⌊
- **Quadrants** for *comparison* ⊞

Non-directional Lines for Associations

When we are connecting shapes that don't have a sequence or flow in the way that they are attached, we can use non-directional lines.

The types of relationships that are best represented this way are called **associations** or associative relationships.[9] When we associate something with something else, both things exist and can exist without the other.

But this pattern offers the user little signal as to what type of association these two objects have, so labeling of non-directional lines is often imperative. It all depends on the degree to which their association is obvious to your audience.

In the diagram shown here, the association between "That Table" and "These Chairs" is more obvious without line labels than the association between "That Table" and "That Dress."

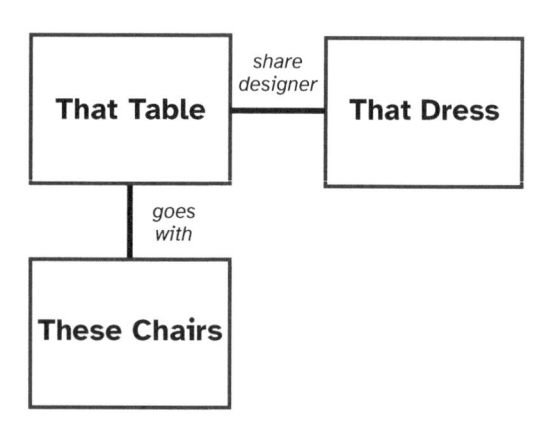

---

[9] "This relationship covers associations between terms that are neither equivalent nor hierarchical, yet the terms are semantically or conceptually associated." See ANSI/NISO Z39.19-2005 (R2010), "Guidelines for the Construction, Format, and Management of Monolingual Controlled Vocabularies," National Information Standards Organization, May 13, 2010, http://www.niso.org/publications/ansiniso-z3919-2005-r2010.

[10] In the 18th century, directional arrows first made their way onto European civic maps to represent the direction and flow of rivers and streams, and they remain a visual element in common universal use today to mean direction and movement. See Robert J. Finkel, "History of the Arrow," American Printing History Association, April 1, 2015, https://printinghistory.org/arrow/.

124 | STUCK? Diagrams Help.

One-Way Lines for Sequences →

When we are connecting shapes that come into existence or focus in an order, or we are representing a path through an experience, we can use one-way lines.[10] The types of relationships that are best represented with one-way lines are called **sequences**, or sometimes **flows**.

When we put things in a sequence, we are prescribing how the audience is meant to use or experience it.

There are two additional common uses of one-way lines in diagrams.

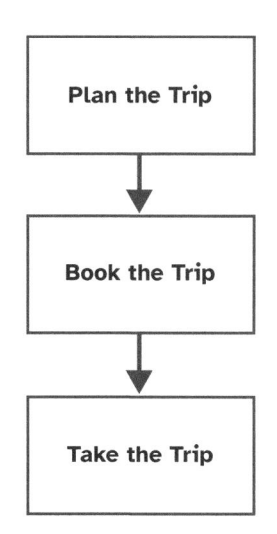

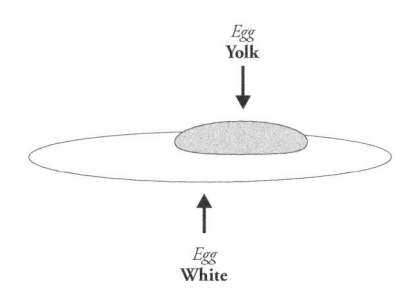

The first is as **pointers** to shapes for the purpose of labeling, as shown in this simple diagram of the parts of an egg.

The second is to create an **axis** on which shapes can be compared on any range of qualitative or quantitative rubrics.

For example, a bar chart defines the minimum and maximum value of two axes, x and y, in order to compare shapes based on their quantitative measurement.

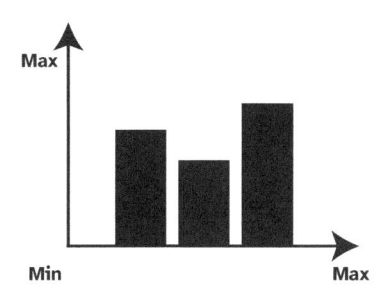

Chapter 2: **Process** | 125

Two-Way Lines for Reciprocation ⟷

When we are representing two or more objects that work together to produce a result, we can use two-way lines. The relationships best visualized with two-way lines tend to be **reciprocal**. You also see this pattern in mathematics to visualize equivalence in nature, meaning that the objects or concepts being represented give to one another or work together in some form.[11]

Reciprocations can be analog, such as people working to achieve a result, or technical, such as a hyperlink between pages that exist on two websites. In the example here, two-way arrows remind us of the reciprocal nature of our relationship with our diagram's audience.

You might not need your audience to make diagrams, but you do need to talk with your audience in order to make diagrams that make sense to them.

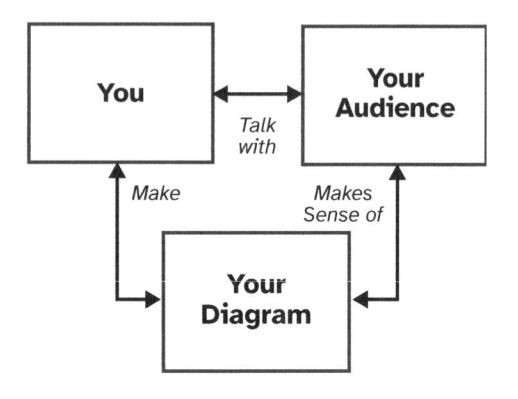

---

[11] The double-headed arrow representing logical equivalence was introduced by Albrecht Becker in *Die Aristotelische Theorie der Möglichkeitsschlüsse* (Berlin, 1933). For more insight into the rich history of arrows, see Finkel, "History of the Arrow," https://printinghistory.org/arrow/.

[12] Visual depictions of tree structures to represent hierarchy date back to 500 CE—for example, the Porphyrian tree. For a rich history of this pattern, check out Manuel Lima, *The Book of Trees: Visualizing Branches of Knowledge* (New York: Princeton Architectural Press, 2014).

Brackets for Hierarchy ∟

When a shape belongs to a group with other shapes, we can use brackets to connect them. The relationships best visualized by brackets are **hierarchical**, meaning that one of the things being connected is the parent to others.[12]

When representing hierarchies with brackets, there are two basic arrangements: horizontal and vertical. When you are representing the top of a hierarchy, and are still only looking to represent things in two levels, a horizontal bracket is most likely to serve you best. But once you hit that third level, consider whether going vertical is the best use of your space.

I once saw a student try to represent five levels deep (!!!) with horizontal brackets, and they had to add color-coding because it got so complex *looking*.

With the introduction of vertical brackets as a pattern, they were able to remove the need for color-coding altogether.

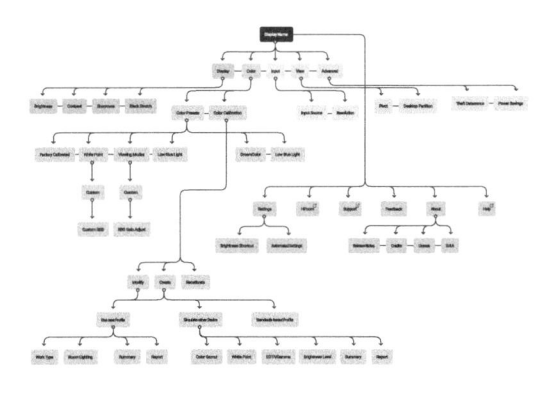

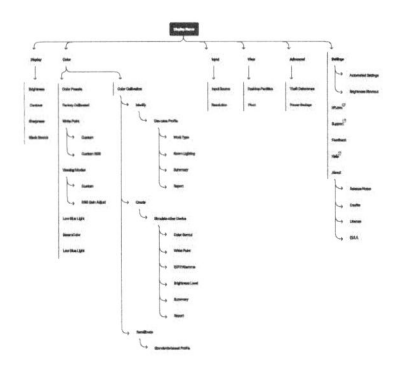

Image source: Trent Lutmer, student at MICA, printed with permission.

Chapter 2: **Process** | 127

There are a variety of ways to draw brackets. Sometimes the tool we are using dictates this decision. Other times we get to choose.

In this section, I provide examples as another reminder that there is no one right way to diagram. There are many ways, and it is up to you to determine your own way, every time. Just because I tend to favor one or another of these patterns in the examples in this book doesn't mean those are superior. So should you have full creative control to do what pleases you most, here are some options to try out.

Here are the most common **horizontal** and **vertical bracket** styles I encounter in the wild.

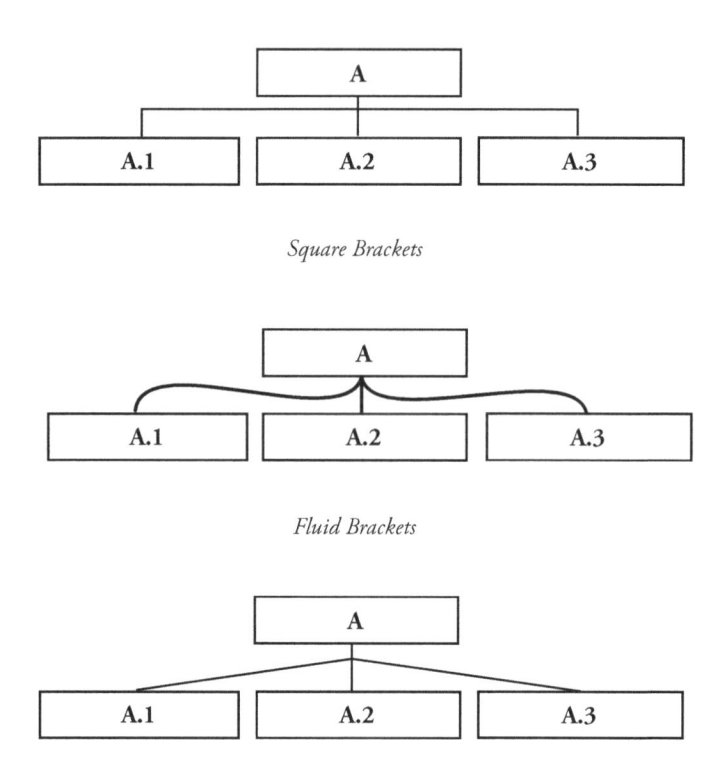

Square Brackets

Fluid Brackets

Diagonal Brackets

128 | STUCK? Diagrams Help.

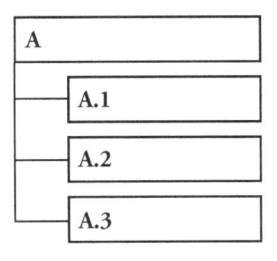

Flush Brackets

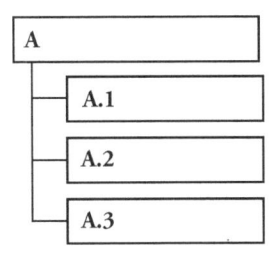

Indented Brackets

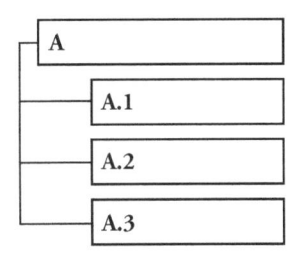

Outdented Brackets

Quadrants for Comparison

In quadrants, a shape is put into a particular spot based on how it relates to other shapes on some established quantitative scale or qualitative rubric.

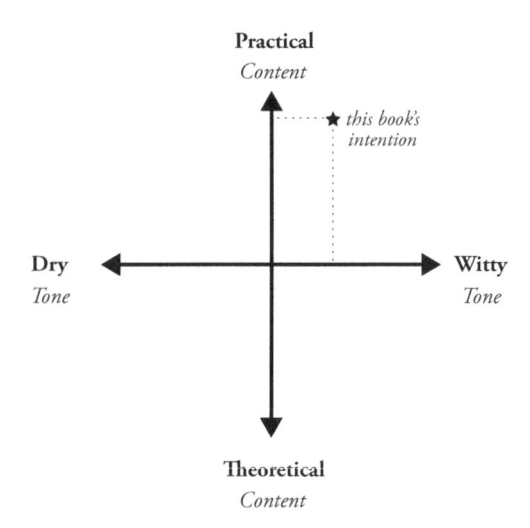

Practical
Content

★ *this book's intention*

Dry
Tone

Witty
Tone

Theoretical
Content

The relationships that are best visualized this way are comparative. These comparisons can be based on quantitative datasets, as you see in the case of numerical graphs in which the location of shapes is plotted on both an x and y axis.

Comparative relationships are also created through quadrants drawn on worksheets or canvases with blank spaces designated to capture certain types of information.

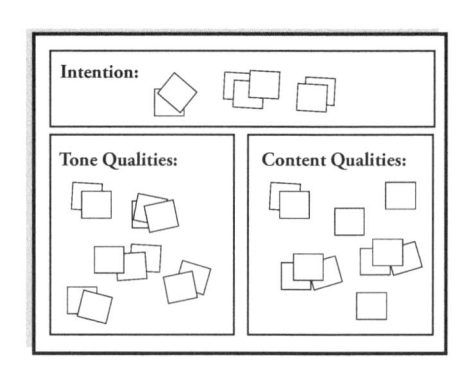

Intention:

Tone Qualities:

Content Qualities:

130 | STUCK? Diagrams Help.

Pop Quiz

Can you name the four patterns you see used here? Bonus points for identifying which relationship types each are meant to represent.

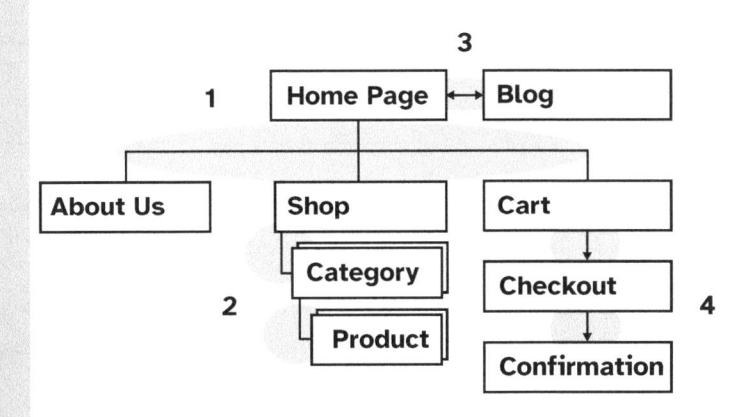

```
                         3
                1   ┌───────────┐   ┌──────┐
                    │ Home Page │◄─►│ Blog │
                    └───────────┘   └──────┘
        ┌────────────────┼──────────────┐
  ┌──────────┐      ┌────────┐      ┌──────┐
  │ About Us │      │  Shop  │      │ Cart │
  └──────────┘      └────────┘      └──────┘
                       ├──┌──────────┐  │
                       │  │ Category │  ▼
                    2  │  └──────────┘ ┌──────────┐   4
                       │  ┌──────────┐ │ Checkout │
                       └──│ Product  │ └──────────┘
                          └──────────┘      │
                                            ▼
                                    ┌──────────────┐
                                    │ Confirmation │
                                    └──────────────┘
```

Answer:

1. *Horizontal brackets* are used for the top two levels of the site's *hierarchical* relationships.

2. *Vertical* brackets are used for the third-level *hierarchical* relationships in the "Shop" section.

3. A *two-way line* is used for the *reciprocal* relationship between the "Home Page" and "Blog."

4. *One-way lines* are used for the *sequential* relationship of the steps in the "Cart" section.

Chapter 2: **Process** | 131

Step 7: Refine Labels

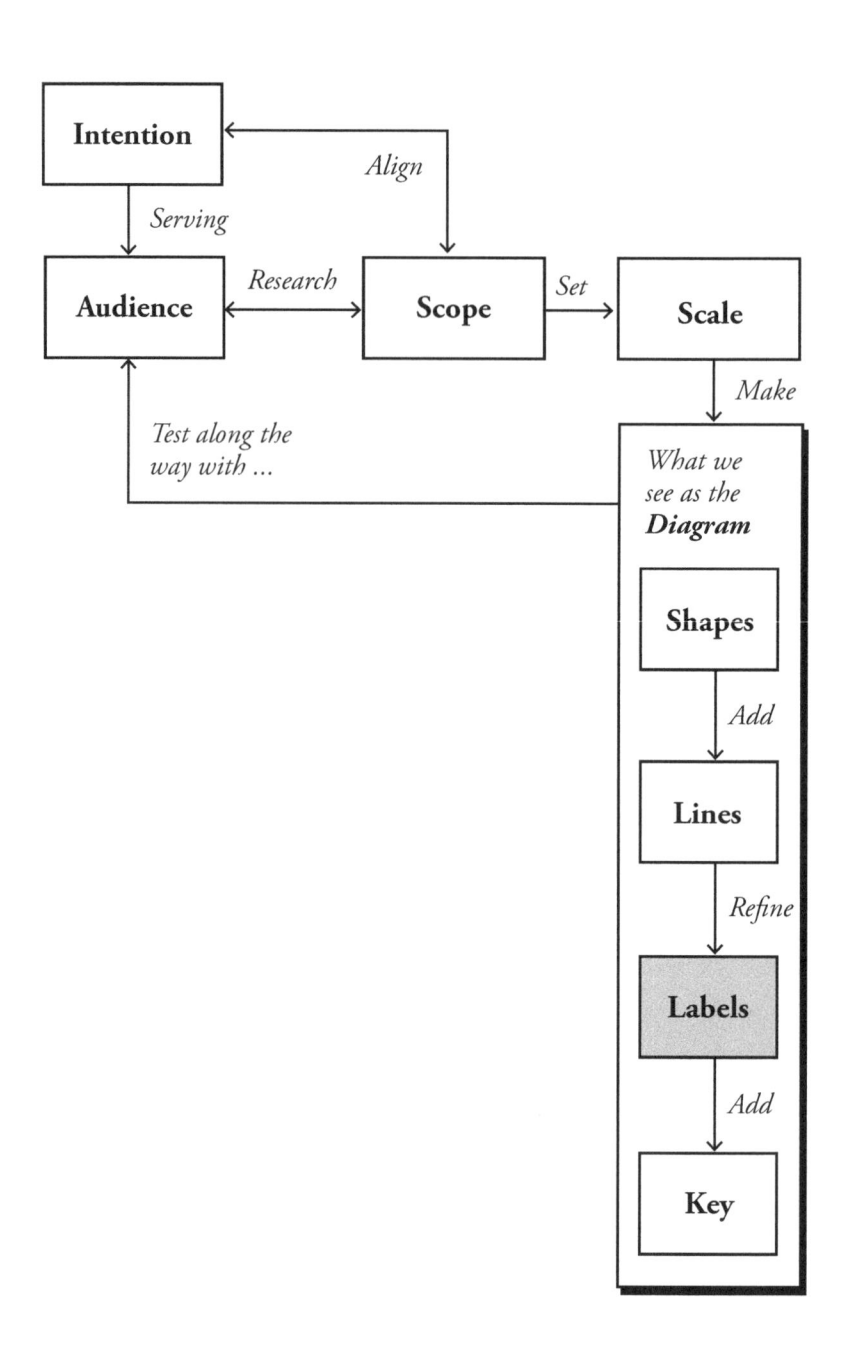

- **Intention** → *Serving* → **Audience**
- **Audience** ↔ *Research* ↔ **Scope**
- **Scope** → *Align* → **Intention**
- **Scope** → *Set* → **Scale**
- **Scale** → *Make* → *What we see as the Diagram*:
  - **Shapes** → *Add* → **Lines** → *Refine* → **Labels** → *Add* → **Key**
- *Test along the way with ...* → **Audience**

As you have been making your diagram all this time, one element has followed you along the whole journey, from the very beginning: the labels.

The words we use to describe the elements of our diagram are critical to getting our point across, but they are also *impossible* to operate without, even for a second, when diagramming.

This creates a quandary of process.

We need labels to do our work, and yet we have to pick out labels so early in the process that we don't actually know that much about our intention or audience when we do this important *deciding*.

In my opinion, the nature of the labels and what we need from them changes quite a lot as we move through each stage of the diagrammatic process.

Exploring	Modeling	Delivering
Labels to *get by*	Labels to *get through*	Labels to *get results*

While Still Exploring, Use Labels to *Get By*

In the exploring phase of diagramming, the labels are really just falling out of our heads, and we are picking them up with our hands and making shapes to represent them.

When we are making these lists of people, places, and things, we don't need to get too bogged down in getting the label *just right*.

In fact, agonizing on the *just right* label at this point is a distraction that captures the attention of many a diagrammer to the detriment of their intention.

Some people falsely assume that if they can't come up with a tight and tidy word for something right now, it might not be worth labeling at all, and … *hey while we are at it, diagramming it actually doesn't sound like much fun either … harumph, why try?*

When we are early in the process, I like to encourage people to choose labels to *get by* with. There is a relief in calling something by a word that you know you can and will change later on. This sets you up to actually go back and refine the labels when you know more about your audience and what you intend to communicate to them with your diagram.

When Modeling, Use Labels to *Get Through*

In the modeling stage of diagramming, we are focused on how our language might support our efforts arranging the content to make sense to our intended audience. At this point, you ideally understand a lot more about your subject matter and what you are diagramming, but you are still doing research with your audience as to the proper modeling of the diagram to make sense to them.

When we are in the middle, we can start to put pressure on our labels to make sense to other people. You will likely (if you are researching your audience) have lots of opportunities to learn about what words and phrases do and do not make sense to your audience.

As you move through this research-heavy stage of the diagramming process, you'll want to refine your labels to remove anything from them that seems to be in the way of reaching your audience. I like to think about these as labels to *get through* with because they are words you are confident will make sense to those you are trying to reach, but the labels can still be messy or clunky or inconsistent at this point, as long as they are pointing in the direction of getting through to your intended audience.

When Delivering, Use Labels to *Get Results*

It is not until this final delivery stage of diagramming that you lean fully on the labels and make sure they are getting the results you are after for the diagram you are making.

At this point in the process, your labels should do two things:

1. Speak for themselves
2. Match your intention

If either of these isn't the case yet, you still have work ahead. The only way to achieve both of these is to have a member of your audience present your diagram back to you and see how they did with getting the message you intended.

- Did they have to ask for clarification on something?
- Did a word or phrase throw them off or give them pause?
- Did any of the labels used feel confusing to them?

The only way to know is to ask. And labels are often the very last adjustments made.

Step 8: Add a Key

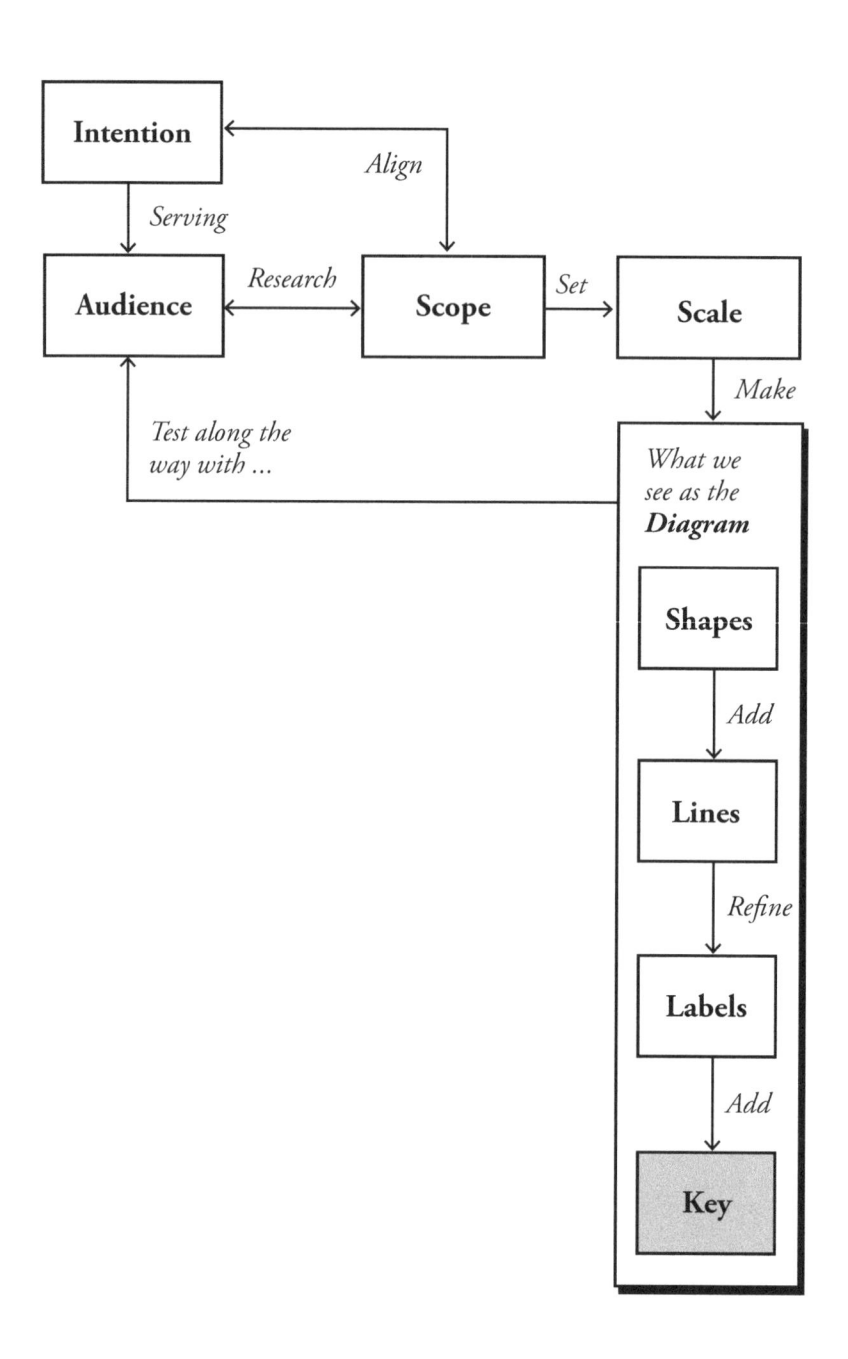

```
Intention ←──── Align ────┐
    │                      │
  Serving                  │
    ↓         Research     │      Set
Audience ←──────────────→ Scope ──────→ Scale
    ↑                                     │
    │                                    Make
    │                                     ↓
    │  Test along the         ┌─────────────────────┐
    └──  way with ...  ───────│ What we             │
                              │ see as the          │
                              │ *Diagram*           │
                              │                     │
                              │      Shapes         │
                              │        │            │
                              │       Add           │
                              │        ↓            │
                              │      Lines          │
                              │        │            │
                              │      Refine         │
                              │        ↓            │
                              │      Labels         │
                              │        │            │
                              │       Add           │
                              │        ↓            │
                              │       Key           │
                              └─────────────────────┘
```

The final step of true finesse of any diagram is the addition of the key. Now, here is where people trip up: *Do you always need a key?*

The answer is yes *but* with a major caveat. You don't always need a little box labeled "Key" in the corner that describes all the visual elements in agonizing detail.

You do, however, need to be assured that every visual element is clear in its intention and meaning. When we are in this final step, we are adding whatever clarity is needed for users to understand the decisions the maker made while construcing the diagram.

Up until this point, we have spent a lot of time thinking about the content of the diagram and how to find the right arrangements of shapes and lines to convey the relationships and context of whatever we are diagramming. Adding the key is the moment at the end when we stand back, skew our vision a bit, step again into our users' shoes, and see what is perhaps not as clear as it could be.

The addition of a box called a key to explain what we mean is an essential pattern in making diagrams, for sure.

But I want to introduce something perhaps controversial that I see all the time: People rely on the key to explain the wrong things.

Here are the very wrong things I see the key trying to do when the diagram itself is actually the one underperforming:

- Explaining overly complexified color-coding and/or iconography
- Defining poorly labeled objects or relationships
- Introducing extraneous information

When we add an element called a *key*, we are trying to do the audience a service by providing them with the information that is key to understanding the diagram. Ironically, for everything our audience has to reference in a key, we are increasing cognitive load and can expect a potential loss of understanding as a result.

To ensure we are using our key wisely, let's explore each of the three common patterns by which cognitive load is added by the key.

Explaining Overly Complexified Color-Coding or Iconography

Sometimes when we are making a diagram, we can get lost in the nuance of the subject we are asking the audience to navigate. In these moments, we can create intricate visual referencing systems that allow us to **encode** loads of information into a single diagram.

Remember my student with the five layers of horizontal hierarchy? The key was trying so hard to make it all clear, but alas it made me dizzy trying to parse what was being communicated.

Each shape or line in our diagram has a fill color, outline stroke, label, and space for other visual indicators. All of these *could* be used to encode a different data point or signal to the audience about that object and how it should be understood or related. Using all these tactics and relying on the audience to untangle what you mean in the overlaps is often lazy diagramming. In order to avoid this, we have to intentionally choose when to add these layers of encoded information into our diagrams. And for each, we have to be clear about how much we rely on a key for helping someone who is stuck.

If you worry your audience might be getting stuck on your diagram due to too much cognitive load, ask yourself the following three questions:

- Have you lost your intention?

- Is this actually *many* diagrams trying to fit into one?

- Are you not quite sure yet what information your audience needs?

People with heavy keys that are more like decoder rings often need to step back and make some tough decisions about whom they are serving and what they intend.

KEY
To properly read this diagram, walk to the southward corner of the room and squint towards the spot where the sun last set in the west.
Also red means maybe and purple means no, and the icons are there because I thought they jazzed up the place.

Defining Poorly Labeled Objects or Relationships

Something I see all the time, especially in student work, is the use of the key to label things because the labels don't fit easily or well into the diagram itself.

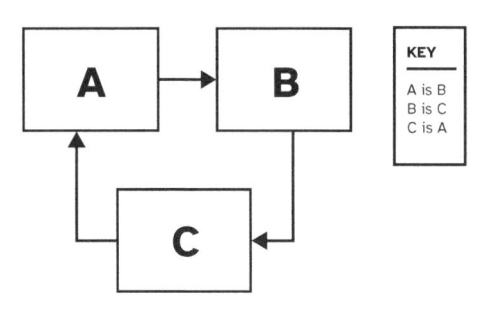

We might, for example, label the elements A,B,C in the diagram and ask that the audience look at the key to see what each of those letters maps to in the diagram's context. When we do this, we are asking the audience to do a lot of work.

They have to remember the arrangement of A,B,C while glancing down at the key to **decode** what it means. Then as they move on in the diagram, they have to remember everything they have decoded.

If you ever have someone write labels on your diagram to avoid looking back at the key, you very obviously have this problem.

This ailment is common in acronym-heavy environments. While depending on the familiarity of the audience with an acronym can be an effective solution for shortening labels, we have to be quite careful about how we define familiarity and try to understand the limits we introduce by relying on our audience to mentally unfurl the acronym.

To avoid leaning on the key when labels would just be better, we have to make space for clearly labeled shapes and lines.

Instead of overloading the key, make room to label *absolutely everything*, then scale it back to what is needed to be understood.

This should leave a clearly labeled diagram and a bonus of plenty of blank space that serves as breathing room for your audience.

Introducing Extraneous Information

The last pattern we will cover regarding overtaxing the key is adding extraneous information to your diagram. I see this all the time, and most often it is a symbol of diagrammatic excitement.

During the diagrammatic process, we are collecting tidbits along the way. We have to learn so much more than just what we are diagramming in order to do it well. So, here is what can happen: We start to convince ourselves that *everyone* will want to get into the nitty-gritty with us, to understand every little rabbit hole and trail of data we followed to arrive at our conclusion.

I'm going to give it to you as straight as I can: No one wants to go down those rabbit holes or inspect those data trails. Let me be clearer: Even when your diagram's intention is to show people how many data trails and rabbit holes you went down or that they will have to travel down with you, even then, no one wants to see all that.

There is a concept in sociolinguistics known as **linguistic insecurity**.[13] It is the fear that stems from feeling like our language or understanding of language is not in line with our current context. You have had this feeling if you've ever thought someone was speaking above your grade level. Many of us have experienced this feeling when navigating foreign countries with a different language than our own.

In my experience, diagrams can elicit a similar kind of insecurity. Diagrams can very quickly turn from a clear and useful object of discourse allowing you to get further with an audience into a brick wall that elicits **diagrammatic insecurity** in your audience, telling them that the diagram is not *for them*.

To avoid this, we have to be sure that every takeaway we have for this diagram is actually a needed one, or else we can end up with a bunch of takeaways missing the mark from sheer overwhelm.

---

[13] One of the earliest uses of the term *linguistic insecurity* appeared in William Labov, *The Social Stratification of English in New York City* (Washington, DC: Center for Applied Linguistics, 1966; 3rd printing, 1982), 52.

If you ever find yourself thinking about how you'll give the tour of the diagram rather than let people engage with it on their own, you likely are suffering from this misfortune.

Start to strip things back to the basics and ask yourself again what intention you have for the diagram's audience.

- How much do they **need to know?**
- How much do they **want to know?**
- How much do they **have time for?**

> **What Belongs in the Key?**
>
> The following three elements are consistently needed in the key. Interestingly, these are also *often* not represented.
>
> - **Explanation of the visual vocabulary in the diagram.**
>   The key should perform the basic function of defining the visual vocabulary choices you made in making the diagram. No one should have to ask why some objects are pink and the others are blue or why some lines are dotted while others are solid.
>
> - **Citations for datasets and manipulative methods used.**
>   The key is the place to include more information as to the origin of the information presented, especially if there was a combination of sources or research methods used. It should be clear where the information for this diagram came from and in what ways it was collected or analyzed.
>
> - **Instructional content built around intention.**
>   The key *can be* a great place to include more information about your intention with the diagram. It is also a place where you can do some editorializing about how you intend for people to read the diagram or what you hope they get out of it. No one should have to ask you why you made this diagram or what they are supposed to do with it. That much should be clear.

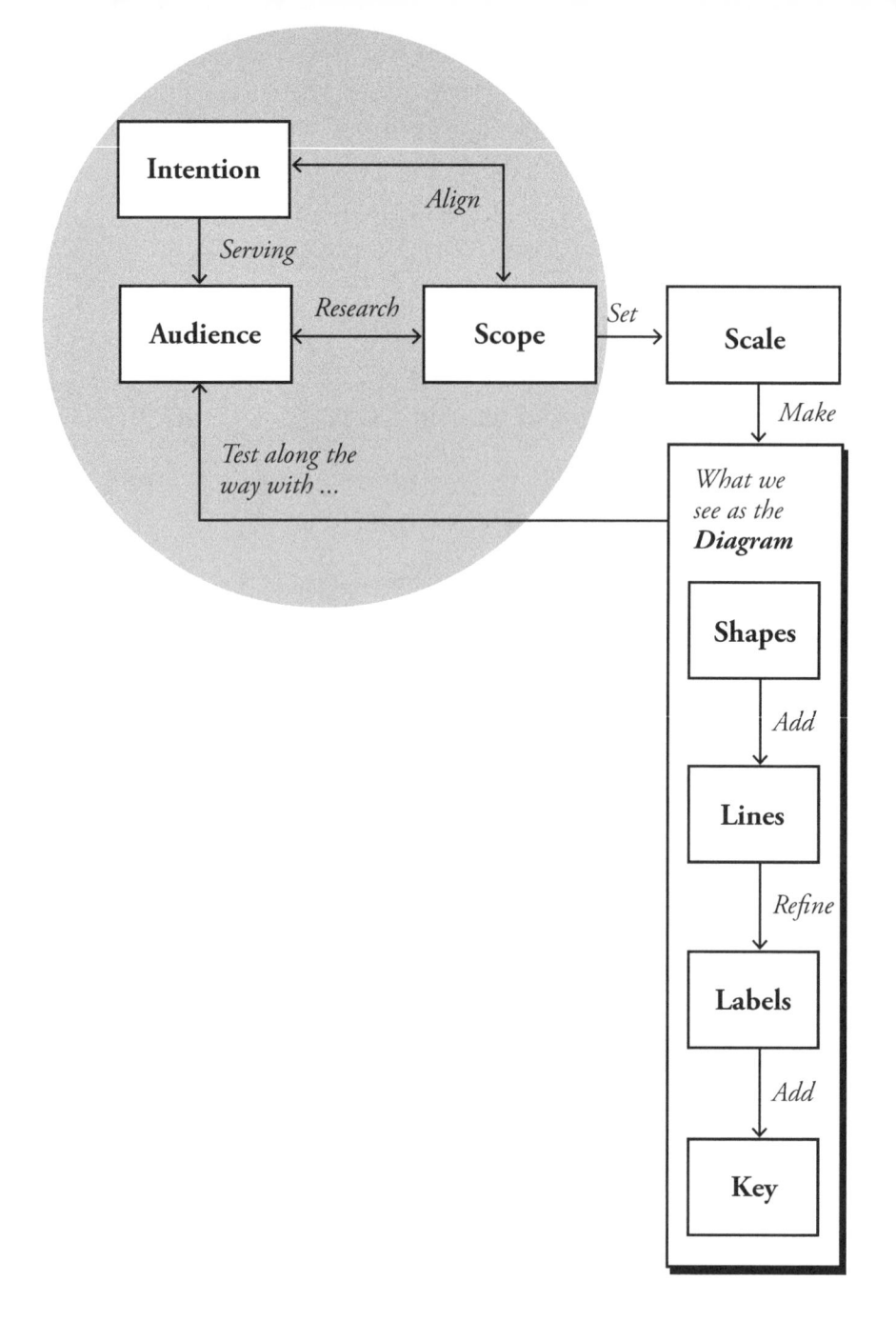

```
Intention
   │ Serving        ↑ Align
   ↓                │
Audience ←Research→ Scope  —Set→  Scale
   ↑                                │
   │ Test along the                 │ Make
   │ way with ...                   ↓
                              What we
                              see as the
                              **Diagram**

                              Shapes
                                │ Add
                                ↓
                              Lines
                                │ Refine
                                ↓
                              Labels
                                │ Add
                                ↓
                               Key
```

Are we *there* yet?

Given that we just moved through this process in a happy linear path, I think it's a good time to talk about loops again.

This time, it's the mechanical loops built into the visual work to check back in with the in-visual work. I also think it's a good time to revisit our two simple criteria for knowing if we have arrived at Diagram Town.

1. Is it a visual representation? *(That's the easy one!)*
2. Does it help someone*?

If you answered yes to both questions but all you have is a coffee-stained napkin with scribbled shapes and lines that helped you explain a concept to your kiddo at breakfast, welcome to Diagram Town. Sometimes it doesn't take much to get there. Other times it's a longer journey we have to plan in advance and pack for. Either way, the goal is the same: Help someone* who is stuck.

*Reminder: You are someone

So, if it *only* helped you, but that's all you intended it to do,

Welcome to Diagram Town

Chapter 1: **Purpose** | 143

3

Craft

In chapters 1 and 2, we talked about the purpose and process of diagramming, and I introduced the series of decisions that we make on the way to Diagram Town. In this chapter, we learn why diagrammatic craft matters and how the contextual nature of diagramming keeps us from having too many tricks that "always work."

To teach you about making diagrams that work in your own context, I will introduce nine principles that I believe determine if a diagram is good.

In each principle, I provide light historical context about what is *known* vs. *unknown* and what is *agreed to* vs. *hotly disputed* about the far-reaching patchwork quilt of a skill set that is diagramming.

If I made only one diagram a week for the past 20 years learning, practicing, and teaching information architecture, then I have made more than 1,000 diagrams in my lifetime, so far. *Heck, I made over 100 diagrams for this book you are reading.*

More than just making diagrams myself, I have had the opportunity to mentor and teach other people about information architecture. Many of these folks end up with a diagrammatic problem to solve as part of the information architecture insight or advice that they seek from me.

I have become quite skilled in looking at a diagram and finding ways it might be improved or clarified from a craft perspective. Now, does this mean that my own diagrams are without flaws?

Absolutely not. In fact, I assure you I have already at this point decided all the diagrams in this book could be improved in one way or another.

This constant search to make *more* sense of the things we make is a journey that is fraught with obstacles. One of the biggest obstacles is a total lack of holistic best practice guidance in the world of diagrams and diagramming.

Where do you go to ask questions about the craft of diagramming? Or to learn the basics about diagramming as a craft and practice? Furthermore, when was the class in which we all sat down and received instruction in this important, human skill?

I mean ... diagrams were all around us that whole time. In every textbook, every lesson plan, every handout, every research report. Diagrams, diagrams, diagrams.

Each of us has a unique patchwork of experience in many, all, or none of these fields. But as unique as our various quilts may be, we all have one critical skill in common.

Diagramming. I forgot the drumroll. My apologies.

Diagramming, like language, is a skill we can all draw from regardless of our walk of life. But because of the wide and deep usefulness of diagrams, not one but several fields of practice and study have developed their own best practices when it comes to diagrams and diagramming.

Over the last two decades, I have diagrammed my way through art school, agency life, corporate technology consulting, teaching graduate school, startups, nonprofits, and billion-dollar businesses.

Each required its own approach to diagramming.

In cooking, there is a concept called *mise en place*. It's French and it means *put in place*. It's the act of gathering and positioning your materials before you dive into cooking.

I feel as if my journey up to this point has been the ideal *mise en place* for me to write this book and specifically this chapter on craft. Let's just say that I made a lot of mistakes so you don't have to.

Here are some of the fields I dipped into while learning to diagram:

- **Cartography:** The study of maps and mapmaking
- **Cognitive science:** The study of how humans think, organize, and learn
- **Education:** The study of how people learn
- **Graphic design:** The art and style of visual communication
- **Information architecture:** The act of deciding which order the pieces of a whole should be arranged in order to communicate the meaning that is intended to users
- **Information design:** The study of how to present data effectively to reach an intention
- **Linguistics:** The study of language and its structure
- **Semiotics:** The study of signs and symbols
- **Typography:** The art and discipline of arranging type
- **Visual explanation:** The study of using graphic props to foster understanding

What Makes a
Diagram Good?

When I started writing about this very squishy and far-reaching topic, I promised myself that I would never leave you with an "it depends" answer ... even if the going got hard.

Well, here we are in the ambigui-muck grappling with the toughest of toughies. What makes this question about goodness tough is the expectation that there is one single list of rules that might always apply to any diagram. As a firm believer in progress over perfection, I do not believe such a list should or could exist.

But lists are useful. Lists keep people from suffering from what they believe is unique pain but in reality is a universal diagrammatic struggle.

And the struggle is *real*. Not much *always* works.

Instead of false promises of things that *always work*, this chapter is merely the tidy ramblings of someone just back from an epic trek of more than 1,000 diagrams.

Think of it like a checklist of things I have learned, trip-ups I can warn you to plan for, and pitfalls I can help you to avoid. I have returned from my trek with nine elemental principles of diagrammatic goodness, under three general themes.

Good Diagrams Are ...

Accessible

1. Easy to Follow — 153

2. Neat and tidy — 159

3. Contrast Aware — 169

Content Driven

4. Clear in tone and timescale — 175

5. Manipulated appropriately — 177

6. Appropriately dense — 179

Visually Supported

7. Typographically sound — 187

8. Effectively encoded — 199

9. Thoughtfully embellished — 202

Good Diagrams Are
Accessible

Accessibility is the access and abilities that you provide to your intended audience. It is also a commitment to understanding and designing for those with potentially different abilities than our own.

Before we get into the three principles that make up this lesson, I want to acknowledge that diagrams are *inherently* difficult to make accessible to some people with visual impairment. There are also neurodivergent folks for whom some forms of visual explanations are not ideal modes of communication or learning.

As someone deeply committed to serving those who have differences that are underrepresented, I want to encourage you as a student of diagramming to think deeply about whom you prioritize as users of your work. I ask you also to consider alternatives to make the information accessible even if the diagram *can't* be.

- **Alternative text:** When the spatial organization part of the diagram is helpful to a user without access to the visual part of the diagram, write short alternative text describing the diagram including any text the diagram contains.

- **Alternative content:** When the message of the diagram would be better reached by a certain audience if presenting the content another way, or if describing it visually doesn't add to the experience for some users, create another way to communicate that message.

If you truly feel your diagram can't serve a specific audience that it would otherwise help, I highly encourage you to make alternative content for them to get the same information in another way. Members of your audience might benefit from a wide range of alternative content types, such as large print, audio, or Braille labels.

And if you are having trouble deciding whether you need alternative text or alternative content, here is a diagram.

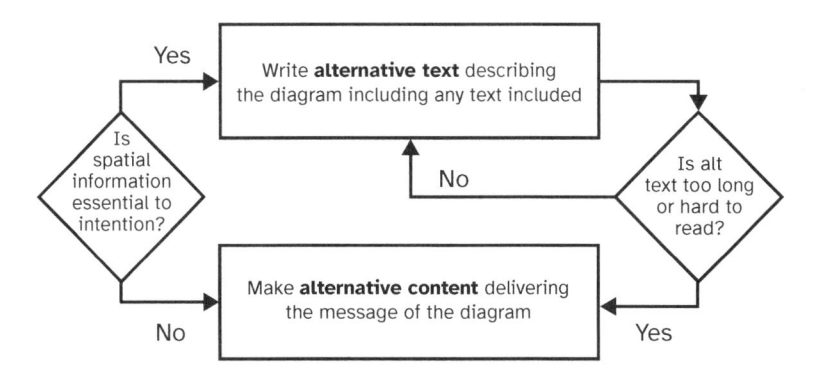

```
                     ┌──────────────────────────────┐
              Yes    │  Write alternative text       │
         ┌──────────▶│  describing the diagram       │──────┐
         │           │  including any text included  │      │
         │           └──────────────────────────────┘      │
    ┌────────┐                      ▲                  ┌────────┐
    │   Is   │                      │                  │ Is alt │
    │ spatial│                      No                 │text too│
    │  info  │                      │                  │long or │
    │essential│                     │                  │hard to │
    │   to   │                      │                  │ read?  │
    │intention?│                    │                  └────────┘
    └────────┘           ┌──────────────────────────┐      │
         │               │ Make alternative content │      │
         │   No          │ delivering the message   │◀─────┘
         └──────────────▶│ of the diagram           │   Yes
                         └──────────────────────────┘
```

When deciding whether you are writing alternative text to describe the image or providing alternative content to deliver the same message, ask yourself whether the audience needs the spatial information that the diagram provides. In other words, does it matter how the elements are arranged visually?

If spatial information *does* matter to your intention, describe the visual part of the diagram in alternative text. But also consider the length of the alternative text needed when describing a diagram. The longer the description, the greater challenge to understanding, creating a secondary reason to instead provide alternative content.

For example, instead of writing a paragraph describing the flow diagram spatially in this section, I wrote the previous two paragraphs as alternative content. I did this because the spatial information is not at all essential to the intention; in fact, it might be distracting if the diagram part is not available.

Providing alternative content is often a kinder gesture than any lengthy alternative text describing a diagram could ever be.

Also don't be surprised when the alternative serves other audiences and abilities that you didn't know you weren't serving well enough or could have better served.

When you get to chapter 4, you will find a dense flow diagram meant to help you identify the right diagrammatic recipe to start from. While thinking through how to handle the alternative text for this diagram, I ended up writing the page that follows it.

In my opinion, the diagram without that text was weaker. I wrote content to make the diagram accessible to users with visual or processing disabilities but ended up with content that made the diagram clearer to all who might encounter it.

When it comes to ensuring that your diagram is rendered accessibly, there are three main challenges in addition to how you approach alternative text or content. I believe these are shared across a variety of people and abilities, including your intended audience.

WARNING: For each of the following principles, the bold words must be defined *uniquely* based on your intended audience's needs.

1. Good diagrams are **easy to follow**.
2. Good diagrams are **neat and tidy**.
3. Good diagrams are **contrast aware**.

#1 Easy to Follow

This bit of wisdom is incredibly simple. Or *cloyingly obvious*, if we aren't being kind today. Good diagrams must (ahead of all other goals) be easy to follow.

As I write these words, dear reader, I sense the eye rolls of the masses. *Of course diagrams have to be easy to follow, duh Abby.*

I know. So why, then, this far along in a book about diagramming, when we are *just* getting into the meat of the craft of diagramming, do I bring up this incredibly obvious morsel from Captain Obvious's latest thought piece titled "Things you already knew and then paid someone to tell you." Why also am I making *such* a big show of calling your attention to how obvious this lesson is rather than just getting into it?

Because too many diagrams are hard to follow for the same freaking reasons. And I'm sick of it. I'm sick of people having to give me a tour of their diagram or move my eyeballs to the right starting place with pointing fingers or mouses or lasers (yes, lasers!). I am sick of being told that I am reading it backwards … or any number of other incredibly frustrating, not user-centered things to hear when struggling with diagrams made by other people.

Diagrams should not need instruction manuals. Diagrams should not need tour guides. Diagrams should be easy to follow.

One tactic to make a diagram easy to follow is to provide an obvious **starting place** or clear visual cues to draw attention to it.

Imagine you are mid-hike and you stop at a trail map to see what's ahead. As you scan the map, you are looking for signals of the right starting place.

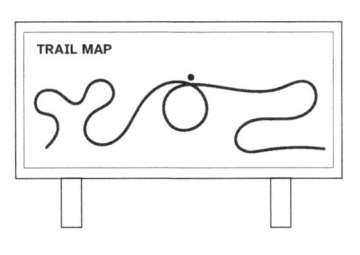

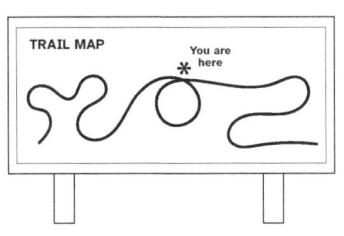

Chapter 3: **Craft** | 153

154 | STUCK? Diagrams Help.

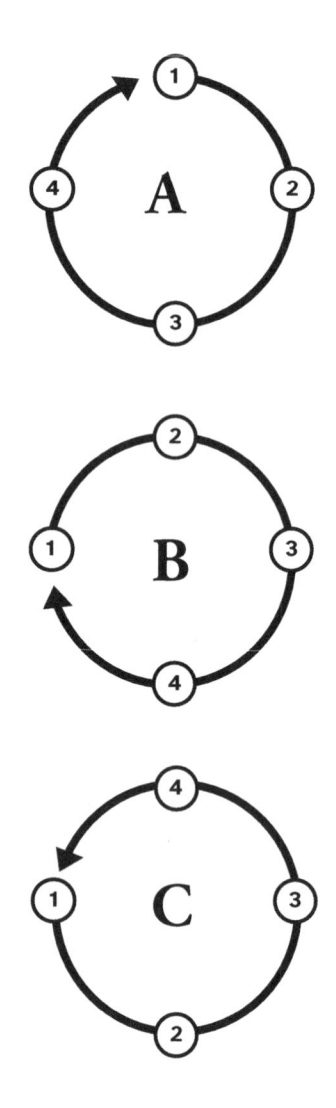

If this starting place is obvious through visual treatment, the map will be easy to follow. This is why you tend to see over-scaled visual markers on maps, because the starting place is less easy to find.

If the marker is not obvious, the map will be harder to follow, as is the case with this first map, where the starting place is marked on the map, but without the large contrasting visual element and label drawing our attention in the second map, it will take a bit more effort to see.

A second tactic when making a diagram easy to follow is to encourage a strong **reading order**, also known as reading direction, especially one in line with a common cultural or contextual pattern.

When it comes to understanding your audience, consider their defaults in terms of reading order. We can use their defaults when making diagrams to help us reach our intention.

All three of the diagrams seen here are circular and in a linear, time-based order.

- Diagrams A and B were both designed to be read clockwise and therefore have a stronger reading order, because they match how people expect to read a circular diagram (since clocks are a common object for most).

- Diagram A is clearer because its starting place is more obvious.

- Diagram C was designed to be read counter-clockwise and has a weaker reading order as a result. Whether you read right to left or left to right, we all agree on clockwise being left to right.

If you ever feel like you need to add additional directional cues, consider whether you're forcing a reading order that is harder to follow. If you are designing a hiking map, you don't get to pick your starting place. But in many diagrammatic instances, we do get to decide where to start our diagram.

Sometimes when I look at diagrams that feel hard to follow, I notice that the starting place or reading order is determined by the strong and scientific forces of *where-I-made-it-fit*. This is often just the first draft of the diagram, fighting to get another chance. Don't take that as a sign this is the only way to arrange it. It for sure is not.

Starting a diagram on the left and flowing to the right is likely to make it more obvious to an audience who reads from left to right. Starting a diagram at the top and flowing to the bottom is likely to make it more obvious to an audience that reads from top to bottom.

It might sound simple, but, as someone who has made a lot of diagrams, I am surprised how often I have to remind myself about these kinds of important details of craft when I'm in the moment.

I must be especially careful to remember details about the audience's context and how those details impact decisions that might feel simple, like reading order.

For example, I was recently talking with someone about a diagram that they found on a blog post. It was a career progression diagram, and at the top was the start of a career, and at the bottom was the end of a career.

This seemed odd to us both at first, because we think of a career as a ladder on which each rung gets you higher. But in talking about it, we wondered if the author chose a top-to-bottom reading order to better match the scrolling behavior of the blog it lived on.

We had expected a bottom-up arrangement of this timeline when looking at it with a fixed viewport. If the blog had used that reading order for the diagram, which is the opposite of a blog's scrolling viewport, the reader would have to read the content in reverse.

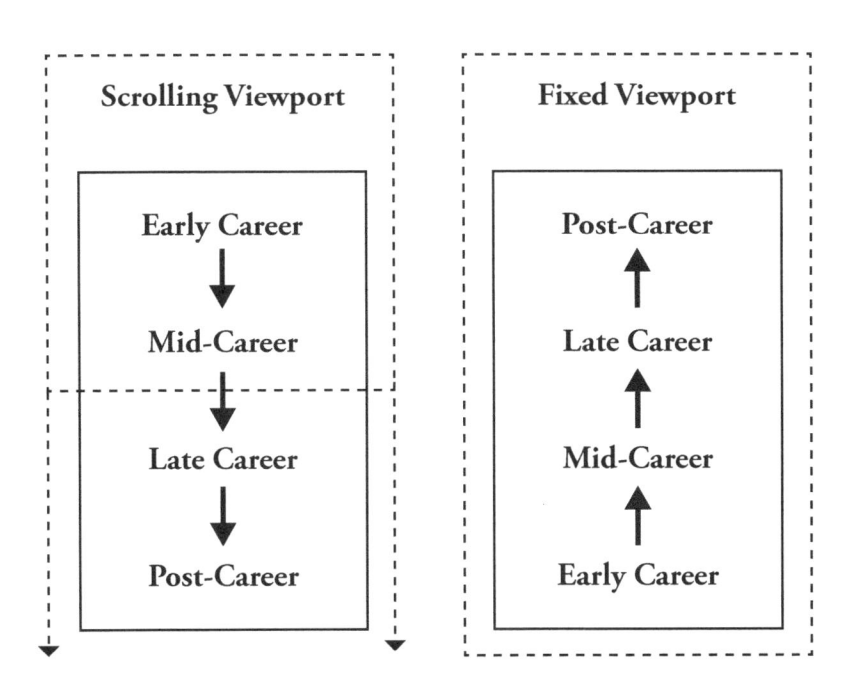

```
┌─────────────────────────┐   ┌─────────────────────────┐
│   Scrolling Viewport    │   │     Fixed Viewport      │
│  ┌───────────────────┐  │   │  ┌───────────────────┐  │
│  │   Early Career    │  │   │  │   Post-Career     │  │
│  │        ↓          │  │   │  │        ↑          │  │
│  │   Mid-Career      │  │   │  │   Late Career     │  │
│  ├───────────────────┤   │   │        ↑          │  │
│  │        ↓          │  │   │  │   Mid-Career      │  │
│  │   Late Career     │  │   │  │        ↑          │  │
│  │        ↓          │  │   │  │   Early Career    │  │
│  │   Post-Career     │  │   │  └───────────────────┘  │
│  └───────────────────┘  │   └─────────────────────────┘
└─────────────────────────┘
```

Now feels like another perfect time to remind you that I expect you to push or decide against what I teach you about diagramming.

Please break my rules (and then email me about it!).

I expect some diagrammatic decisions to be made in the face of choosing an obvious starting place or providing a strong reading order. I can imagine diagrammatic opportunities where each of these might be interesting to explore to get the reader to search or hunt more.

Now that you have read my guidance, perhaps when you do choose to start in a non-obvious place or provide a less strong reading order, you at least understand what you are doing, why you are choosing to do it, and what the balance of rewards and consequences are for that choice. Ultimately, you choose how you make your diagram.

I also (not so secretly since I am writing it here) hope that when you see other people's diagrams that are suffering from these painfully common and easy-to-fix ailments, you pass them the gift of seeing and labeling the problem.

Making diagrams obvious for people other than ourselves is incredibly hard. Be a bud and tell your diagrammatic peer that their diagram, *while valuable AF*, would benefit from a more obvious starting place or a stronger reading order.

Prepare for the thank-you notes, friends. This kind of feedback *makes* diagrams (and, fair warning, sometimes first breaks the maker momentarily).

#2 Neat and Tidy

Not only is this bit of advice also annoyingly simple, but, as we saw in chapter 2 when we introduced the concept of cognitive load, it is also backed by science. Dang.

Keeping your diagrams neat and tidy doesn't just benefit folks like me, your anal-retentive diagrammatic author-teacher-friend. Making sure that our diagrams are neat and tidy is one of the surest ways we can limit the cognitive load we place on our audience when looking at our diagrams.

> You: Wait. What? That's a strong statement, Abby.
>
> Me: Yep, hear me out.

Have you ever opened the instructions for putting something together and felt totally overwhelmed just looking at the pictures? Maybe you even put off assembly for a while until you actually cooled down. In many such cases, the designer of those instructions off-loaded too much cognitive load onto you, the audience.

Many of us have had times when we had to get through someone else's messy diagram to find the meaning within it because they hadn't done that part for us. Here's looking at you, *almost every assembly-required product I've ever bought.*

And it's important to note that as the diagrammer, you can't always choose your way out of all cognitive load. Some subject matters come with a higher load than others. And it's definitely not just visual messiness that causes cognitive load to be high.

I can assure you that there are diagrams in which the content, no matter how tidy, will always elicit a ton of cognitive load to consume.

For example, take the work of Erin Malone, an information architect who worked for the Anti-Defamation League to diagram the origins and social structures surrounding online hate speech.

Given this kind of emotionally charged subject matter, Erin could not have eliminated the weight of the subject matter from the cognitive load required of her audience, but she was able to identify ways to make the diagrams neat and tidy so as to not add any extra weight to an already packed docket.

There are two examples shown here from Erin's work.

First is the messy diagram made just for her; next is the tidied and simplified diagram meant for a wider audience. Her finished diagram is not printed to a readable scale here but is available at the link below.[14]

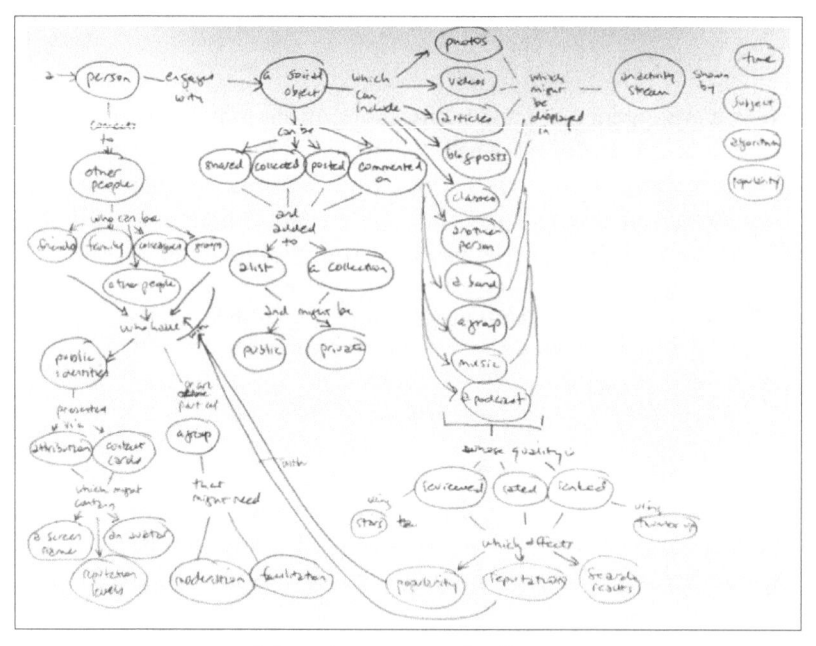

Messy diagram just for Erin

---

[14] For more information on this project, see https://www.adl.org/online-hate-ecosystem-primer. These figures are reprinted here by permission of the Anti-Defamation League.

Relationships in the Cyber Hate
Ecosystem Between the Main Actors

ADL. CENTER FOR TECHNOLOGY & SOCIETY

Before - not aligned to grid

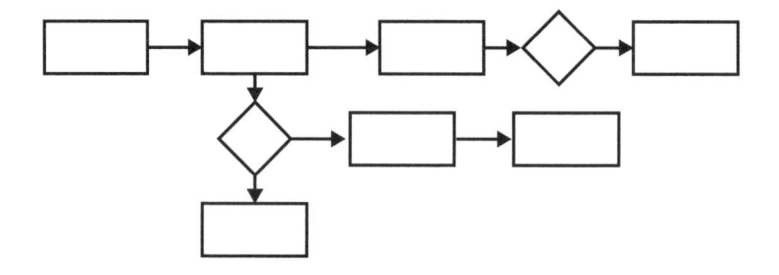

After - aligned to grid

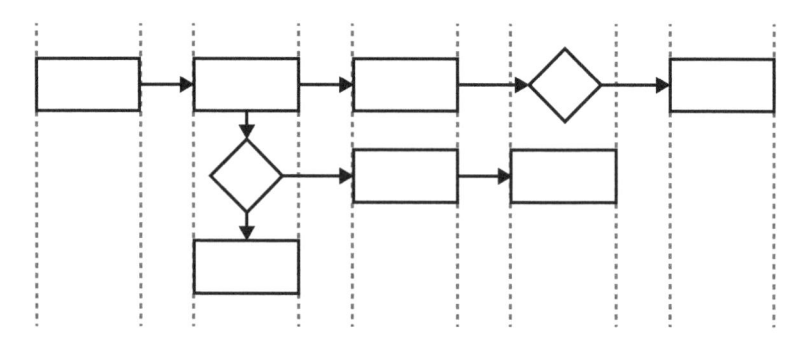

When we encounter diagrams that are neat and tidy, we get to skip one layer of the anxiety of other people's diagrams. It's an immediate lessening of the cognitive load.

While I can't necessarily help you make the subject matter you are diagramming less complex or less demanding, I can urge you to do everything in your diagrammatic power to reduce the cognitive load your diagram requires by eliminating as many distractions of clutter, sloppiness, and detritus as possible.

One way to make things neat and tidy is to use a **grid** when defining the spacing of our diagrams. With a grid of guidelines for ourselves, we can use alignment to lessen our audience's cognitive load.

It continues to amaze me how much grids help and how many people have yet to receive the gift of this valuable but basic graphic design lesson.

What Do I Use a Grid to Align?

In addition to providing visual order to the flow of diagrams, a grid can (and should) be used to determine:

- **Alignment** of shapes, lines, and labels
- **Spacing** between shapes, lines, and labels
- **Width** of shapes, lines, and labels
- **Placement** of headlines, key, and marginalia

164 | STUCK? Diagrams Help.

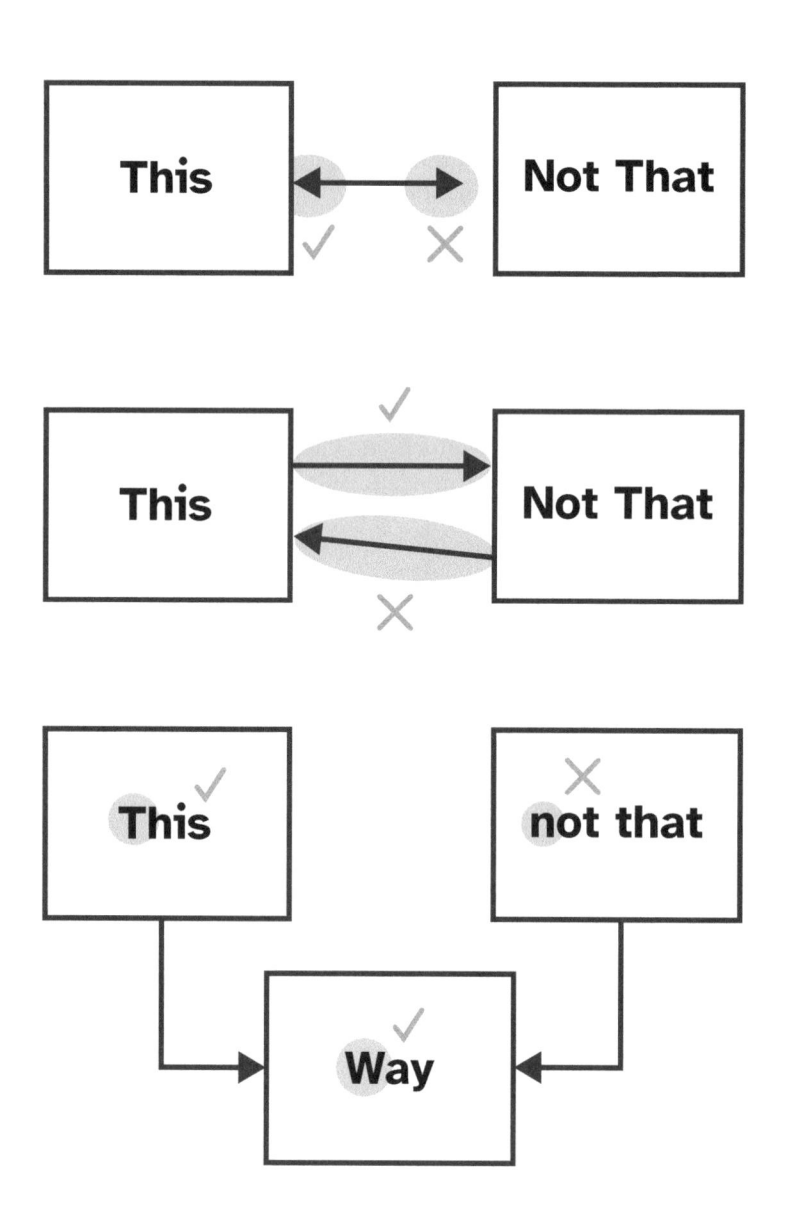

Once you have a grid in good use, there are three issues of neat-and-tidiness to add to your diagrammatic preflight checklist:

- Ensure lines touch shapes they are meant to connect.
- Straighten lines and/or alignment.
- Implement consistent casing for labels.

What About When Lines Have to Cross?

… dun dun DUN!

If you spend some time digging into the how-to guides for many diagramming tools, you will inevitably end up running into guidance about how to deal with crossing lines. Most state clearly that if you cross your lines and don't make a visual choice so that the relationships are clear to viewers, then things could get diagrammatically complicated.

Through a broad survey of these tools and that guidance, there are two solutions that propose to deal with **line-crossing**:

- **Bumps**, in which you make a shape out of the intersection
- **Spaces**, in which you break a line to give space to another

Some of these diagramming tools even give you options to easily make bumps and spaces along with the ability to set how rounded or squared off your bumps should be. The magic of software!

The problem I fear with these innocent solutions is that they are often used to solve the wrong problem.

In many diagrams I have made, or reviewed, I have noticed that if we just spend a bit more time moving things around, we can often avoid the lines having to cross at all.

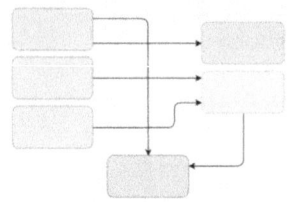

Before line jumps – a confusing diagram.

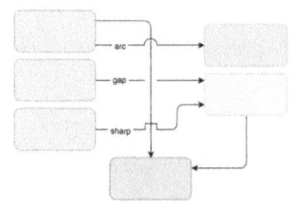

After line jumps – much easier to 'read'!

I want to show you an example from a tool called draw.io.[15] In a help article, they compare a diagram made without line jumps to one made with line jumps.

This team is obviously trying their best to show the power of the software that they provide.

And there are times when the lines *will* have to cross, in which case, the three kinds of bumps they offer are generously thoughtful to our graphic needs.

This example, however, is in my humble opinion not a good case for showcasing this feature because with less than one minute of effort, I was able to see an alternative way to place the lines that maintained all the relationships being expressed.

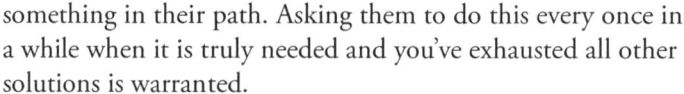

When we cross our lines, we have to ask our users to do a little hop over something in their path. Asking them to do this every once in a while when it is truly needed and you've exhausted all other solutions is warranted.

But asking users to jump over things in their path over and over because you didn't take the time to move things around until they were more settled is placing cognitive load onto your users unnecessarily.

And should you really go overboard on obfuscating their path with too many of these little hops, you should not be surprised

---

[15] Kymberly Fergusson, "draw.io Now Supports Line Jumps," draw.io, September 7, 2017, https://drawio-app.com/draw-io-now-supports-line-jumps/.

when you pay dearly for that decision in loss of understanding, engagement, and/or recall of your diagram from those you intended to serve with it.

I will admit that moving the shapes and lines around until they feel *just right* is a wild and unpredictable adventure into minutiae that many lack the patience for. At times, it can feel like the shapes are set in concrete, unable to logically occupy any other arrangement than the one we are clinging to that isn't *quite* working but is currently housing our madness.

We can start to believe that these intricate laces we have tatted between the shapes hold the true power of understanding the complexity within the thing we are diagramming. If this feeling ever finds you, beware.

Diagrams love to trick their makers into thinking they are as simple as they can be far before they actually are.

When the line-jumping tools try to tempt you away from trying again, try again, friend. Always hit *duplicate, save as,* etc. first, then do your worst, and don't be surprised when it becomes your best and you never go back to the original again.

- Swap everything dramatically to opposite sides.
- Flip the orientation from portrait to landscape.
- Make what had been linear wildly non-linear.
- Try out a visual metaphor you thought of in the shower.

Get your brain out of the structure you had made before, even for an hour, and it will do wonders for your own cognitive load. If you spend the extra time moving things around so your users have less path interruption, thereby reducing their cognitive load, it will do wonders for your intention to serve them.

More Contrast ↑

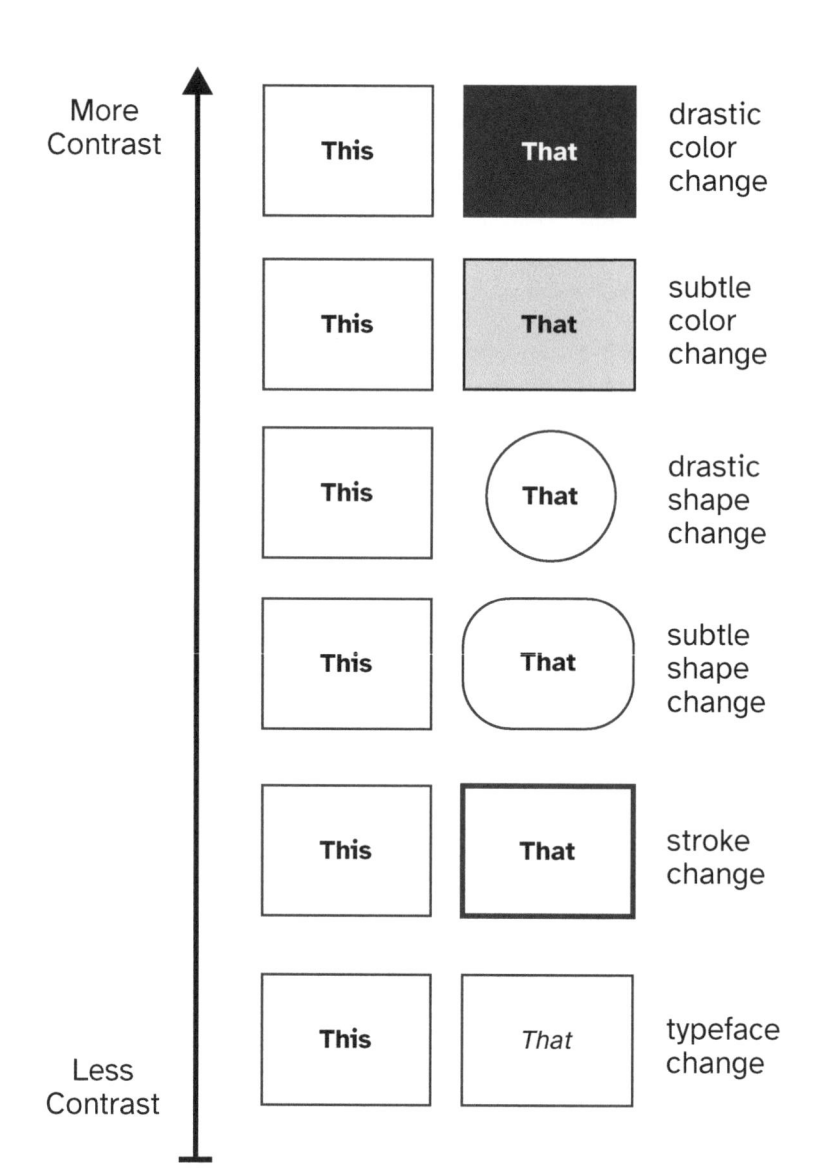

This	That	drastic color change
This	That	subtle color change
This	That	drastic shape change
This	That	subtle shape change
This	That	stroke change
This	*That*	typeface change

Less Contrast

#3 Contrast Aware

When diagramming, we often venture off into the world of varied type sizes and/or colors for our content. When we do this, we ask for a whole new set of challenges when it comes to rendering a diagram accessibly.

Size, color, and differences of typography can all be great differentiators. We can use the contrast of color, size, or typography to communicate some things easily. These differentiators can also add pizzazz to a diagram and give it more style or visual interest.

The most important thing to keep in mind when thinking about varying color, type scale, and type is contrast. **Contrast** is difference that can be perceived.

When we use colors or sizes that have differences that we (the makers) can perceive, we may not realize that to others that same contrast is perceived differently.

Good diagrams have people behind them who have worked to eliminate potential for the information to be lost should contrast not be perceived as designed.

- The option with the most contrast in this diagram is the one that uses a drastic color change.
- The one with the least contrast uses **bold** vs. *italic* type to differentiate.

I can promise you that some people looking at this book will see those two bottommost boxes as identical with no contrast at all.

If you *don't* see them as identical, this lesson in contrast is even more critical for you to pay attention to.

Your radar for contrast differences, especially in subtle design cues, might be very different from that of the audiences you diagram in service of.

There are two types of contrast to keep in mind:

- **Legibility:** Is the contrast between elements and their backgrounds high enough to be legible?

- **Comparability:** Is the contrast between elements and *other* elements high enough to effectively encode a difference of meaning?

Contrast often comes down to math, which means we have no excuse to muck it up. A contrast ratio between two colors can be measured, and defined levels of adherence are well researched and widely available.[16]

Be careful not to accidentally add contrast through inconsistency. Even though many people are not highly attuned to the subtle contrast of some design changes, other unintended contrasts such as inconsistent type styles or line weights seem to just jump out at many people.

In reviewing this book, Noah Iliinsky, an author who writes about information visualization, pointed me to two established principles that support paying attention to the unintended contrast that can be introduced by inconsistency.

---

[16] W3C, "Understanding Success Criterion 1.4.3: Contrast (Minimum)," https://www.w3.org/WAI/WCAG21/Understanding/contrast-minimum.html.

[17] "Readers ... expect any change in a pattern to mean something. ... When things stay the same, there is no new information; when something changes, there is—or should be—new information." Stephen M. Kosslyn, *Elements of Graph Design* (New York: Freeman, 1994), 26.

[18] "Entities that appear alike in some way, for example, in their style, location, size, orientation, color, and so on, will be grouped together in a viewer's mind. Entities that appear unalike will be separated." Patrick Moore and Chad Fitz, "Gestalt Theory and Instructional Design," *Journal of Technical Writing and Communication* 23, no. 2 (1993): 149.

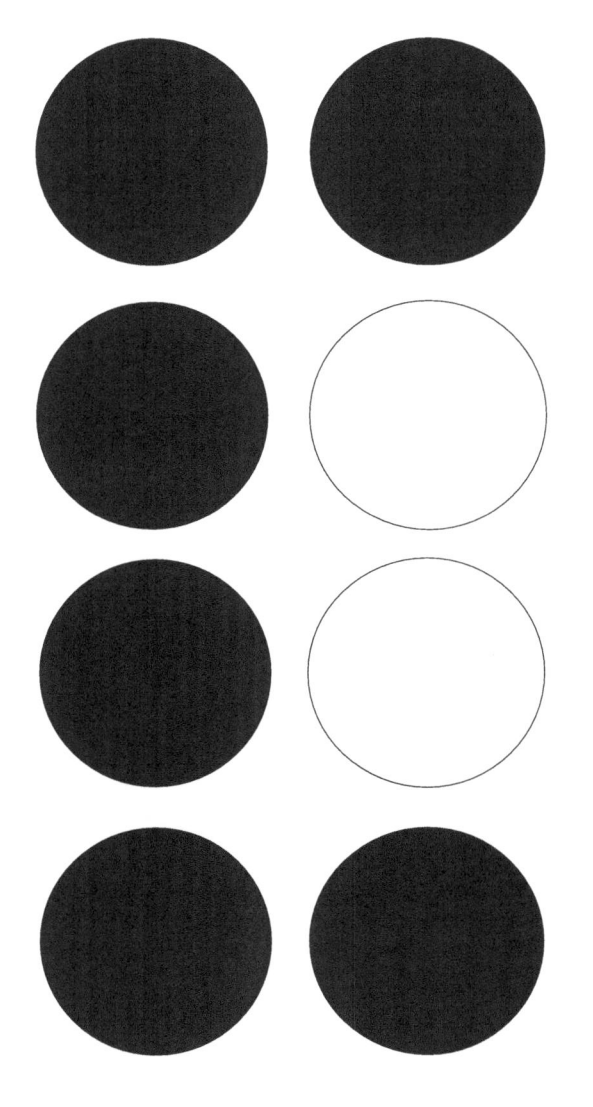

The first principle is from neuropsychology. It is called the **principle of informative change** and states that when something changes, people will want to interpret the new information introduced.[17]

The second principle is the **Gestalt principle of similarity**, which states that when things appear alike, people are more likely to group them together, and when things don't look alike, they can assume the difference means something.[18]

Are you trying to *not* group the circles here by color and struggling?

When we make visual decisions about how to style the elements of our diagram, we must first ensure that the contrast we intend is legible, but we must also ensure that no unintended contrast has been introduced.

When you are ready to get into the work, see my recommended resources for properly checking and understanding your contrast, color, and type scale accessibility, which are provided in the back of the book.

Chapter 3: **Craft** | 171

Questions to Ask Yourself

In closing this lesson on making diagrams *accessible*, here are some questions I hope you are asking yourself:

- For whom am I intending to make this diagram accessible?

- What decisions am I making that need to be thought through differently based on my audience's abilities?

- How much cognitive load does this subject matter require of the audience?

- How can I remove unnecessary cognitive load through the design decisions I make?

- What are my audience's unique and varied needs and abilities that I can pay attention to especially when it comes to the perception of contrast between colors, tones, and type sizes?

I hope you are leaving this section with a broader perspective on what it means to think about making diagrams *accessible*.

Accessible Diagram Checklist

- ☐ Create an alternative way to communicate the information if the diagram can't be accessible.

- ☐ Provide an obvious starting place or clear visual cues to draw attention to it.

- ☐ Encourage a strong reading order, especially one in line with a common cultural or contextual pattern.

- ☐ Ensure lines touch the shapes that they are meant to connect.

- ☐ Straighten lines and/or alignment.

- ☐ Implement consistent casing for labels.

- ☐ Reduce cognitive load by assessing the need for line-jumping or extraneous details.

- ☐ Eliminate places information might be lost should contrast not be perceived as intended by those with different visual abilities.

Good Diagrams Are
Content Driven

The second lesson and set of principles I want to explore with you about diagrammatic craft concerns the way that content is chosen, framed, and developed.

Let's return to the definition from the start of the book.

A diagram:

- Is visually represented
- Helps someone

Content is obviously critical to both of these parts of a diagram. Without good content, a visual representation cannot help someone who is stuck.

When a viewer approaches our diagram, we have to have made the right decisions about what to include, what not to include, and how to frame what is included.

In looking at ways that content decisions lead to the success or failure of diagrams, three principles add up to what I think it means to be content driven.

4. Good diagrams **have a clear tone and timescale**.
5. Good diagrams **manipulate content appropriately**.
6. Good diagrams **are appropriately dense**.

#4 Clear in Tone & Timescale

There is an artfulness to the tone you choose for your diagram. For example, the following two diagrams differ only in label. The top diagram is meant for a general audience, whereas the lower is meant for a specialized audience.

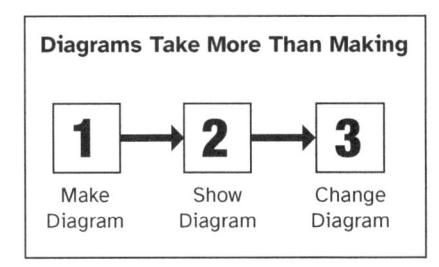

Diagrams Take More Than Making

1 → 2 → 3

Make Diagram — Show Diagram — Change Diagram

Directive & Simplified Tone for General Audience

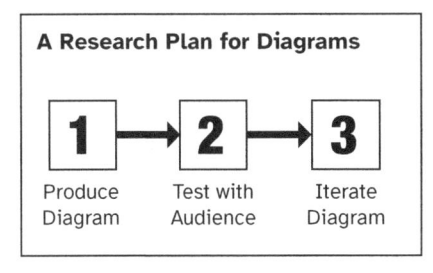

A Research Plan for Diagrams

1 → 2 → 3

Produce Diagram — Test with Audience — Iterate Diagram

Declarative & Authoritative Tone for Specialized Audience

Whether for the labels for a flow diagram or for each of the continuums that define a quadrant diagram, the words you choose matter deeply for the clarity of the diagram.

When paired with the visual elements of the diagram, the words you choose become the **tone** of the diagram. Some diagrams are silly. Some diagrams are serious. Whatever the tone, it is imperative that the words, images, and embellishments chosen support the intention of the diagram.

In my experience, the consistency with which words are finally delivered helps strengthen the tone. When we use a grammatical mishmash of label styles, it can get in the way of our audience picking up on our intended tone.

Another related decision about content framing that I want to be persnickety-particular about is the timescale (or, in too many cases, lack of timescale) of diagrams.

Timescale is the period of time represented by the diagram. Diagrammatic timescale is a critical decision point for any maker, and the ability to represent multiple timescales in a single diagram is an advanced move you should at least know if you are making.

In critiquing the diagrams of others, I find too many makers are stuck between two timescales in the diagram they are wrestling with and not making that clear to either themselves or their audience.

They are often trying to make sense of what *is* while also finding places to put their hopes and dreams for what *is possible* or what *could change* under the right circumstances.

Tale of Three Timescales

In *How to Make Sense of Any Mess*, I propose a taxonomy of three timescales that I believe diagrams can be presented in.

- **Then:** Diagrams about how things used to be, such as a diagram of the coastline 30 years ago
- **Now:** Diagrams about how things are, such as a diagram of the same coastline today
- **When:** Diagrams about how things could be, such as a diagram of a projected coastline 10 years from now

Tips for Timescale

- Include timeframes for sources and any data in the key or marginalia, especially if time is not represented as an axis of your diagram.
- Frame the headline of the diagram to reinforce the timescale.
- Pay attention to the use of past vs. present tense in labels.

#5 Manipulated Appropriately

If the safety sirens in your head are already going off because I used the word *manipulate*, get ready to get uncomfortable as we close our discussion about content by talking about the role of manipulation in diagramming.

Whether we are cleaning up a dataset or deciding what content to include or not include, we are making decisions that are manipulating content, ultimately to serve the intention we set.

Words sometimes contain within them the answer to why they feel so fraught. In this case, we can find that the root of the word *manipulation* is from the Latin *manipulus*, or handful.

When we are making diagrams, we are taking a handful (or several handfuls) of messages, data points, insights, and actions and manipulating them into a crystallized form to help our audience.

A balance can be found in understanding that appropriate manipulation comes down to protecting the energy of the audience while keeping them deeply informed on why they can trust what they are consuming.

Precision is the level of exactness or specificity at which data is presented. Sometimes the diagrammer has decided to provide us with extraneous details through a lack of precision.

Richard Saul Wurman coined the term *unnecessary exactitude* to describe when a data point is needlessly precise for its intention.[19]

---

[19] Richard Saul Wurman, *Information Anxiety* (New York: Doubleday, 1989).

Consider these percentages:

3% vs. 3.1% vs. 3.18%

Each of these data manipulations could be judged as either a kind gesture or a gross manipulation depending on the context of presentation and intended use.

What is an appropriate level of precision changes if we are communicating the chance of rain this evening vs. the blood lead level of a community's children.

Saying there is a 3.1% chance of rain tomorrow is, for most audiences, unnecessarily exact. But saying that 3.1% of children over five years of age from Flint, Michigan, had concerning levels of lead in their blood before Flint switched its water source from the Detroit Water Authority to the Flint Water System as compared with 5% after the switch feels appropriate. Unlike the weather, in this context, rounding down to 3% would be an obvious manipulation towards mistruth.

The way you manipulate your diagrams' content says a lot about you, what you know and think about your audiences, and what your intentions are. Don't water down your data to make it fit. Don't leave your data raw just because you like decimal points.

The real work is communicating the truth with the appropriate level of precision.

[20] Chinaro Kennedy et al., "Blood Lead Levels among Children Aged <6 Years—Flint, Michigan, 2013–2016," *Morbidity and Mortality Weekly Report* 65, no. 25 (2016), https://www.cdc.gov/mmwr/volumes/65/wr/pdfs/mm6525e1.pdf.

#6 Appropriately Dense

Lastly let's dig into how to best craft content by thinking about the concept of *diagrammatic density*.

When I say **density**, I am technically referring to the ratio of blank space to content on a diagram. But I am also artistically referring to the feeling of balance that you can strike with a diagram where the eye is both pleased and rested.

There are four basic levers of craft that we have as diagrammers when determining the density of our diagram.

- **Amount of content.** How many objects and relationships are you representing? How many data points are you layering on?

- **Type size and style.** Have you thought about your type from a readability standpoint?

- **Line length and label length.** How wide are your containers for type? How long are your labels?

- **Leading (line spacing).** Have you allowed enough space between the lines of text?

Amount of Content

Like *good*, the concept of *right* is fraught with difficulty from both a scientific and artistic standpoint. There is no definitive guidance for how dense a diagram should be to be most effective in the way there is for checking the contrast ratio between two colors to ensure that text on screens is readable for everyone, including people with color vision deficiency.[21]

Instead, this is an area of diagrammatic craft where the maker must face a reckoning. As we spoke about in chapter 2 in our discussion about scope, this is the part where we look at all the elements of the diagram, and we identify the role of each.

Then we determine who is a core member of the team and who needs to be removed, for understanding's sake.

So, what content can go?

There are two tactics I turn to when juggling too many elements but not sure what to remove.

- Have someone else (ideally an audience member) give you a tour of the diagram and describe each element to you. Then have them create a list of the elements in rank order of (1,2,3,…) based on how important they are for them to understand the diagram. Repeat with as many people as you need to in order to know what to remove.

- Ask yourself which element of the diagram would make a good character for a whole spin-off diagram. Maybe there is a dataset that could be entirely removed and given its own spotlight and space to shine.

---

[21] See, for example, Lea Verou, Contrast Ratio, accessed August 10, 2021, https://contrast-ratio.com.

Type Size & Style

Along with the content you choose to include, one of the biggest determiners of density in your diagram is the sizing and styling of your type.

Making decisions about how many different sizes and styles of type to have in a diagram is critical to determining how to set the right line length and line spacing. All of these decisions are connected to one another. By keeping a tight set of type sizes and styles, we can better focus on centering the value of the diagram.

If you find yourself spending a lot of time on this part, up front especially, beware. I often find that people spending a lot of time thinking about type scale and styling are trying to make a diagram work that just isn't working.

If you know your intention and have followed that intention through the process of setting your shapes, adding the lines, and refining your labels, this part should come together pretty easily.

Line Length & Label Length

When setting the type of a diagram, most of the line length, or measure, is determined by the width of the shapes and their labels. The world of typography provides strong guidance about readable body copy being set between 45 and 75 characters per line.[22]

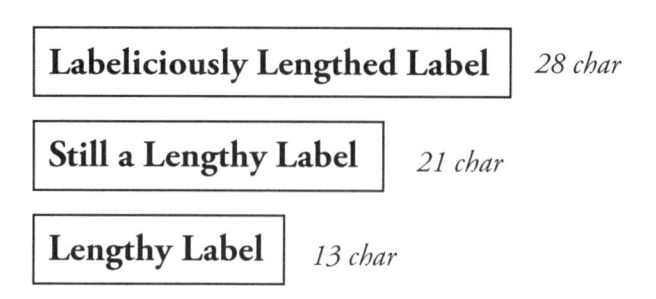

Labeliciously Lengthed Label	28 char
Still a Lengthy Label	21 char
Lengthy Label	13 char

There are also warnings of the impact to readability of overly short line lengths.[23] We can use this guidance to make sure any blocks of text are set at a readable line length in our diagram.

But we have to think about the line length of our diagram labels a bit differently. Because unlike for body copy, the ideal density for a label for a shape in a diagram is much shorter than 45 characters. I aim for under 25 characters max for most labels.

---

[22] See, for example, Robert Bringhurst, *The Elements of Typographic Style*, 2nd ed. (Vancouver, BC: Hartley & Marks, 1997), 26. "The 66-character line (counting both letters and spaces) is widely regarded as ideal."

[23] Bringhurst, *Elements of Typographic Style*, 27.

Leading (Line Spacing)

Another consideration of diagrammatic density is how much space, or leading, you allow between the lines of text in your diagram. If you have labels that wrap or longer blocks of text as part of your diagram, you will want to pay attention to not have too much or too little leading.

If you are new to typesetting, I would suggest being extremely cautious when setting the leading or line spacing to dramatically more or less than the type size in pretty much any context.

Depending on type size and the amount of elements in the diagram, it can exhaust the eye to look at wrapped labels with tight line lengths and even-scaled leading.

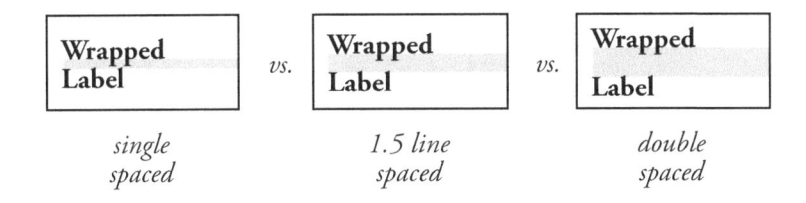

Wrapped Label	vs.	Wrapped Label	vs.	Wrapped Label
single spaced		*1.5 line spaced*		*double spaced*

In this diagram, I think the 1.5 line spacing is more pleasing than the single- and double-spaced lines. This is my opinion and call as a craftsperson. There is no typography boss to say which wins.

You might look at these three boxes and have trouble discerning the difference between them. Or you might think the spacing on the single- or double-spaced option is more pleasing. All are valid.

When it comes to your unique diagram, take a step back, squint, and go with your gut. Then test it with your audience.

Do I sound like a broken record yet?

Questions to Ask Yourself

In closing this lesson on making diagrams *content driven*, here are some questions I hope you are asking yourself:

- Is the tone of this diagram aligned with my intention?
- Do I have a clear timescale in mind? And is that timescale obvious to my audience?
- Have I thoughtfully balanced truth and necessary precision?
- Have I thought through what is too much when it comes to diagrammatic density?
- How much have I played with the typographic levers I have to work with?

I hope you are leaving this section with a better understanding of the important role that content plays in a diagram's ability to be helpful.

Content Driven
Diagram Checklist

- ❑ Experiment with your approach to tone until it feels right and tests well.

- ❑ Make sure a clear timescale is communicated with the content that is shown.

- ❑ Ensure you aren't stuck between two timescales or trying to represent too many timescales.

- ❑ Manipulate the content to properly balance intention and precision based on your audience.

- ❑ Consider the right balance of content to have an ideal diagrammatic density.

- ❑ Play with the three typographic levers (type size and scale, line length, and line spacing) to determine diagrammatic density.

Good Diagrams Are
Visually Supported

We can't discuss diagrammatic craft without taking a good, hard look at the wisdom that has been provided through the decades of work done in the field of graphic design.

The good news is that you don't need to know everything. Instead, there are some critical things to be aware of.

The big takeaway for this principle is that the visuals must be in support of the diagram, not a decoration or coloring book layer on top. Our type must be readable and visually interesting enough that our audience will want to engage with it—but not so expressive that it will steal the limelight or distract the audience. Our intention mustn't be obfuscated by an arbitrary or purely decorative use of visual symbols, icons, or colors.

In my estimation, "being visually represented" is at least one-half of the magic of diagrams, but visual design being done heavy-handedly or unnecessarily is the plight of many diagrams that couldn't serve their full intention as a result.

There are three principles of craft that I want to break down about what it means for a diagram to be visually supported.

7. Good diagrams are **typographically sound**.
8. Good diagrams are **effectively encoded**.
9. Good diagrams are **thoughtfully embellished**.

#7 Typographically Sound

In my last year of design school, I was a teaching assistant for a required course for all graphic design students, Typography 1. It was my job for several semesters to gently force graphic design students to learn about the basics of typography with hopes that they would go on to careers of respecting the beautiful medium that the printed letterform is.

Covering all of typography is not my plan here, but in this section, I have included the level of consideration and understanding of type that I feel you should have top of mind if you are taking on the responsibility of rendering type for an audience other than yourself.

Choosing the Right Typeface

Diagrams can be a challenging environment for type. In choosing the right typeface (or font) for a diagram, you will want to focus on identifying the characteristics that make a typeface legible and readable at whatever scale and in whatever context this specific diagram will be.

The diagrams in this book are set in a variety of typefaces; each was chosen with care. In a few, I even got to use a typeface called Abby Covert New Regular, which was designed by Joe Kowlaski based on my handwriting.

Choosing a typeface is a personal choice, as is most of the craft part of diagramming. It comes down to the context you find yourself diagramming in. Sometimes you are making something special enough to warrant purchase of a special typeface, or a friend will gift you with one that will delight you. Other times you will have to make do with what you have installed on the machine you are using or the way letters look when rendered by your own hand.

As long as you keep readability and legibility at your intended scale in mind, you will make the right choice. This former typography TA totally trusts you to make the right decision.

The following are the basic typographic concepts you should start to make yourself comfortable with. If you are looking for more, I have suggested some deeper typographic resources in the back of the book.

Serif vs. Sans Serif

One of the important choices to make is whether to use a serif or sans serif typeface. In the following example, the sans serif typeface (Helvetica) lacks the flourish of a serif on each letterform seen in the serif typeface (Garamond):

Neither is right or wrong, but there are a lot of opinions on which is best for what.

Understanding Spacing within a Typeface

When determining if a typeface can meet the diagrammatic challenge, you first have to understand just a *little* bit about how letterforms are constructed and what they are and are not designed to do well. Below is a diagram pointing to six core terms you should become familiar with. Each is additionally defined in the indexed lexicon.

Learning what these typographic terms mean and how they affect readability will help you make the best choices for your diagram.

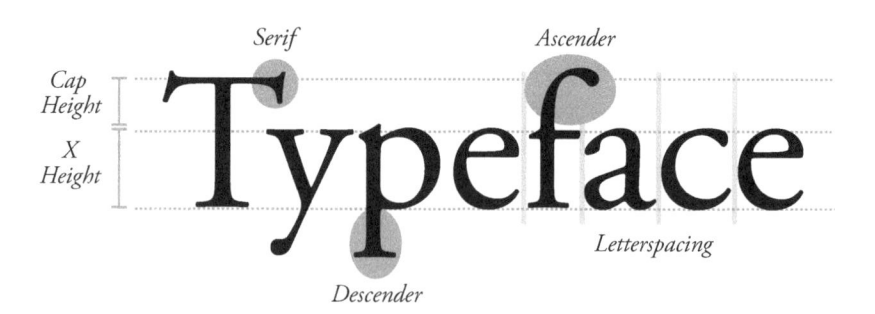

Serif   *Ascender*

Cap Height
X Height

Typeface

Letterspacing

Descender

188 | STUCK? Diagrams Help.

Typographic Hierarchy

An important determination for choosing a typeface is the smallest setting it can handle in the context you will be using it. When we make diagrams, the typographic hierarchy is the visual order that we instill through our typographic choices.

Determining your typographic hierarchy is the key to figuring out whether you have chosen the right typeface to support your intention.

When diagramming, our **typographic hierarchy** most commonly involves defining the type style for the following elements:

- **Headlines** *(or Title)*
- **Shape labels**
- **Line labels**
- **Explanatory content**
- **Key headline**
- **Key content**
- **Marginalia**

When we decide how to style the type of each of these elements, we are deciding where in the typographic hierarchy we want our audience to place this kind of content.

Headlines

The headline type style establishes a lot about a diagram. Is it a quiet diagram or a loud diagram? Is it asking us a question or delivering a recommendation? The way you choose to frame and style that headline makes a difference. Experiment with various typefaces and styles (weights and widths) to get a sense of how the choice of headline typography can further strengthen or weaken the tone of your diagram (see #4 Clear in Tone & Timescale).

Shape Labels

Whatever decisions you make, be consistent. To aid in consistency, I have learned to identify the longest label and start by styling its type first. Then I find the shortest label and style its type next.

By styling the type of those two extremes to feel harmonious, I am more likely to have a resulting style that will work for all the labels.

I learned this trick after too often having almost all my labels styled consistently only to run into one that looked weird because it was too long or too short. Learn from my mistakes, spend the time up front—especially with BIG diagrams.

The final decision in regard to shape labels is their **alignment**. While things such as alignment matter a good bit to how your diagram is perceived and understood, I can assure you that there is no right or wrong answer here from a typographic standpoint.

In fact, here are six perfectly fine variations for horizontal and vertical label alignments.

While issues might be raised in some typography classes about a few of the examples here (several made me feel squicky to set), none of these decisions are wrong or bad.

There are a few typographic decisions to make in regard to shape labels:

- **Type:** What typeface, style, and size will you use to label your shapes?

- **Padding:** How much room will the shape have around each label?

- **Horizontal and vertical alignment:** How does the label sit in relation to the shape?

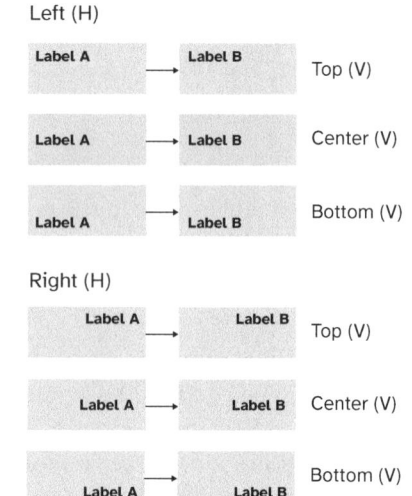

Left (H)

Label A → Label B	Top (V)
Label A → Label B	Center (V)
Label A → Label B	Bottom (V)

Right (H)

Label A → Label B	Top (V)
Label A → Label B	Center (V)
Label A → Label B	Bottom (V)

I tell you this because I think many people need permission to play and decide for themselves what is good for their diagram. I don't care what you choose, but for the audience's good, either be consistent or intentional in your inconsistency.

Line Labels

There are a few typographic decision points to consider when labeling lines:

- **Type:** What typeface, style, and size will you use to label your lines?

- **Reading order:** Which reading order is the label's direction encouraging? *Left to right, right to left, top to bottom, bottom to top?*

- **Alignment:** What is the relationship of the label to the line? *Above, below, alongside?*

Shapes often find their permanent place only after the line labels are typographically styled. Lines can be finicky to label, and sometimes I have to add more space between the shapes to get the type right. This can be like a loosening before a final tightening of the typographic bolts.

Before

[Label A] ➡ [Label B] ➡ [Label C]

After

[Label A] —*Label*→ [Label B] —*Label*→ [Label C]

Label Orientation

You may eventually experience a moment when you believe that a label might need to be rotated to best fit into the diagram that you are making. At this moment, a seemingly basic question is, What is the proper direction to rotate a text label in a diagram?

We humans have been doing this diagram labeling thing for a long time, and there are really only so many possible degrees you might rotate text in one of three ways. Surely someone must have decided.

- **Top to bottom** (also known as *descending*) is any angle where the start of the phrase is above the end.

- **Bottom to top** (also known as *ascending*) is any angle where the start of the phrase is below the end.

- **Stacked** (also known as *marquis*) is where the word or phrase is set with one letter per line.

If you were trained to make process diagrams, you were maybe handed a standard to follow that says bottom to top is always the way to rotate your line labels.[24]

And if you make charts of quantitative data, you might also believe that bottom to top is the only way to rotate type because of your ideas of proper axis-labeling.

---

[24] International Organization for Standardization, "ISO 15519-1:2010 (en) Specification for Diagrams for Process Industry—Part 1: General Rules," ISO Online Browsing Platform (OBP), accessed August 10, 2021, https://www.iso.org/obp/ui/#iso:std:iso:15519:-1:ed-1:v1:en.

[25] See Henry Petroski, *The Book on the Bookshelf* (New York: Knopf, 1999).

If you work in wayfinding and signage, the advice is generally that for signs read from the ground, set the label bottom to top, and for signs someone approaches at eye level, top to bottom.

If you are someone who academically studies readability, you might warn us that the proper rotation of a label should be determined based on the ideal reading order of the intended audience.

And should you google it, you will find many people in message boards and blog comments assuming that there is a "well, duh" standard to rely on here:

And should you look further into the "because reasons" of book spine rotation, you will find all sorts of nifty background tidbits as to why different languages think about the orientation of books differently—resulting in spine design (and opinion) differences across cultures.[25]

While I can confirm that this contextual knowledge about book spines in different locales is indeed interesting and a rabbit hole, I can also confirm that it is absolutely not the right way to think about rotating your diagram labels.

"Just use the rotation of book spines in the local culture or language of the intended audience."

—says everyone without thinking too hard about it

I'll be honest, I could have let this go. I could have gone with an "it depends" response and moved on with my life. But here's the thing—people feel anxious about this choice (or mess it up for their users) all the time.

People don't mess up label orientation because they want unreadable or less clear labels.

Chapter 3: **Craft** | 193

People mess up label orientation because it's a consideration set that hasn't been made clear for them yet or because they trusted strangers-on-the-internet's bogus advice to always mimic book spines, like I did for years.

When making things for humans to read, it is kind to prioritize readability. Diagrams are no exception.

Rotation has consistently proven to have an impact on the readability of text in short and long form. Studies of this date back to the late 19th century.[26]

Interestingly, neither top to bottom nor bottom to top has been proven to be "better" from an academic standpoint. So, if you, like many, assume that your default is the default, remember that you are not your user.

Rather than one standard default to apply to all contexts, mediums, intentions, and cultures, text content has been proven more recently to be most readable when set to meet the specific readability needs of specific users in specific contexts.[27]

In other words, science tells us to do everything in our diagrammatic power to not rotate our labels at all, and if we do, either way we go, we better pay attention to our user and their context.

Let's talk about the line length of the label you are setting because line length matters when deciding how to set the label.

---

[26] "90 degrees in either direction is 205% slower on avg." Edmund B. Huey, "Preliminary Experiments in the Physiology and Psychology of Reading," *American Journal of Psychology* 9, no. 4 (July 1898): 575–586, https://doi.org/10.2307/1412192.

[27] "[T]he major factor determining reading speed was the mismatch between the orientation of the text and that of the reader." See Nicolas Davidenko and Alexander Ambard, "Reading Sideways: Effects of Egocentric and Environmental Orientation in a Lexical Decision Task," *Vision Research* 153 (2018): 8.

Label Length (char)

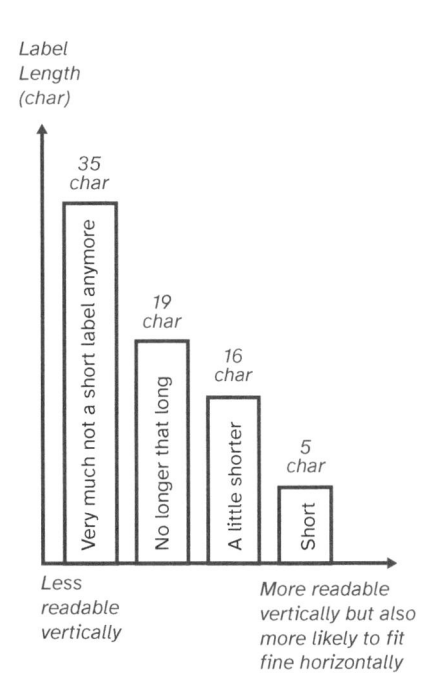

- 35 char — Very much not a short label anymore
- 19 char — No longer that long
- 16 char — A little shorter
- 5 char — Short

Less readable vertically ← → *More readable vertically but also more likely to fit fine horizontally*

The longer your label, the harder it will be to read when set vertically.

And the shorter the label, the more likely it will be to fit horizontally without too much more design finesse than rotation would take.

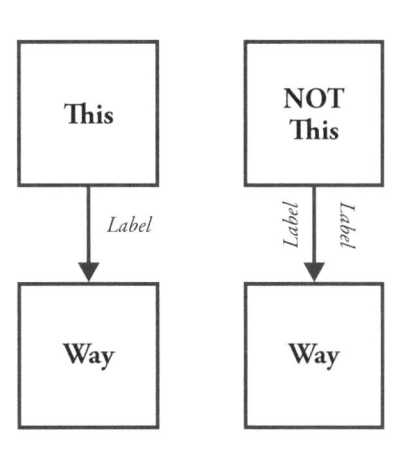

This
↓ *Label*
Way

NOT This
Label *Label*
Way

Chapter 3: **Craft** | 195

Edge direction &
baseline direction
are **aligned**

Edge direction &
baseline direction
are **reversed**

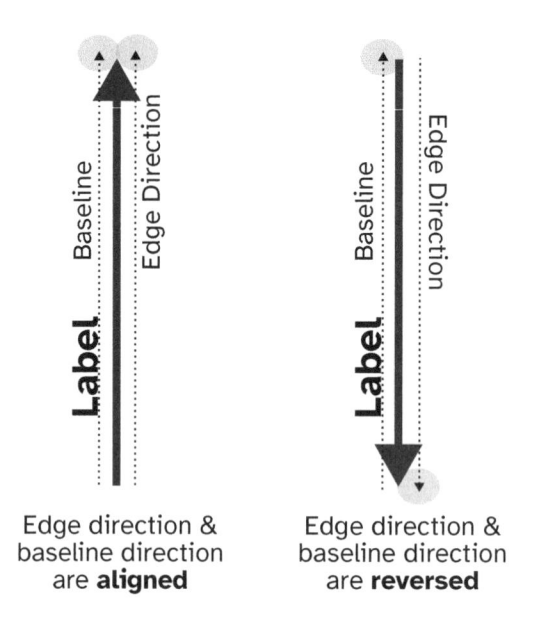

But I will admit there are times when I have had to rotate a label. So to be helpful to you when doing the same, I will now introduce a concept that I call an **edge direction**, or the directional rotation of a line label's **baseline** in relation to the direction of the line being labeled.

I want to define this concept because in my experience there are directional cues in a diagram that need to be considered in addition to the habits or preferences of the viewers' language or cultural context.

Diagrams have directional cues both in the lines being labeled and in the directional connections between elements.

When we reinforce these directional cues by aligning our edge directions and baselines, we make for more understandable diagrams.

When we reverse the baseline direction of a label to oppose the edge direction of the line it labels or to oppose the general flow of the diagram, we can lose understandability as a result.

When we align a baseline to the edge direction, we might end up rotating labels in opposite directions from one another, as in this first example.

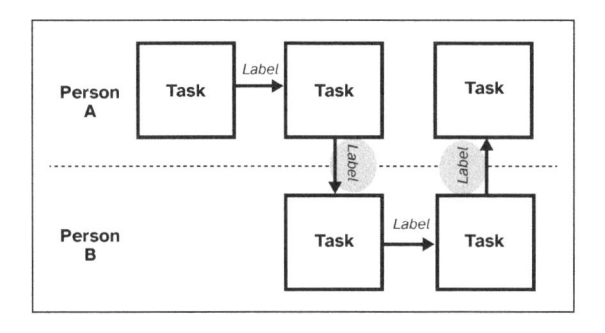

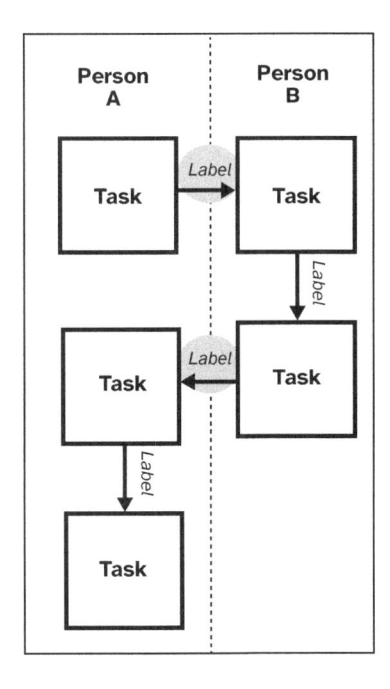

There will also be times when the baseline is not best aligned with the edge direction of the elements you are laying out.

In this second example, you would have to set one of the labels upside down to align the baseline to that of the edge direction.

Standards do exist for some contexts (such as diagrams for the process industry), and while some people report that rotating their head to the left to read bottom to top feels more natural, others report the opposite is true. Science says that either direction is equally impactful on readability and a concept such as "proper" heavily relies on context.

Where I have landed is that deciding on the proper orientation for your diagram labels depends on the audience you want to reach, the context of reaching them, and the risks you are willing to take on reducing readability and understandability.

My advice on label rotation comes down to this:

- Try everything in your power to not rotate the label at all.

- If you *have to* rotate a label, make sure you aren't obfuscating the edge direction without intention.

- Don't turn your labels upside down; it's almost always unreadable.

Styling Explanatory, Key & Marginalia Content

The final set of typographic decisions often comes in the styling of the content that supports the diagram's shapes and lines.

This content is not to be trifled with in terms of typographic styling. The way you choose to style these elements says a lot about them. It communicates how much you value and prioritize that content and ultimately how important you think the audience should believe that those elements are.

I recommend setting yourself a minimum type size based on the accessibility needs and reading context of your audience. When we are setting this kind of content, we need boundaries to make sure we don't accidentally make something inaccessible in trying to make it harmonious with the overall hierarchy.

Editing will also be your good friend at this stage. If you have been writing tiny novellas in marginalia and are now considering sending magnifying glasses with the diagrams to justify the use of type at increasingly smaller sizes, I see you. Try harder.

#8 Effectively Encoded

When we use color, pattern, or iconography to "mean something," we **encode** our diagram with a new layer of information. But as viewers, using a diagram that requires us to decode what a color, pattern, or icon means can be downright confusing.

In my estimation, the effective encoding of information comes with more baggage than any of the other visual tricks of the diagramming trade.

I want to focus on why these choices can be tricky when you desire a consistent interpretation of your diagram.

When we make diagrams that incorporate color, especially when we try to encode information using color, we must remain aware that some colors and combinations of colors have associations, either culturally or situationally.

Perhaps the most common example of color to encode information in a business context is the use of red and green to indicate status or quality.

In this schema, red is often used to mean "in jeopardy," "behind," or "off track," and green is used to mean "going well" or "on track," mirroring the international standard for traffic lights, which seems basic enough for most people to "get."

But in Chinese culture, both colors have positive connotations, with red used to mean celebration and green to mean prosperity. In South America, the color green is most associated with death, and the color red is associated with life.

The international standard of red and green traffic lights wasn't even introduced to China or South America until the 1950s. These colors had whole and rich lives in these cultures before the invention and conglomeration of the automobile industry.

My point here is not to tell you to avoid red and green color-coding for cultural reasons. (I have better reasons to tell you to avoid this, which we are going to get to in the next section!)

My objective is to convince you that when we choose to use color to encode meaning, there are often cultural or situational connotations that come with the colors we might choose for our diagrams. And with knowledge of those meanings, we can do better and make lots more sense.

Along with the cultural and situational implications of the colors we are using, there are accessibility challenges that come with color use in diagrams.

Color use can impact accessibility when:

- People are unable to differentiate between certain shades.

- Complex encoding of meaning through color is too heavy a cognitive load.

Several good friends of mine are people who cannot see the difference between red and green. This form of color vision deficiency is incredibly common, occurring in an estimated one out of 12 men and one out of 200 women.[28]

Imagine you are in a boardroom presenting your diagram to 24 people. If you use red/green colors in your diagram as the sole way of encoding meaning, at least one person might not be able to decode that meaning. And this is just one form of color vision deficiency that impacts people's ability to distinguish shades.

---

[28] National Health Service, "Colour Vision Deficiency (Colour Blindness)," accessed August 10, 2021, https://www.nhs.uk/conditions/colour-vision-deficiency.

Always back up your encoding.

The good news is that there is an easy solution here. Anytime you find yourself leaning on the use of color or a shift in styling to mean something, make sure there is an alternative way to get that same information.

Bonus: When I find an alternative, I often end up with a better singular way to serve more people. Boom.

For example, in the first three drafts of this book, I had planned to use red and green throughout several of the diagrams to mean *good* and *bad*. At this point in the text, I even had a statement about how I had checked to ensure there was *backup encoding*, knowing that ultimately color was limiting in terms of whom I might reach.

The next time I edited the diagrams, looking to ensure that promise of backup encoding, I found instead that the red and green were no longer even needed to make the point clear once alternatives were put in place. *And a spoiler alert: The most common backup is unsurprisingly … labels!*

To close this section, I want to revisit our conversation on cognitive load in the context of using color in diagrams.

I fear that too many people ask colors to do too much heavy lifting in diagrams. Just because we *can* **color code** something doesn't mean we *should*.

When we ask our audience to decode meaning through translation of a color into a concept, we are requesting space in the temporary memory of their minds.

Before taking up that precious space, make sure that the value you are delivering is worth the energy it requires of the audience.

As with type and typography, there is much to learn about color and color theory. I have provided some resources for further study in the back of the book, should you want to learn more.

#9 Thoughtfully Embellished

Good diagrams use visual embellishment to enhance the meaning of the diagram, not to obfuscate it.

Whether it be the icons or imagery or the colors, layout, or any decorative or branded elements, we must ensure none of it actually ends up getting in the way of the helpfulness.

Images

Including images in our diagrams is an important tactic, especially when we want to draw out a specific emotion from our audience. A box labeled "Manatee" is never going to make the emotional connection that a labeled photo or illustration can.

In some diagrams, the box can suffice. In others, adding the image creates a needed connection to what is being diagrammed.

Imagery can be a shorthand with an audience if we are sure it will be understood. In cases where we make that bet and fail, understanding is lost. Depending on how critical the misunderstood element is, the level of misunderstanding or lack of understanding differs.

I was once on a project for which the designer insisted that "everyone knows the *film* icon" and that it could stand without further explanation or labeling. Then his own kid guessed first that it was bunk beds and second that it was a ladder.

I live by this common wisdom when it comes to imagery in my diagrams:

- Always label icons—start by labeling them all, then remove the ones that feel repetitive.

- Avoid encoding information into complex iconography schemas that your audience has to decode using a key (or perhaps you provided a decoder ring?).

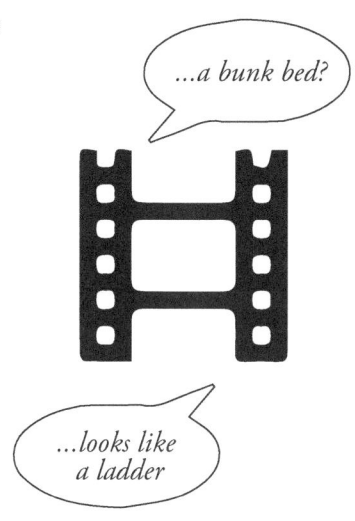

- Be careful when adding embellishment to your diagram that doesn't carry some information or meaning that helps reach your intention.

But, dear reader, less is not always more.[29] There are some contexts, culturally or situationally, for which decorative embellishment and graphic flourishes might help the diagram to feel like it belongs.

There are many others for which the use of embellishment is far less thoughtful and detracts from the meaning.

---

[29] Many Western design philosophies profess visual simplicity as the only way to good design, perhaps most recognizably summed up by Mies van der Rohe as "less is more." When aesthetic preferences such as simplicity are standards by which all work should be judged, we can lose valuable shape, color, texture, and flavor in our work. This was the goal of explicitly anti-ethnic fascist design philosophy, and it doesn't need to always guide our choices.

Chapter 3: **Craft** | 203

Questions to Ask Yourself

In closing this lesson on making diagrams *visually supported*, here are some questions I hope you are asking yourself:

- For whom am I intending to make this diagram accessible?

- What decisions am I making that need to be thought through differently based on my audience's abilities?

- How much cognitive load does this subject matter require of the audience?

- How can I remove unnecessary cognitive load through the design decisions I make?

- What are my audience's unique and varied needs and abilities that I can pay attention to especially when it comes to the perception of contrast between colors, and type styles and sizes?

I hope you are leaving this section with a better understanding of the balance between making something look pleasing and having it actually deliver on your diagrammatic intentions.

Visually Supported Diagram Checklist

- ❏ Establish typographic hierarchy (typefaces, sizes, styles).
- ❏ Consider how visual embellishment helps (or hurts) your intention.
- ❏ Include branding elements to establish authorship and trust in your presentation of the diagram to others.
- ❏ Ensure your color use is accessible and understandable to the audience whom it is meant to serve.
- ❏ Consider how any use of color is impacting cognitive load—be *extra* careful encoding meaning with color.

> "You can't teach the poetry, but you can teach the craft."
>
> David Hockney

Craft Is About
Right Now

Remember that 96-week journey diagram that took me nine months to research and develop for Nike?

Ten years later, I regret relying on a complex color-coding schema to encode multiple roles onto each step of the flow. I added initials in addition to the colors to back up my encoding, but I see now how I could have avoided the color-coding entirely if I had just dwelled longer on the form the diagram ultimately took.

I want to be clear, this diagram was a success. It solved the problems it set out to solve and became an important object of discourse for a change management initiative taken on by a billion dollar company. It did its job during its career and now lives happily in retirement on a file server in Portland.

That doesn't mean that diagram was perfect or that I would do it the same way now should I run into a similar challenge.

When I interviewed people about making diagrams that impacted their lives or work in some way, I was shocked by how precious their diagrams had become to them in hindsight.

Very few of the interviewees I recruited were able to come up with one *single* thing that they would change about their diagrams in hindsight. Many of them would change the circumstances that made the diagram necessary, but many of their diagrams remained these untouchable heroes that had saved them from themselves and then gone into proverbial cold storage thereafter—never to be questioned, only revered.

Each diagram I saw in these interviews was special in its own way, each had its own look and feel, and each came wrapped in the unique background and experience quilt of the person who made it.

In each I saw places I could interject to improve their craft and make their diagrams stronger, and more clear. And yet, by the end of each conversation, I also found myself seeing these diagrams in that same precious, museum-quality way as the makers seemed to.

Who am I to question the *craft* of the diagram when it was finally able to bring a team together around a mission or explain a topic in a way that opened up new ways of understanding? Who am I to critique the line spacing or color choices of a diagram that was able to connect dots that felt chaotically disconnected for people until the diagram swooped in to make sense of them all?

As we close this chapter on diagrammatic craft, here is the message I hope you are taking away: There is no right or wrong in diagramming; there is only *better* and *on purpose*.

We make diagrams for *right* when they are needed. Sometimes we are given months and a creative team to make these diagrammatic decisions. Sometimes we are walking up to a whiteboard on fire from a moment of misunderstanding.

We can always make diagrams better from a craft perspective, but we don't ever have to make them perfect. Instead, we make decisions about how the diagram is made on purpose and with our intentions and audience in mind. That's how we get to know what our version of *good* looks like.

When I was writing this book, most of the diagrams and sentences were bad the first or 10th time. Some still are, surely. Diagrams are tricksters. We can make a diagram we find helpful and clear at the end of an afternoon toiling on it, only to wake up to a nonsensical garbage pile not living up to the challenge the next morning.

When it comes to craft, what we need most often is time. Time to sit with things, time to ask other people, time to iterate, time to noodle. The first three chapters of this book were written to *prepare* you to take the time you need to make better diagrams.

First we learned in chapter 1 the *purpose* of diagrams and the role they play when we are stuck. Then we took a bumpy and emotional road trip in chapter 2 through the *process* of diagramming.

With purpose and process in the rearview, chapter 3 provided some guardrails and three checklists to help you ask yourself the right questions of *craft* as you diagram and determine what good means in context of your intention.

But, dear reader, none of this matters at all if the only diagrams you make are in your head. In order to see how and why these lessons matter, you have to do a whole lot of diagramming.

The best way to learn about craft is to practice.

To ensure you have a wide variety of diagram types to explore as you start to apply this skill set to different contexts, chapter 4 provides 12 diagrammatic recipes to try on your own, and chapter 5 shares eight stories of sensemakers learning what it takes to diagram with other people.

To make sure you revisit craft as you work, next is a BINGO card with 25 diagrammatic violations taken from this chapter.

If you are feeling especially brave, try teaming up with a partner to see who can rack up the most points of critique on your next diagrammatic endeavor!

Diagram
Critique
BINGO

The lessons of this chapter have been conveniently distilled into this BINGO card of the 25 most common issues of diagrammatic craft mapped to the five diagrammatic superpowers of STUCK.

This was designed to aid you in critiquing your diagrams in process.

S Stability	T Transparency
Contrast ratio issues p. 169	Unclear timescale p. 176
Unneeded line jumps used p. 165	Inappropriate manipulation of data p. 177
Baseline and edge directions are reversed p. 196	Data is too precise p. 177
Not accessible to intended audience p. 150	Data is not precise enough p. 177
Unclear encoding p. 199	Ineffective or lack of branding p. 202

U Understanding	**C** Clarity	**K** Kindness
Unclear logic or reading direction p. 155	Tone doesn't match the intention p. 175	Not tidy p. 159
Unclear starting place p. 153	Unclear audience p. 70	Encoding lacks a backup p. 201
Too much information p. 86	Icons lack labels p. 203	Too much cognitive load for the value delivered p. 86
Too little information p. 87	Ineffective use of visual embellishment p. 202	Labels are too long p. 182
Not the right information p. 88	Unclear or ineffective typographic hierarchy p. 189	Line length and/or line spacing issues p. 183

Chapter 3: **Craft** | 211

4

Recipes

Rather than simply dump a collection of diagrammatic recipes on you, I thought it might be helpful to give you a starting place based on your current need. What question(s) are you stuck on?

At the end of chapter 1, we learned about the three common centers that diagrams have. I want to revisit that conversation as we start to look at recipes for common diagrams because understanding what is at the center of the question(s) you are stuck on is a good place to start when picking a recipe that will have the highest chance at being helpful.

The decision flow in the following diagram leads you through a series of questions to identify a type of diagram to start from based on what is at the center of the question you are stuck on and what you are trying to visualize.

Which Recipe Should I Try *First*?

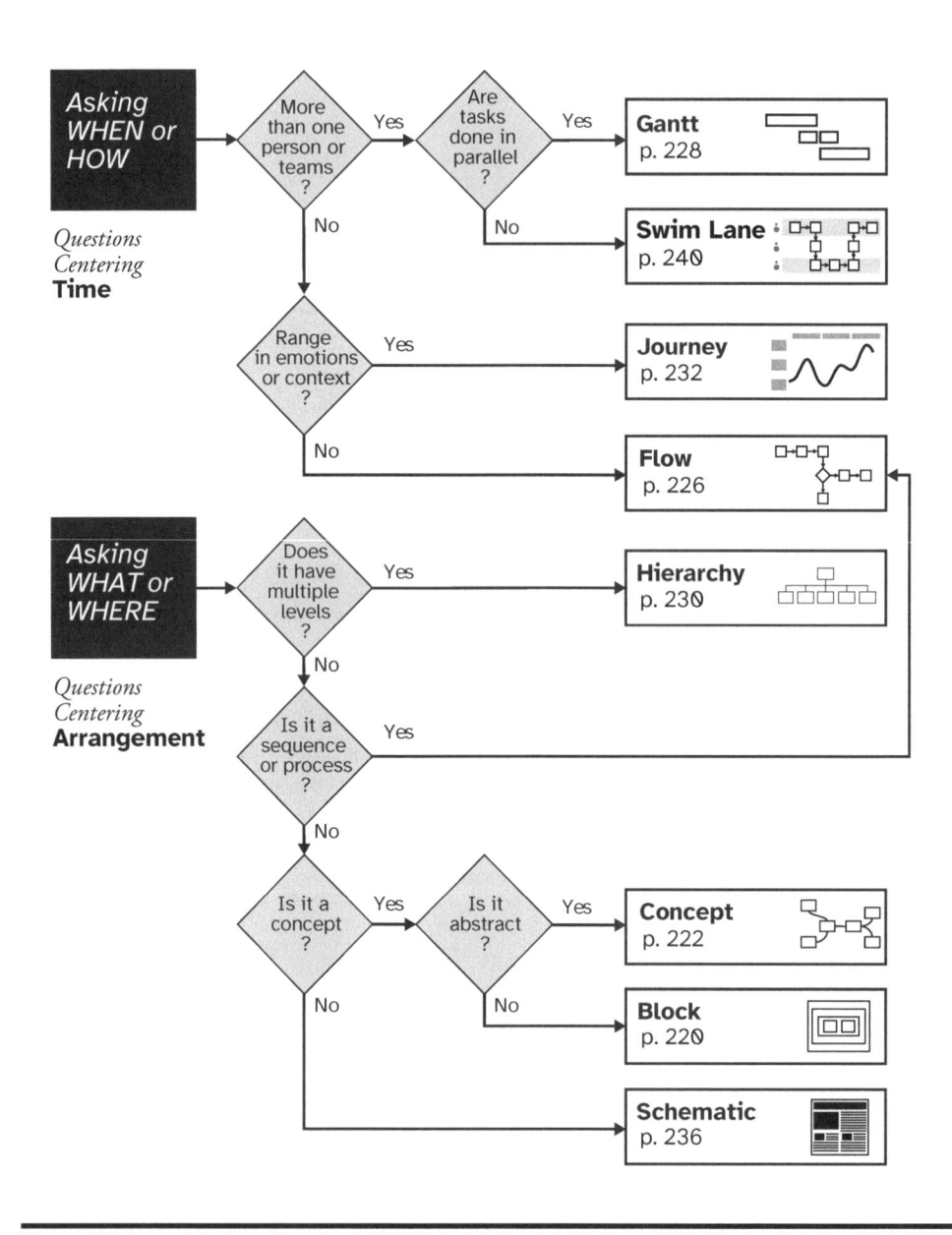

Asking WHEN or HOW

Questions Centering **Time**

- More than one person or teams?
  - Yes → Are tasks done in parallel?
    - Yes → **Gantt** p. 228
    - No → **Swim Lane** p. 240
  - No → Range in emotions or context?
    - Yes → **Journey** p. 232
    - No → **Flow** p. 226

Asking WHAT or WHERE

Questions Centering **Arrangement**

- Does it have multiple levels?
  - Yes → **Hierarchy** p. 230
  - No → Is it a sequence or process?
    - Yes → (Flow p. 226)
    - No → Is it a concept?
      - Yes → Is it abstract?
        - Yes → **Concept** p. 222
        - No → **Block** p. 220
      - No → **Schematic** p. 236

214 | STUCK? Diagrams Help.

Asking WHY or WHICH?

Questions Centering **Context**

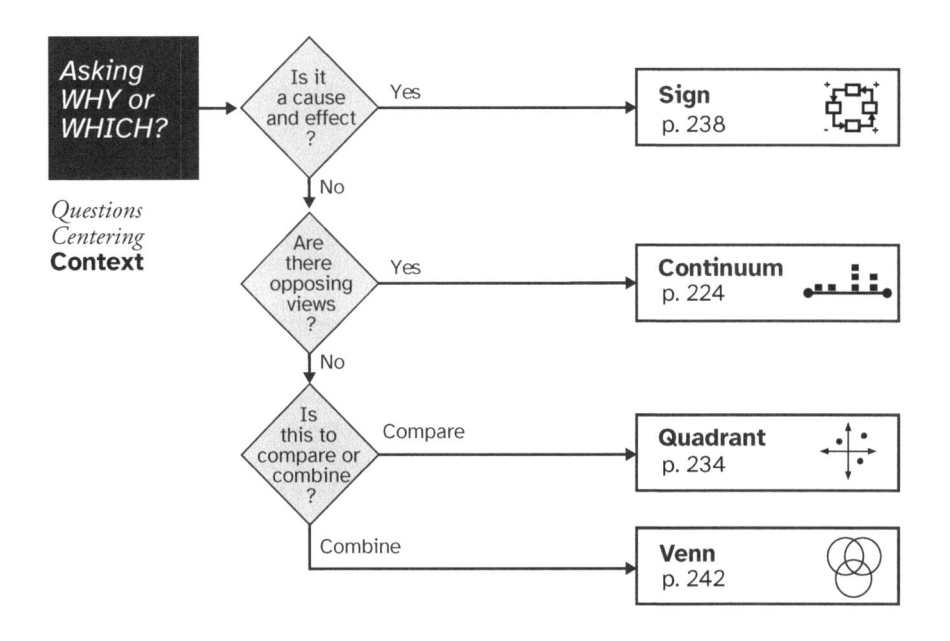

- Is it a cause and effect? — Yes → **Sign** p. 238
- No ↓
- Are there opposing views? — Yes → **Continuum** p. 224
- No ↓
- Is this to compare or combine?
  - Compare → **Quadrant** p. 234
  - Combine → **Venn** p. 242

Since this is the most complex diagram in this book, and the logic of this diagram could be tedious to follow for some readers at this scale, I have written out an alternative on the next page to present the same questions that the diagram asks.

You might remember the lesson we learned about the importance of providing alternatives when diagrams are critical and accessibility of the content is of concern.

Chapter 4: **Recipes** | 215

If your questions center *time*, such as *when* and *how*, the first factor to consider is how many people or teams you have to represent. If more than two, you could be deciding between a **Gantt** and a **swim lane diagram**. Gantts are better for visualizing tasks done in parallel, whereas swim lanes are better for visualizing tasks done with hand-offs.

If you are only representing one role, or a single person or system's experience, then you are deciding between a journey and a flow diagram. A **journey diagram** will better allow you to show the process over time but with the added ability to layer on emotional or contextual range. The **flow diagram** will be more prescriptive on capturing logic and the flow of data.

If your questions center *arrangement*, such as *what* and *where*, you are often deciding between showing things hierarchically or experientially. If you are showing how a place is divided into multiple levels, a **hierarchy diagram** will serve as a good starting point. If you want to create a diagram of the lower level of the *parts* of an object or interface, then a **schematic**, **block**, or **concept diagram** might serve you best.

Schematics, I find, are more useful for the physical (non-conceptual) experiences that people have with objects and systems, whereas block and association diagrams are better for the more conceptual information we need to communicate. I tend to turn to block diagrams when the way the parts are assembled into a whole is more concrete. Associations I tend to reserve for when things assemble in more abstract ways.

Lastly, if your questions center *context*, such as *why* and *which*, and you want to show things that have a cause and effect on one another, a **sign diagram** is a wonderful recipe to explore. If you are seeing a lot of opposing views on important questions of which or why, try making a **continuum**. If you need to compare things, a **quadrant** is a great starting place. If you want to show what happens when things combine, a **Venn diagram** might serve you well as a start.

The Trouble
with Examples

In my experience teaching diagramming, I have found that there is always a risk of providing too many examples.

While examples show a beginner the results of diagrammatic theory in practice, they also often gloss over the process that was needed to get there. As the first three chapters have taught us, it takes a lot of work *behind* the diagram to get to good.

Showing a swim lane diagram of an overly simplified process for the purpose of teaching this template will not properly prepare someone to make a swim lane in their actual context. Kind of like how showing you a picture of a chocolate soufflé does not mean your soufflé will rise or taste good given your unique context and skill level with the materials and techniques involved.

You can't learn to speak a language by memorizing phrases to get you through expected interactions; instead, you must understand the grammar and proper syntax. Whether it's cooking, speaking, or diagramming, how you handle the *unexpected* moments determines how well your skill set serves you and your current intentions.

As you look through these recipes, remember that their purpose is to expand your toolkit when it comes to diagramming. These recipes are meant to reveal a grammar with which you can construct infinite sentences—not to limit you to templates that you can only use in limited contexts.

In this chapter, you will find a dozen tried-and-true, step-by-step recipes for you to experiment with as you learn to diagram.

Origin Stories

All of the diagram types I have written recipes for existed before my career as an information architect even began. The majority were invented a hundred or more years ago and still serve as critical tools in multiple fields of practice today.[30]

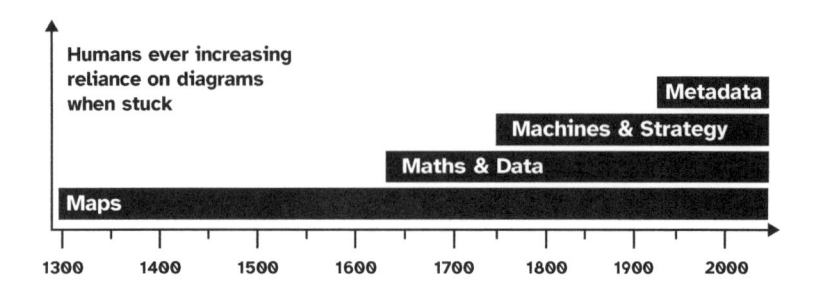

```
Humans ever increasing
reliance on diagrams
when stuck
                                            Metadata
                                Machines & Strategy
                        Maths & Data
Maps
1300  1400  1500  1600  1700  1800  1900  2000
```

Where possible, I have included a brief historical perspective on the origin and development of the diagram type behind the recipe.

If you want a fuller historical perspective of diagrams and why their attribution is so fraught, the literature review in the back of the book has a perspective to share.

---

[30] The above simple diagram is based on an amazingly deep resource. When you are ready to dig into the mind-blowing history of diagramming and diagrammatic thought, this website is a great place to start: Michael Friendly, and Daniel J. Denis, "Milestones in the History of Thematic Cartography, Statistical Graphics, and Data Visualization" (2001), http://www.datavis.ca/milestones/.

218 | STUCK? Diagrams Help.

Diagram
Recipes

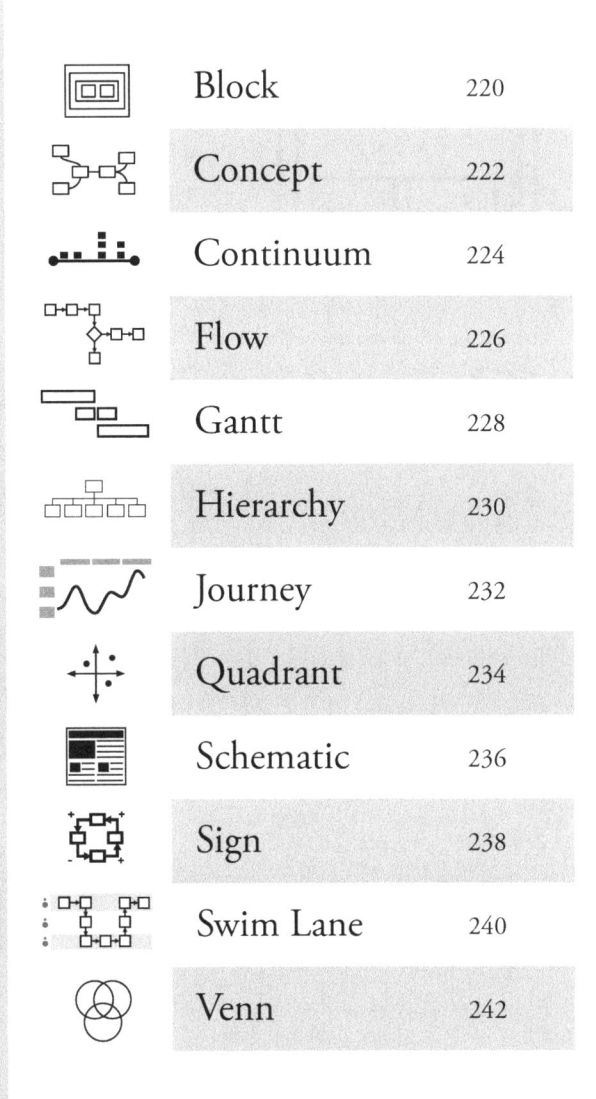

	Block	220
	Concept	222
	Continuum	224
	Flow	226
	Gantt	228
	Hierarchy	230
	Journey	232
	Quadrant	234
	Schematic	236
	Sign	238
	Swim Lane	240
	Venn	242

▣ **Block**

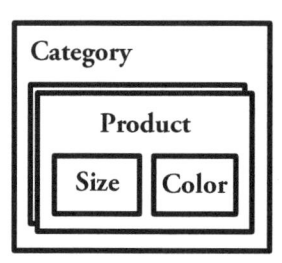

A simple block diagram of a catalog model for thinking about product metadata.

When concepts, objects, or systems are composed of smaller concepts, objects, or systems, block diagrams are good for understanding the interdependence amongst parts.

While the origin of this format is not well documented, block diagrams are most often historically seen in circuits and electronics.

In modern contexts, they are most commonly found in engineering and data schema design.

What to Expect

In the example, all three shapes (A, B, and C) purposefully have different type alignment.

While this is not consistent, it is more harmonious and tidy than if they are the same for the sake of consistency vs. aligned to make sense as a set. Leave label orientation for after the shapes' alignment to one another is set.

Ingredients

- ❑ A list of the pieces that make up the whole

- ❑ Research into understanding how many layers deep the objects nest

Ideas for *Block Diagrams*

Diagram categories that you need to contain in a closet, cabinet, or file system and what might be in nested containers.

Diagram how core people, places, and things in a business relate to and are contained within one another.

220 | STUCK? Diagrams Help.

also known as black box, top down, nested shape

Step 1:

Make a shape for each concept, object, or system in your scope. Arrange the shapes to understand their relative specificity to one another, from broad to narrow.

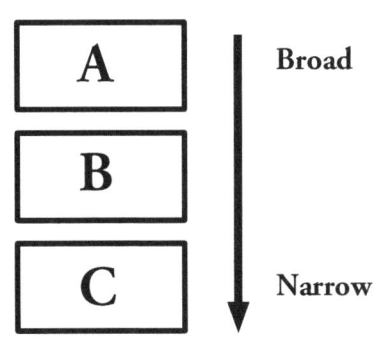

A

B

C

Broad

Narrow

Step 2:

Change the shapes' sizes to better represent the objects' relative size to one another.

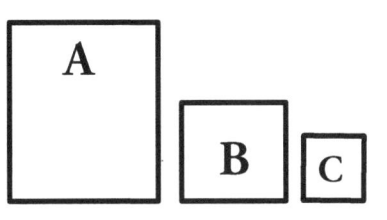

A

B

C

Step 3:

Nest shapes to reflect their interdependence.

Add definitions if the labels aren't enough.

Also, if you want to indicate that multiple instances of an object exist, consider stacking, as is seen here.

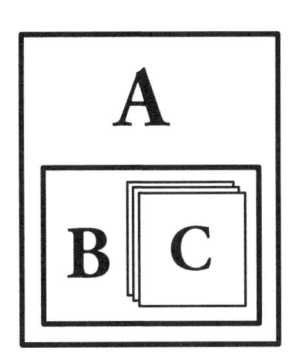

A

B C

Chapter 4: **Recipes** | 221

Concept

When concepts, objects, or systems have a variety of relationships that are not just hierarchical in nature, concept diagrams are good for understanding those relationships and how objects relate to one another in a given context. This type of diagram, which puts words into boxes and then connects those boxes with lines, has found its way into many fields because of its broad applicability to many different types of contexts.

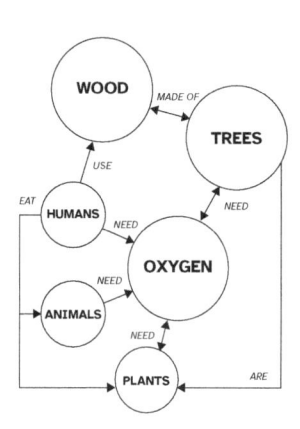

A simple concept diagram about how we relate to trees

Ingredients

- ❑ An audit of concepts, objects, or systems that exist in the context and scope

- ❑ Understanding of how the objects connect or relate to one another

Ideas for *Concept Diagrams*

Diagram your values, dreams, and goals to your actions and thoughts.

Diagram informal and formal working relationships, shared resources, and connections within an organization of which you are a part.

What to Expect

Concept diagrams can get wild quickly!

If you are struggling to get the shapes into an arrangement that feels *right*, try:

- Rotating the diagram's orientation from portrait to landscape

- Moving the shapes to opposite sides of the diagram.

also known as entity relationship diagram (ERD), mind map, bubble chart

Step 1:

Make a shape for each concept, object, or system in your scope.

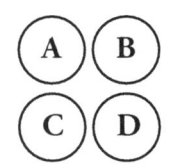

Step 2:

Arrange shapes using three of the line patterns that we learned in chapter 2:

— **Non-directional lines**
 for associations

→ **One-way lines**
 for sequences

↔ **Two-way lines**
 for reciprocation

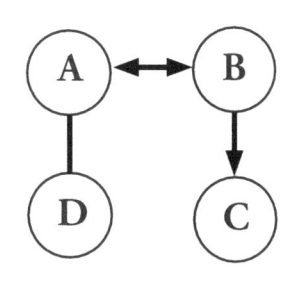

Step 3:

Once the shapes are in a solid arrangement, label the lines describing the relationship, ideally creating readable statements with shape labels.

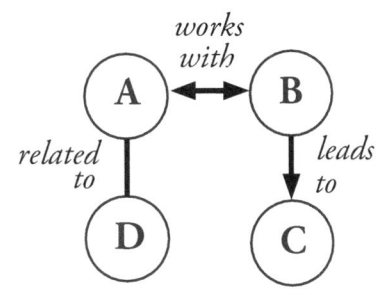

Chapter 4: **Recipes** | 223

Continuum

When there are potentially *differing* opinions on the direction or tone to take, continuums are a stellar format for both gathering data and presenting differences once gathered.

Our focus in Q4

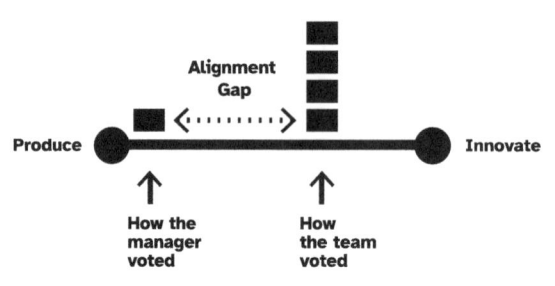

Produce ←———■——⟨·······⟩——■———→ Innovate

Alignment Gap

↑ How the manager voted

↑ How the team voted

A continuum of a major disconnect on a team.

This type of diagram, which really is as simple as a line with each end labeled, provides directional clarity without a ton of heavy cognitive load.

What to Expect

Continuums are a writing exercise more than anything else. How you define the ends of the spectrum matter greatly to the usefulness of this exercise.

To make a strong continuum avoid using overly negative or positive words for either end. Each should feel like a valid direction.

Ingredients

- ☐ Two competing directions
- ☐ Disagreement on which way to go or how to balance
- ☐ Permission, time, and space to gather opinions

Ideas for *Continuums*

Diagram the ways in which your personal style, ideology, or identity exists on a spectrum.

Diagram two potential directions for a project to take. Then gather votes from your teammates and visualize any gaps you find.

also known as performance continuum, spectrum

Step 1:

Identify the directions that are opposing or competing and find the right set of words to express the distinction without judgment on either end.

Common Continuum Pairs

- Optimize vs. Add
- Maintain vs. Improve
- Engage vs. Convert
- Service vs. Product
- Acquire vs. Build
- Scale vs. Hone

Step 2:

Draw a line and label each end. Then ask each person involved to mark their opinion and/or preference on the line.

Have each person vote without seeing others' votes; power dynamics can and will alter the results.

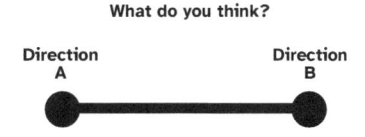

What do you think?

Direction A — Direction B

Step 3:

Gather all the data points and assemble the continuum. Lastly, decide the right headline and points to call out about the data as presented.

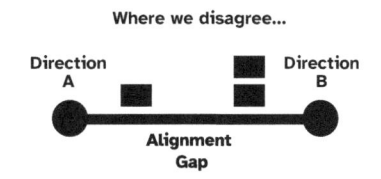

Where we disagree...

Direction A — Direction B

Alignment Gap

Chapter 4: **Recipes** | 225

Flow

A simple process diagram of my mornings

When there is a specific sequence or process, flow diagrams are good for understanding the detailed steps and choices involved by a single actor or system. Flow diagrams can be found in areas as far afield as user experience design and cancer research.

The rich and confusing history of flow diagrams serves as a primary example of the complex historical lineage of diagram types (see the literature review).

What to Expect

As you start to diagram using a flow, ask yourself if you are diagramming the process as it is or as it could be.

I recommend starting with mapping the as it is, which gives you the best chance to understand the process enough to make meaningful and holistic changes to it.

Ingredients

- ☐ A list of the steps of the process
- ☐ Understanding of the conditions or decisions that change the path or sequence of that process for specific users
- ☐ Research into the ways the process or sequence varies by context or user

Ideas for
Flow Diagrams

Diagram your daily routine, identifying the tasks and decisions in a typical day, looking for time for <insert goal>.

Diagram a process that feels needlessly complex or time consuming. Use a flow diagram to identify and point out potential improvements.

226 | STUCK? Diagrams Help.

also known as decision flow, question flow, structogram, functional band

---

Step 1:

Make a list of the steps and decisions in the process. Then make a shape for each step. Identify any that differ based on a decision, factor, or condition.

| Step 1 |
| Step 2 |
| Step 3a or Step 3b |
| Step 4 |
| Step 5a or Step 5b |

Step 2:

Arrange the steps into rows, making a new row (see dotted line) every time a major decision or choice determines the path.

Step 1 — Step 2 — Step 3a
....
Step 3b — Step 4 — Step 5a
....
Step 5b

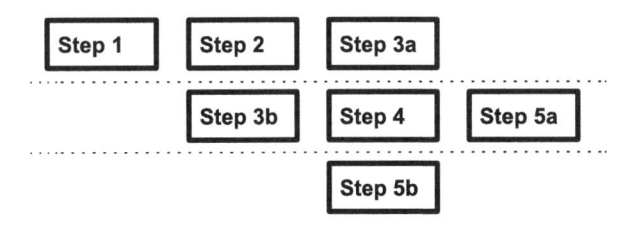

Step 3:

Add and label lines and decision points (see the discussion about decision diamonds in chapter 2) each time the actor or system makes a choice that splits the path.

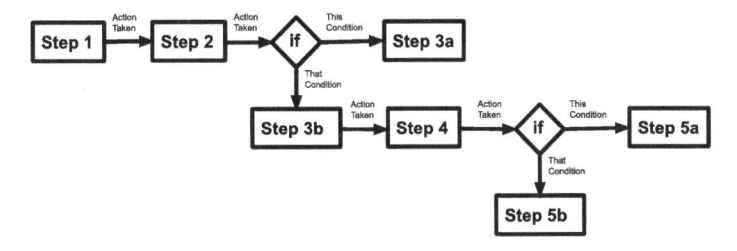

Step 1 —Action Taken→ Step 2 —Action Taken→ if —This Condition→ Step 3a
                                              ↓ That Condition
Step 3b —Action Taken→ Step 4 —Action Taken→ if —This Condition→ Step 5a
                                              ↓ That Condition
                                            Step 5b

Chapter 4: **Recipes** | 227

Gantt

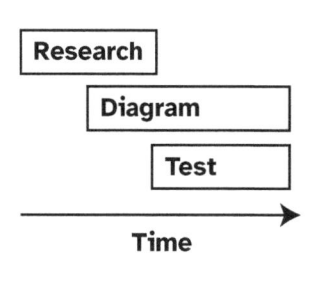

A simple Gantt of the ideal relationship between research, and diagramming, and testing

When tasks are dependent on one another to reach a goal or set of goals, Gantts are commonly used to visualize processes and projects at the task level.

Henry Gantt, a management consultant, invented this type of diagram between 1910 to 1915 to better track and manage the productivity of major infrastructure projects like the Hoover Dam.

More than a hundred years later, we still use this diagram type to manage project task dependency.

What to Expect

Gantts are finicky to manage if made manually in a drawing tool.

If you are managing something actively using the diagram, consider better tooling such as a spreadsheet or project management software. But if you are just visualizing an established high-level process, those same tools might feel like too much.

Ingredients

- ❏ List of tasks
- ❏ Understanding of each task's relationships to other tasks
- ❏ Understanding of the level of effort and ownership of each task

Ideas for *Gantts*

Diagram a moment-by-moment Gantt of a meal involving multiple dishes that need to be served at the same time.

Diagram a week-by-week or day-by-day Gantt of a project you are taking on with others at work.

228 | STUCK? Diagrams Help.

also known as project plan, task flow, dependency flow

Step 1:

Make a row for each task and a column for each increment of time you want to diagram tasks to (moment-by-moment, hourly, daily, weekly, monthly, etc.).

              Week 1   Week 2   Week 3
      Task 1
      Task 2
      Task 3

Step 2:

Add an indication for every column that a particular task requires (either for timeliness or dependence; if dependent, use a bracket to connect tasks).

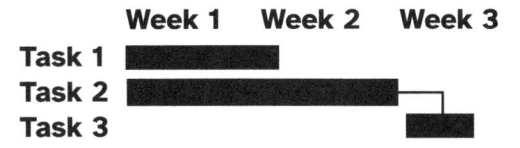

              Week 1   Week 2   Week 3
      Task 1 ▬▬▬▬▬
      Task 2 ▬▬▬▬▬▬▬▬▬▬▬▬┐
      Task 3   ▬▬▬

Hierarchy

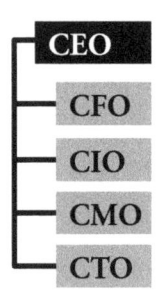

```
├─ CEO
├─ CFO
├─ CIO
├─ CMO
└─ CTO
```

A simple hierarchy diagram of an executive team

When there is ownership or categorization between people, places, or things, hierarchy diagrams are good for understanding the levels of something that exist.

Hierarchy diagrams are used for things as far afield as family trees and navigation planning for software and systems.

Examples of branching tree structures representing hierarchies date back to 500 CE with the Porphyrian tree.

What to Expect

When you diagram a list of multiples of a single type (e.g. articles, products, jobs, pages, books), pay attention to the level of detail to share based on your audience. A stacked shape (like C1 in Category C) represents a group of like objects in minimal space (see the discussion about collapsed vs. spread stacks in chapter 2).

Ingredients

- ❏ A list of objects to be represented hierarchically

- ❏ An understanding of the objects' ownership or categorization

Ideas for *Hierarchies*

Diagram the hierarchy of categories you use or might use to organize a personal collection that currently lacks order.

Diagram the hierarchy of how you organized something. It could be a document, a website, a file system, or anything with groupings.

230 | STUCK? Diagrams Help.

also known as tree map, org chart, navigation map, site map

Step 1:

Start with a nested list.

Use this list to find out how many levels you need.

```
<Thing We Organized>
Category A
Category B
        Sub Cat B1
        Sub Cat B2
Category C
        Sub Cat C1
```

Step 2:

Determine the layout of shapes and lines to represent each category and subcategory. There are two common approaches to hierarchy diagrams: horizontal or vertical. (See the discussion about bracket styles in chapter 2.)

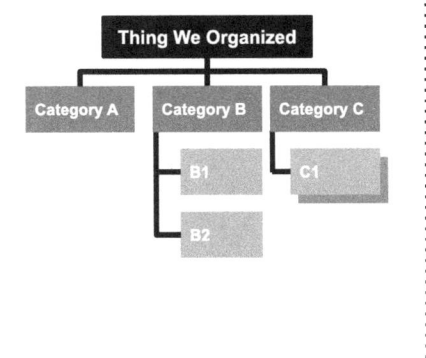

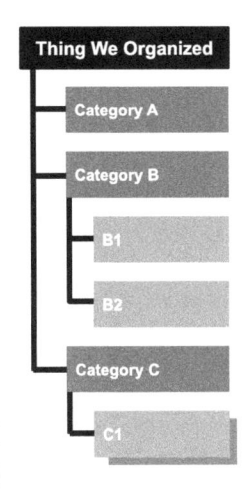

Chapter 4: **Recipes** | 231

〰️ Journey

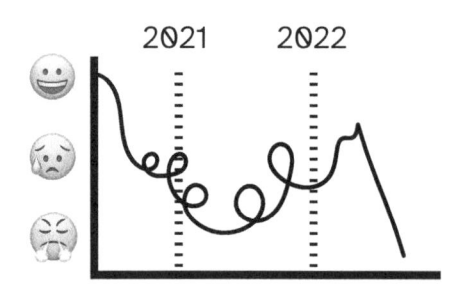

A journey diagram of the emotional experience of one person living through a global pandemic

When time is an element of the problem space and qualitative insights must be gathered along the way, journey diagrams are good for understanding the sequence and quality of an experience.

The customer journey mapping approach for service design was first introduced by OxfordSM in 1998, but there is evidence of similar techniques used much earlier. An example are service blueprints seen in the *Harvard Business Review* as early as 1984.[31]

What to Expect

This method requires research and/or experience on or observing the journey.

When made from our gut about someone else's experience, journey diagrams are often not helpful and can even be harmful if used to make critical decisions.

Ingredients

- ❏ Understanding of the time considerations of an experience
- ❏ Consideration of how unique each experience can be

Ideas for *Journeys*

Make a journey map of your life so far. What have been the major steps along the way that led you to where you are?

Diagram a journey of a customer going through a cycle of using something you work on.

232 | STUCK? Diagrams Help.

also known as journey map, customer flow, experience flow

Step 1:

Determine contexts and phases for the journey. Common contexts are where the user is or how the user feels. Phases group parts of the journey sequentially. Make a row for each context and column for each phase. This example has two contexts and three phases identified.

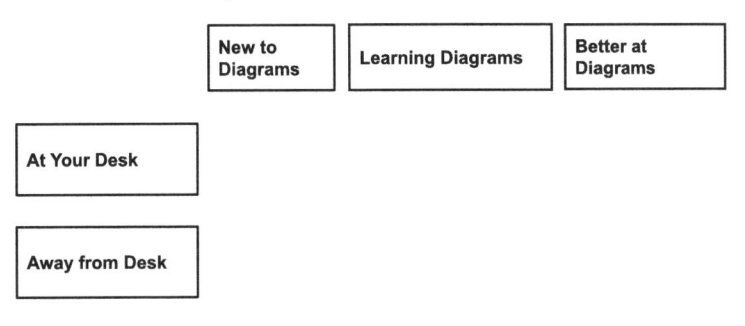

	New to Diagrams	Learning Diagrams	Better at Diagrams
At Your Desk			
Away from Desk			

Step 2:

Map each step or milestone in the journey to the appropriate phase and context.

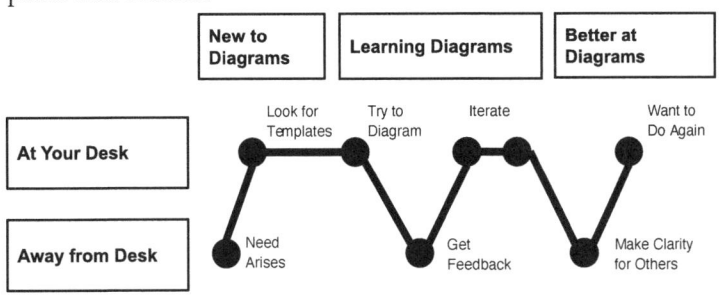

	New to Diagrams	Learning Diagrams	Better at Diagrams
At Your Desk	Look for Templates	Try to Diagram — Iterate	Want to Do Again
Away from Desk	Need Arises	Get Feedback	Make Clarity for Others

Chapter 4: **Recipes** | 233

⁃⁌⁃ **Quadrant**

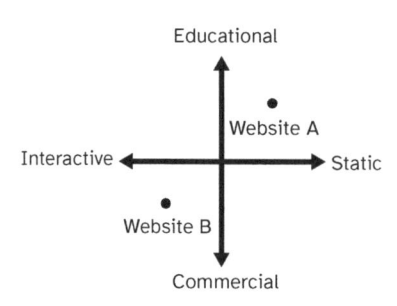

A simple quadrant diagram comparing two websites

When comparing things using two qualitative continuums or established quantitative spectrums to form value-driven groups, quadrant diagrams can visualize difference as well as identify clusters of similarity. Quadrants may have started as a Cartesian system for comparing quantitative coordinates, but they are just as useful when used to compare qualitative continuums.

What to Expect

If working with quantitative spectrums, make sure you include demarcation of the increment used.

Also, it is sometimes helpful to users to add the coordinates to the label of each item.

Ingredients

- ❏ A list of things to be compared
- ❏ Understanding of the continuums or range on which you want to compare them

Ideas for *Quadrants*

Make a quadrant diagram comparing your food takeout options, drawing useful distinctions (fastest, tastiest, cheapest, etc.).

Make a quadrant diagram comparing projects you or your team might take on. This is a great exercise for scoping what is important vs. urgent, as an example.

also known as four-up, graph quadrant, Cartesian coordinate system

Step 1:

Decide on the qualitative continuums (perceived space between ideas) or quantitative spectrums (actual measurable space between quantifiable things) on which you want to compare things.

See the continuum recipe on page 224 for more on writing qualitative continuums.

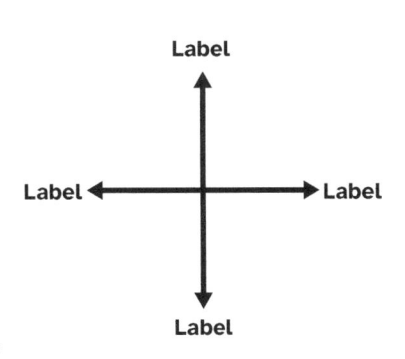

Step 2:

Add a labeled shape for each thing being compared at the intersection of each spectrum or quadrant. Optionally label the quadrants or highlight a goal (see shaded circle as an example).

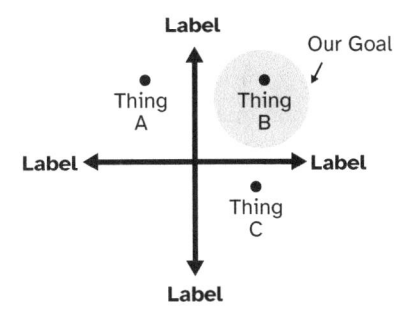

Chapter 4: **Recipes** | 235

Schematic

Living Room	Kitchen
Entry / Bath	Bedroom / Porch

A schematic of the floorplan of an apartment

When there is a (digital or physical) interface that is or will be used by end users, schematic diagrams are good for communicating how parts of a whole come together. They represent the elements of a system using abstract, graphic symbols and usually omit any details that are not pertinent to the intention. They may also often include oversimplified elements in order to make the essential meaning easier to grasp.

Schematics are so old and fundamental to human communication that it was impossible to actually track down their lineage—but the earliest cave paintings of animals were perhaps the earliest schematics, because they were likely intended to help people understand which animals were worth eating (or likeliest to eat them).

What to Expect

The rooms of an apartment are more *figured out* than the sections on a webpage. If things are still being figured out, make sure the schematic is clear about what decisions are still being made. The closer the schematic looks to the real user experience, the more likely people will think it is figured out.

Ingredients

- ❑ Understanding of the parts and whole of an interface
- ❑ Details about the materials that the interface is made of and how it works

Ideas for *Schematics*

Diagram a schematic of a meal, family tradition, or celebration in a culture of interest. What are the elements and how are they presented?

Diagram a schematic of an interface that you use to do your job. Use this schematic to design the dream interface you wish you had to do that same job.

also known as wireframe, blueprint, sketch, outline drawing

Step 1:

Draw a simple picture of the thing you are diagramming.

Step 2:

Label the pieces and parts.

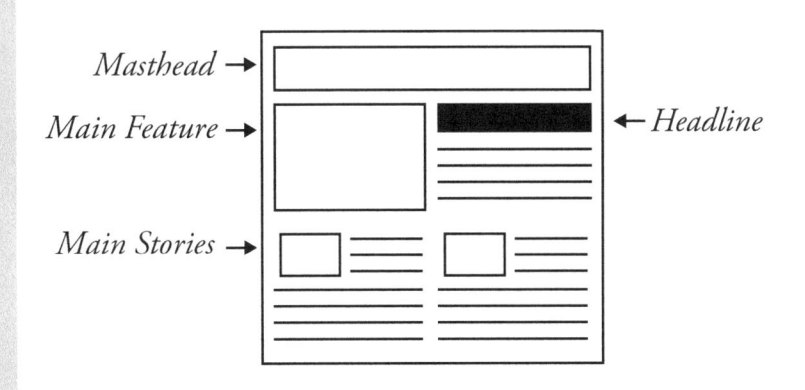

Masthead →
Main Feature → ← *Headline*

Main Stories →

Chapter 4: **Recipes** | 237

Sign

When there is a cause-and-effect relationship between people, places, or things, sign diagrams are an easy-to-use format for exploring the system effects that are created as a result.

We can use positive (+) and negative (-) to represent either qualitative or quantitative changes within systems.

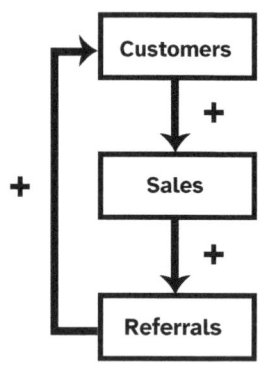

A sign diagram showing a healthy selling cycle

The origin of this diagram type is not clear, but this recipe was inspired by Malcolm Craig's *Thinking Visually*, which is where I first saw instructional content on this diagrammatic form.[32]

What to Expect

This is a powerful structure to create because it visualizes the levels you have to work with to impact the system as a whole or in parts.

The only way to have that impact is to remain neutral in your labeling of those levers. Avoid including labels such as *less*, *more*, *increase*, or *decrease*. A good trick is that you should be able to turn any + to a - and still have a system that makes sense.

Ingredients

- A list of people, places and things that impact one another
- Understanding of the positive or negative quality of that impact or the ability to measure it

Ideas for *Sign Diagrams*

Make a sign diagram of the impact your personal habits have on your mental or physical health.

Make a sign diagram to explore the influences you have on a system you work on or within.

238 | STUCK? Diagrams Help.

also known as systems diagram, cause and effect, multi-cause

Step 1:

Start with list of the factors you think matter to the problem space you are diagramming.

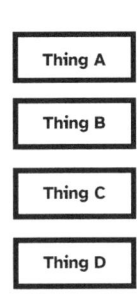

Step 2:

Start to group things from the list into couplets where the positive (+) or negative (-) impact in at least one direction is clear.

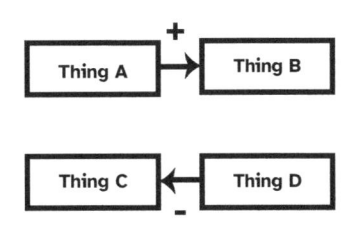

Step 3:

Add any less obvious impacts that reveal themselves now that these couplets have started to do their magic.

Now move the shapes into the best arrangement to better express your intention.

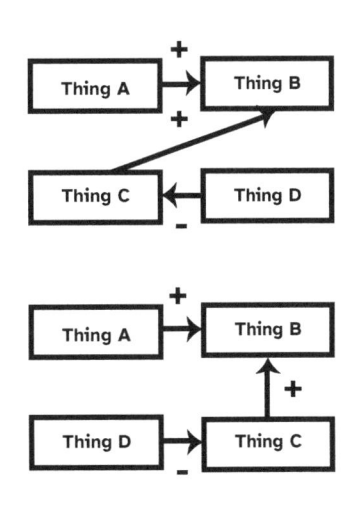

Chapter 4: **Recipes** | 239

Swim Lane

A swim lane diagram of a hand-off between sales and service staff

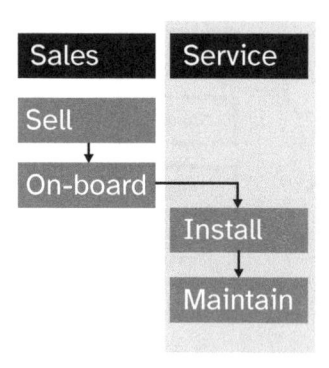

When there is more than one party involved, swim lane diagrams are good for understanding the hand-offs between multiple parties in a singular process.

Swim lanes were first discussed, under the moniker *multi-column process charts*, in a riveting 1945 pamphlet by the United States Bureau of the Budget called "Process Charting: Its Use in Procedural Analysis."[33] Despite their bureaucratic origins, swim lanes can be quite useful in everyday life.

What to Expect

The order of your columns really matters quite a bit to how neat and orderly the flow comes out appearing across roles. Test a few options to determine which is most readable and pleasing to the eye. I often start with the *origin* role for the process as the first column and add columns in the order of the hand-offs.

Ingredients

- List of tasks by role
- Understanding of the sequence of hand-offs

Ideas for *Swim Lanes*

Diagram a swim lane of a shared process in your household or community. Write out the roles involved and the discrete steps that every role does to make something big happen.

Diagram a swim lane of a work process that you are a part of with other people. Write out the roles involved and the discrete steps that every role does to make something big happen.

240 | STUCK? Diagrams Help.

also known as multi-user flow, team flow, multi-column process chart

Step 1:

Make a column for each role in the process.

| Role 1 | Role 2 | Role 3 |

Step 2:

List out the tasks under each role, in rough order of how they are undertaken.

I suggest vertical running swim lanes for longer processes and horizontal for shorter, but either works just as effectively.

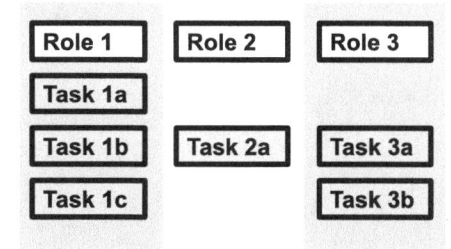

Role 1	Role 2	Role 3
Task 1a		
Task 1b	Task 2a	Task 3a
Task 1c		Task 3b

Step 3:

Use arrows to connect the tasks across roles as they work as a single process. Use a diamond anytime there are multiple paths based on a decision or condition.

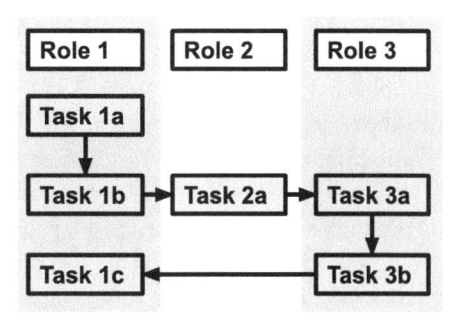

Role 1	Role 2	Role 3
Task 1a ↓		
Task 1b →	Task 2a →	Task 3a ↓
Task 1c ←		Task 3b

Chapter 4: **Recipes** | 241

Venn

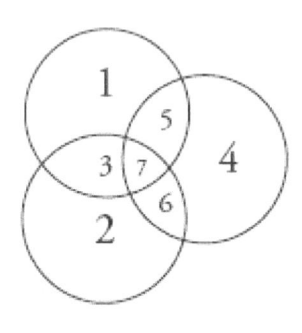

A simple Venn diagram about the fun of maths.

When concepts need to be related to one another, Venn diagrams are good for understanding how overlaps result in novel outcomes. This popular diagram style was introduced by John Venn in the 1880s.[34]

More recently, Venns have stayed busy enabling the creation of hilarious memes. Do yourself the favor of typing "funny Venn" into any image searching engine and then prepare to be delighted.

What to Expect

Venn diagrams can make things feel overly simple or tidy. Challenge yourself to label all the overlaps and then get ready to learn something new. A Venn is best used as a thinking tool when you are working through what the perceived or actual overlaps might mean for your intentions. If a Venn diagram feels a bit constraining for your intention, do a search for Euler diagrams. They are more free form but based on the same premise as Venn in terms of visualizing overlaps and groupings.

Ingredients

- ❏ List of concepts
- ❏ Understanding of the concepts' relationships to one another

Ideas for *Venn Diagrams*

Diagram a Venn of your inspiration, style, or personal influences. Use this to better understand what you uniquely bring to the overlaps of things you have interest or experience in.

Diagram a Venn of how roles overlap at your job. Perhaps there is a task that people of different roles work on together or a role in which two specialties situationally overlap for meeting the needs of your organization.

also known as Euler, overlapping circles, concept mash-ups

Step 1:

Draw circles for each concept.

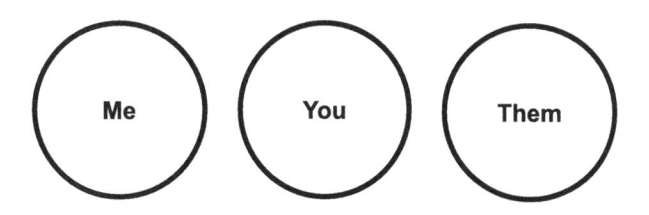

Step 2:

Overlap the circles and label the places where the overlap creates additional or different meaning.

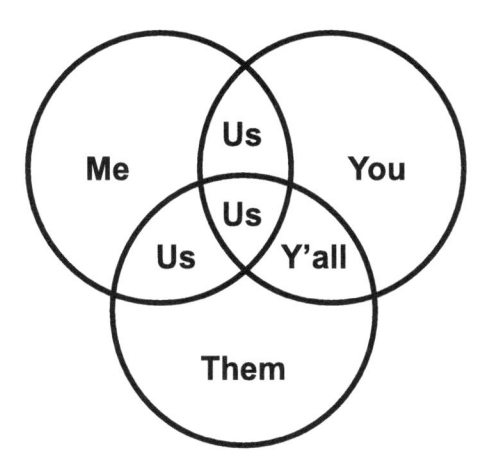

Chapter 4: **Recipes** | 243

Don't Let Templates Constrain You

One of the hardest parts about teaching these recipes for common types of diagrams is a fear that I am limiting your creative potential by showing these examples.

By laying out a flow diagram guiding you to the most obvious diagrammatic outcomes, I might be further perpetuating the suburbanality that Diagram Town has these days, where everything looks the same.

If you aren't careful, by relying solely on existing recipes of other diagrammers, you can entirely miss realizing the power that diagramming holds.

When teaching diagrammatic technique in a classroom, I have the students recite what I call the diagrammer's pledge.

Find a mirror and read the next page aloud.

Recipe End Notes

[31] See, for example, G. Lynn Shostack, "Designing Services That Deliver," *Harvard Business Review*, January 1984, https://hbr.org/1984/01/designing-services-that-deliver. Interestingly, the term *service blueprint* makes an early appearance in Shostack's essay. The service blueprint has since evolved to include the journey element as just one of the layers. See Sarah Gibbons, "Service Blueprints: Definition," Nielsen Norman Group, August 27, 2017, https://www.nngroup.com/articles/service-blueprints-definition.

[32] See Malcolm Craig, *Thinking Visually* (London: Continuum, 2000).

[33] United States Bureau of the Budget, "Process Charting: Its Use in Procedural Analysis" (Washington, DC: US Government Printing Office, 1945), 1.

[34] John Venn, "On the Diagrammatic and Mechanical Representation of Propositions and Reasonings," *London, Edinburgh, and Dublin Philosophical Magazine and Journal of Science* 10, no. 59 (July 1880): 1–18.

The Diagrammer's Pledge

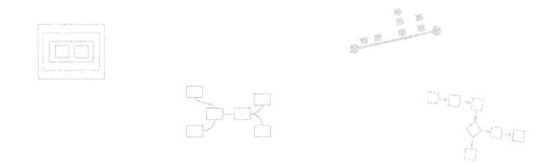

I hereby swear to not let the diagrammatic recipes taught to me or the stories told to me convince me that all diagrammatic options are out there to be copied.

They are not.

I will seek to learn from the diagrams of others while leaving enough room to make my own decisions about meeting my unique intention.

5

Collaboration

Throughout this book, we have explored how the *intra*personal dynamics of your emotional journey impact your experience with the mechanical process of diagramming.

In this final chapter, we will more deeply explore the messy and strange *inter*personal dynamics that go into making good diagrams when collaborating with others.

I saved this for last because it is the sweet ending I think this book deserves. I want to close our time together by dwelling on what happens at the intersection of people and diagrams.

Being helpful to someone who is stuck is at the heart of diagrammatic purpose, process, and craft. Sometimes the someone stuck is the maker themselves; other times the someone is an external audience for whom it is clear there is a need for *more than words*.

Either way, we can't ever make the mistake of thinking we can skip the people part of diagramming. People are the essential ingredient to how diagrams work.

Allow me to introduce you to a cast of characters who are each experiencing their own unique diagrammatic circumstances.

Every story is based on at least one real person who has chosen to share with me their experience with a diagram they have wrestled with and lived to tell about. I have changed the names, contexts, and details in each story to mold it into a lesson about collaboration.

Now that we have talked through the purpose, process, and craft of diagramming, I am hopeful that if you still feel stuck, one of these stories will feel enough like your own story to inspire you to use the skills you have learned thus far.

The most important lessons of these stories, at least to me as a teacher, are the paths the diagrammers did not go down and the mistakes they did not make. My analysis of how they could have screwed up the people part follows each story.

Cast of Characters

Wren: Changing the Center	249
Oli: Agreeing on Definitions	254
Randi: Addressing Collective Anxiety	258
Kris: Expanding the Assignment	262
Ilhan: Struck by a Vision	268
Lee: Provoking Conversation	274
Dani: Asking Obvious Questions	280
Cyd: Changing the Metaphor	286

Wren: **Changing the Center**

When Wren was hired, there were 36 people on the production team they would be managing. The hiring manager failed, however, to mention the 22 people who had been recently let go or how toxic the team's prior manager had been leading up to the layoffs.

For the first few weeks on the job, Wren tried to listen to the concerns and experiences of the team and work on confidence that the near future would not include any further layoffs.

Along with the mood on the team, which was downright sullen, Wren also identified that there was a lack of understanding about what the structural changes to the team actually meant for the day-to-day work. There were way fewer people but, as is so often the case, not any less work to get done.

At first, Wren felt defeated by all this. As a young manager, only in their first role managing a team this large, it was a hard way to start. In the first meeting with the team, someone had to leave the room overcome with grief talking about the layoffs.

It was clear to Wren that a new tack needed to be taken with this team, one that didn't center *management* or how insignificant the team had come to feel in the larger organization. The new approach would instead center the process that the team was so skilled at delivering and the results they were after for their efforts.

The plan was to have a team meeting to level set with everyone and present Wren's vision for how the team could operate. In preparing for the meeting, Wren remembered a diagram that Disney Studios used for its organizational chart when it was still just a small animation studio.

Always the innovator, Disney had proposed a process-centered map of roles within the studio and how they worked together to get things done rather than a traditional hierarchy-based org chart.[35]

Wren wasn't running an animation studio, but the context felt so similar to the group of production artists and craftspeople in this department that it felt useful as an exercise to give this format a try. They set out to work with pen and paper, making a version of the Disney diagram translated to this organization and team.

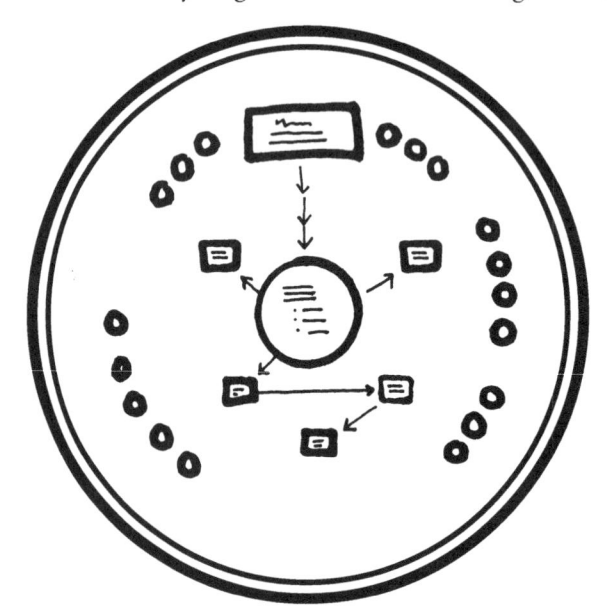

Within the first few moments of working with the new diagram, Wren liked how it decentered management and put focus on enabling, not controlling, the team. Wren decided that if Walt Disney was in charge of stories, an equivalent here might be being in charge of *setting audacious goals*.

With that decision, the tone of the diagram and the management approach Wren was after became a bit clearer. Wren then worked on a taxonomy of skills and roles that made up the team. Wren decided that getting agreement on such a list would be a perfect team activity, so they made a draft version based on listening to team members and set aside time on an upcoming meeting agenda to talk about the taxonomy and gather people's interest in making the right call on how to break down what the group does.

---

[35] Alyssa Carnahan, "Artifactual: The Disney Family Map," The Walt Disney Family Museum, March 16, 2012, https://www.waltdisney.org/blog/artifactual-disney-family-map.

250 | STUCK? Diagrams Help.

Next was the process flow at the center. Once again, that felt like a good exercise for the team to talk through and design together. But Wren knew how hard it would be to get this team talking without something to react to. So based on best guesses, good intentions, and observation of the team the last few weeks, Wren took a shot at how the process *could* go.

With a straw-diagram in place, Wren crafted a short presentation around the idea of the Disney diagram and what it meant about this new approach to managing the team.

The meeting was sullen to start, as all team meetings up to this point had been. Wren confidently went through the short presentation and then put the strawman diagram up on screen. Then, shocking to all involved, Wren stated that they would be dedicating the remaining 80% of the meeting to work as a team to critique and solidify the taxonomy of skills and the process by which work is taken in, defined, and delivered.

By the end of the hour, there had been a ton of great discussion and even a few people who had offered to help push the diagram further along after the meeting.

Wren knew how big a turn this was for this team and tried to not jinx it with the wrong kind of smile or remark. When the meeting was over, team members lingered instead of darting out. There was even a sigh and two giggles of relief, each bringing needed levity and brightness to a dark-for-too-long place.

The diagram didn't change everything, but it was a moment when things took a turn for the different.

What If Wren Made the Diagram without Input?

Wren was hired as a new manager for a team that had been decimated by layoffs and organizational restructuring, leaving them in a state of mistrust and grief.

A few weeks into surveying the situation and coming up with a plan, there was a big meeting with the whole team. Instead of unveiling and dictating a plan, Wren used a diagram inspired by Disney Studios to invite the team's collaboration on two important topics that seemed in deep need of attention: roles and process.

Think about how the results could have been much different had Wren become overly confident about what the roles and process should be and just presented that to the team as a diagrammatic directive instead of a collaboration invitation.

Wren was facing the kind of uncertainty that breeds mistrust. When diagramming in an environment that is emotionally charged with change and fear, like Wren was in, swooping in from the outside to *should* all over everyone would have brought a much different result. Likely more mistrust and fear.

Same diagram, different approach to the people part.

Lessons from Wren's Story

Instead of bravehearting towards the fear and uncertainty alone, be like Wren. Find places to bring others into the diagrammatic process. When we include other people in our process, the results are always better.

In the case of Wren's meeting, the culture of the team and the level of trust that they have in their new leader was on the line; the stakes were high. It was not just about a diagram.

Diagrams are just objects of discourse. They only matter as much as the discourse that is spurred by them. As we bring people into our diagrammatic process, it's important to take with us the following lessons from Wren's story.

- Clearly identify places in your diagram that you want to work on with other people and use larger group time together to gather interest. Assign pieces of the workload to specific people or small groups to build cross-functional trust in the diagrammatic process.

- Try a new format or out-of-the-box way of visualizing something old, tired, or triggering as a way to get people to actually look at the content with new eyes.

Chapter 5: **Collaboration** | 253

Oli: **Agreeing on Definitions**

As a data scientist turned UX designer, Oli got a dream assignment working on a team responsible for the search experience of a product that was incredibly search dependent.

The team was implementing a new approach to knowledge management called an ontology. It would help the search algorithm to have a more human understanding of how terms relate to one another.

Oli decided to start by interviewing their teammates, who had all worked on this for a lot longer but all from different angles, backgrounds, and skill sets.

From the interviews, Oli came away with a great overview of ontologies from each person's perspective and area of expertise. But everyone also seemed to have a slightly different definition of the pieces and parts of an actual ontology, which might be fine except that they also seemed to deeply disagree in ways that might impact the product they were making together.

Oli saw the issue from a business user standpoint; clearly, there was a mismatch in the language that the team was using, and this made sense given the diverse experience and background of the team. Oli knew that there were important building block concepts that everyone would be better off being on the same page about, so they got to work making a list of definitions.

In the next team meeting, Oli shared the list and had a good start to a discussion about whether they could get alignment on the definitions. No one seemed too engaged with the subject. One machine learning engineer snarked that *"the words don't matter as much as the use cases and the training set."*

For the next meeting, Oli tried something new. Instead of just the list of definitions, they made a simple block diagram of how the concepts related to one another.

For each element, the definition from the prior meeting was also shown, but no one focused on that part yet. This simple visualization energized the room, mostly about what Oli had totally-gotten-wrong-ZOMG, but still it was progress! The next meeting, another diagram, this one showing the elements of another data structure within the search algorithm that was confusing.

Then another showing the types of relationships in the ontology. Meeting after meeting, diagram after diagram, Oli tackled the list of definitions visually.

Oli became known as the bringer of diagrams—even earning the nickname OliGrammer over time. And the diagrams of core vocabulary did get the team through the exercise of agreeing on all those verbal definitions after all.

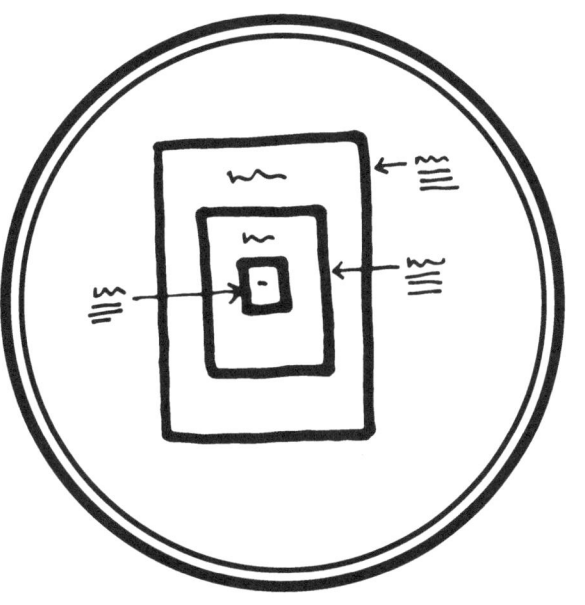

Not only were these simple Oligrams™ useful for the team to get on the same page about the words they use to do their work, they also became the central visual prop when the team was called into the boardroom to give a quarterly progress briefing on the search product.

Oli proudly presented a selection of four Oligrams™ that the team had chosen for the executive audience. The CEO said it was one of the clearest presentations from a search team they had ever seen and congratulated Oli and the team on being the first to teach them how the search algorithms actually worked!

Was it the diagram that made it clear? Nah. It was Oli knowing that when it comes to working with other people, we can get further with diagrams than with words alone. But still, a pretty good day for diagrams.

Chapter 5: **Collaboration** | 255

What If Oli Hadn't Interviewed Coworkers?

The initial spark of insight that led Oli down the diagrammatic path was choosing to interview coworkers in an effort to better understand the problem space of ontologies from multiple angles. All of the power in Oli's story roots from this decision to dig deeper.

Think about how the results could have been much different had Oli not had that interviewing experience. There is another version of this story in which Oli just started working on the end user's experience, never even fully aware of the linguistic and structural misunderstandings that were at the center of every team interaction and output. Perhaps that would have remained the reality through to this project's completion.

Oli had a choice to make at the beginning—the choice to seek understanding from others rather than just leaning solely on their own expertise. If Oli had come onto the team merely focused on being an expert in UX, they would not have had the new person perspective to point out the flaws of the ontology being built by a smart team that was just missing one another in terms of shared meaning.

Lessons from Oli's Story

Instead of deciding to play expert and stay in your lane, when you find yourself on a cross-functional team trying to achieve something big, take a beginner's approach. Ask the questions that others are afraid to ask or that are the hardest to answer clearly.

Oli didn't make diagrams to be well known in the organization. They made them for the most important reason one can diagram: to lessen the suffering of not knowing. In this case, the not knowing was a common varietal: not speaking the same language as someone while attempting to work on the same thing as that someone.

When we talk, we don't often go in a straight line. We meander, we stumble, we edit in flow. When we talk using a diagram, we can follow a straighter path to better orient, instruct, and contextualize. As you dig deeper, keep in mind these lessons from Oli's story.

- Talk to people one-on-one. In groups, we hear the edited version of the truth too often. By meeting each person alone, Oli was able to see the differences between people's perspectives without creating conflict.

- When words get hard, turn to pictures. If group members are frustratingly missing one another's points, use a visual to reorient them towards a shared model.

Randi: **Addressing Collective Anxiety**

When Randi arrived in Tulsa, they knew they were in for a dramatic week at a client site. Their program manager had been on a few sales calls to this same organization and described the meetings as "pretty combative."

Randi's assignment was straightforward in Tulsa that week. They needed to present a navigation system redesign proposal that was based on months of user research and auditing work on the current website for a national insurance company in the middle of acquiring a network of local insurance agencies.

On the first day of the trip, Randi started out the day by presenting a research and audit recap. They then presented the proposal for how a user would potentially see the proposed and tested navigation options.

They found out quickly what the program manager had warned about in terms of expectant combat. Before the first coffee break, there was already a heated argument to break up between two department heads over how prominent they were compared to each other in the navigation proposal.

On top of the combative atmosphere, Randi picked up a sense of collective anxiety, it seemed, about the workload involved in this redesign. Everyone was anxious amidst a lot of change and trying to figure out what the change meant to them or their teams.

That night back at the hotel, Randi had an idea while ironing a shirt for the next day's trip to that same nondescript Tulsa conference room. *What if this simple sitemap could better prepare the team for the work of this redesign?*

Randi made a mental list of the things everyone was seemingly the most anxious about after reviewing the proposal:

- How many pages do we need to review, rewrite, or create?
- Who gets the final say on each page?

Randi opened up the sitemap they had presented earlier that day and added a few new layers onto it:

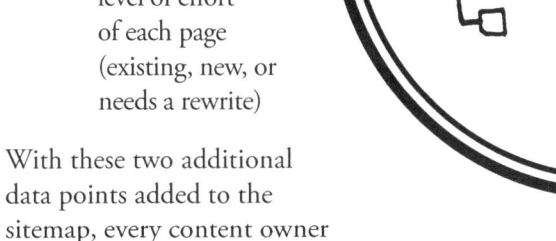

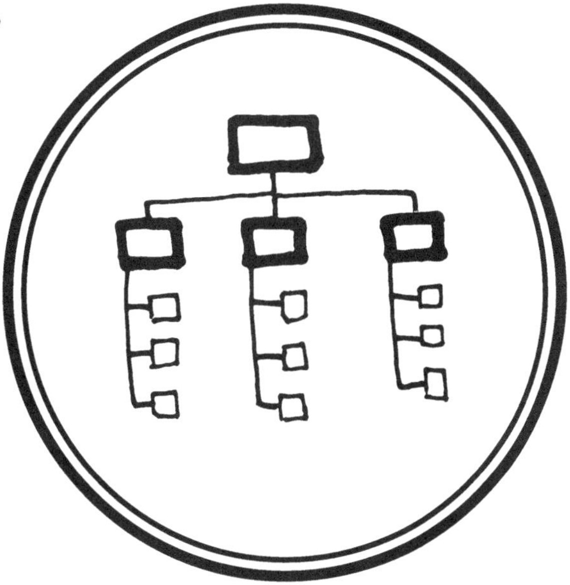

1. Color-coding designating "ownership" at the page level

2. Iconography for level of effort of each page (existing, new, or needs a rewrite)

With these two additional data points added to the sitemap, every content owner in the organization (there were 18 owners across >1,000 pages) could easily see the pages they were responsible for. They could also see the level of effort expected for each section they owned, so they could start to think about staffing.

The next day, Randi showed the diagram to a sea of interested faces. The content owners got it and knew what they needed to do. There were still arguments to be had about prioritization within the navigation, but now that there was clarity about the ownership and level of effort, it felt less like a battle and more like a set of needed negotiations for the team to make along the way.

It wasn't just the diagram that made the change. Before revealing the diagram, Randi gave an impassioned speech to the group about the importance of working together to get through this period of change.

But once there was a diagram of the work to be done that also created a clear understanding of who would be doing that work, the fights stopped and the work really started.

What If Randi Had Ignored the Collective Anxiety?

A consultant is ironing their shirt in a Tulsa hotel room, in preparation for the big meeting the next day. Suddenly it hits them that perhaps they could reduce a lot of anxiety for the client team if content ownership and status were added as a layer onto the sitemap being argued about passionately.

By adding this extra information, Randi was able to better handle an objection that was getting in the way of talking about the navigation proposal: Who is going to do all this work?

Think about how the outcome could have been different had Randi just gone in for day two of battle with only the same old sitemap to protect them.

Randi's ability to quell the client team's collective anxiety about workload is what makes this story interesting; otherwise, it's merely any other sitemap presentation in a featureless boardroom.

When we are diagramming, understanding our audience involves understanding them enough to know how their emotions, context, and mentality are likely to impact their ability to use the diagram as we intend. By seeing this collective anxiety and meeting it where it was, Randi was able to break through and finally discuss what they were actually there to discuss.

Lessons from Randi's Story

If you are trying to make a point using a diagram and another related point keeps coming up, figure out if it's in need of addressing to discuss what you are *actually* there to discuss.

If Randi didn't think bigger than the assignment, the assignment could not have gotten done. Without this pivot for day two, Randi was probably heading back to Tulsa to that same nondescript boardroom to do this whole thing all over again. I'm not saying I am Randi, but I will say I have been Randi with the same old sitemap and a request for a return visit to "iron everything out."

When we are making diagrams, sometimes other issues come up. Over the course of getting to know your audience in an effort to better meet them where they are, keep in mind these lessons from Randi's story.

- Consider calling an audible. To be effective, this diagram pivot had to be contextualized and connected to the issue by that issue being called out.

- Instead of sticking with the plan, read the room. Randi was ironing a shirt for this big meeting and still had the bravery to change the sitemap to better serve the group. The lesson is not to burn the candle at both ends on client trips, friends. The lesson is to leave room in the plan to change it.

Chapter 5: **Collaboration** | 261

Kris: **Expanding the Assignment**

When Kris got a job as a product manager for a university, they had no idea how much they would end up improving life on campus for 40,000 students and a whole department of customer service representatives.

Kris's first assignment was to redesign the online student handbook containing all the content a student would ever need to know regarding systems, processes, and various deadlines for programs, benefits, and other assistance made available to students on campus and online.

In the first few weeks on the job, Kris asked to take a tour of the call center and interview some of the customer service people who take calls from students all day answering questions.

In these interviews, Kris learned that over the years the process for enrollment and financial aid had complexified so much you needed an advanced degree to figure it all out. Many customer service agents had sticky notes and scribbles on note pads all over their desks reminding them of things that were otherwise buried or hard to find in the handbook.

On the first day of interviews, Kris learned the call center was nicknamed the we-have-jobs-because-the-handbook-sucks department.

On a typical day, 70% of the customer service calls received were about confusion regarding the handbook. Most of the calls were some variety of "*Where to find something in the handbook*" or "*How to understand some long convoluted paragraph in the handbook*" about something simple to explain in … er, human.

Kris decided on the second day of customer service interviews to leverage the collective knowledge of the student experience that could be found in the customer service reps' stories to make a diagram.

They had a hunch something was off. They created a journey map in which the x axis was the span of the full academic calendar year and the y axis was the sections of the handbook.

AUG	SEP	OCT	NOV	DEC	JAN	FEB	MAR	APR	MAY	JUN

| Student Life |

| Finances |

| Housing |

| Academics |

| Events |

Using the handbook, Kris unpacked and mapped every event, milestone, deadline, and date-based insight to be found onto the diagram. They printed the partially filled-in diagram big on a plotter in the print department and hung it in the room where the interviews with customer service reps were taking place.

With each rep, they added sticky notes about things that always come up at points in the year and any other details that had been missed from reviewing the handbook.

The reps commented on how helpful it was to see it all laid out this way. A few reps ran back to their desks to grab hand-drawn diagrams of processes that students called about all the time to share with Kris.

At lunchtime, a manager popped in to see the diagram that had been the buzz of the breakroom all morning. The manager had just had a discussion with a few team members who thought it would potentially help them to better prepare for what to expect from a call volume and content training perspective throughout the year.

The manager asked if they could take a picture of the map and if Kris could follow up on if anything is done with this work.

Kris had learned some critical insights through this effort about the way deadlines and events piled on top of one another without insight and oversight and how that wrought havoc on teams and resources, especially those in customer service.

While Kris felt like the customer service reps were newly inspired to better tackle the havoc with more foresight and better sticky note explanation arsenals, it felt important to tell others on the team who might be able to help change the student experience to reduce the pressure on certain time periods.

Within the first few conversations with colleagues responsible for the digital student experience for financial aid and the housing department, Kris knew that the solution was more than just clearer communication in the handbook or better training for customer service reps. This was a system with a set of clear and potentially preventable and predictable overloads.

One afternoon, Kris ordered pizzas and invited counterparts from each major department to a meeting to discuss the "student experience."

A journey diagram was hung prominently, showing how certain parts of the academic year were *pile-ons* from the student perspective.

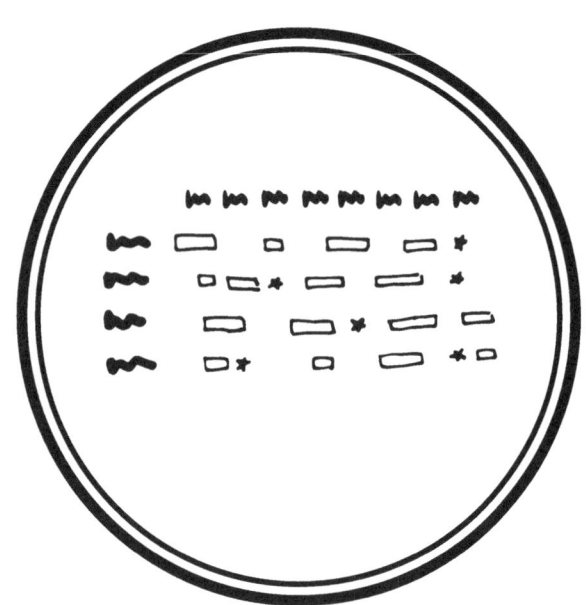

264 | STUCK? Diagrams Help.

The diagram also illustrated how ineffective things such as marketing and customer service were in the face of those pile-ons.

The problem was clear, and the question was simple:

Do all these dates need to stay as is?

The discussions started about what was possible in each department. Maybe this deadline *could* get moved, whereas this one *had to* stay put, "because reasons." Slowly, deadline by deadline, date by date, milestone by milestone, the leading was loosened between all the milestones and deadlines. The student experience (and, by extension, that of the customer service reps) started to feel less brutal.

Now all that had to happen was individual lobbying at the department level to make changes to the schedule. Some changes were bigger requests than others; many were expected to take time to get changed.

Kris made a document containing the journey diagram and the needed changes by department, and the work began.

Kris had spent a few days not *technically* working on the digital student handbook, knowing that the deeper work on understanding the intricacies and overlaps of student experience was foundational to really helping students.

And they learned, *as they had a few other times before*, the power of showing, not telling.

What If Kris Hadn't Pushed for Change?

Kris's story is a stellar example of diagramming for a group to discuss how to improve what's happening for the user based on how the system is designed, or not designed as the case may be.

By getting people together and using the journey diagram as a tool to stay on message, Kris was able to get them to explore the problem together and negotiate a realistic plan to lobby for real change.

Think about how the outcome could have been different had Kris just used the journey map to document what was going on for the student handbook to be clearer, instead of bringing others in. Perhaps a funny way to think about this is, *What if Kris just did their actual job?*

When we diagram things as they are, we have to be prepared to see things we don't want to see. And once you see a mess, it's hard to unsee it. By going past the assignment to push for change, Kris was better able to serve the end users of the student handbook. Could they have made the handbook easier to understand without changing the system itself? Surely. But without pushing for change, all Kris had the ability to do was write and edit around these preventable and repetitive stress-filled valleys in the student (and customer service rep) experience.

Lessons from **Kris's Story**

If you are minding your business, doing your work in your silo, and a research finding or insight hits above your level to tackle properly, figure out the right people to absorb this insight and make that happen.

Diagrams are a great way to shortcut a lot on the way to a big conversation. Pizza helps, sure. But starting a conversation by saying "I think there are times when the students are overwhelmed" would not have yielded the results Kris achieved with the aid of the diagram.

By introducing the diagram as a territory to explore with the group on a well-defined quest, Kris was able to move a big conversation forward quite quickly. Let's take from Kris's story a couple of lessons on how diagrams can help us go further.

- Use a diagram when you need to move quickly through a territory but want to make sure your audience doesn't get lost along the way to your actual point.

- See something, say something. If you are making a diagram in one context and see a problem at a different level that impacts your ability to serve your audience, say something.

Ilhan: **Struck by a Vision**

When Ilhan finally grasped what their jazz guitar teacher, Michel, was trying to teach, it changed how they played guitar forever.

Ilhan, a talented technical writer, became intrigued with the idea that Michel could help so many more people if only the wise old teacher's brilliant ideas weren't only accessible through limited private lessons with Michel in a tiny town 30 minutes outside Sydney, Australia.

Their lessons began after Ilhan had been given a business card at a local Sydney music shop, almost under the table, when inquiring about assistance leveling up in jazz guitar.

One day, after a lesson, Ilhan asked Michel if they would ever consider or had ever considered writing a book. Michel giggled and blushed, saying, "Write a book? I play guitar, not keyboard."

"What if I were to help you by ghostwriting the book?" Ilhan bravely asked. Michel looked intrigued and replied, "Hmm … I guess you start writing, and we will see how we go."

They started to have a coffee after their lessons to review what they had just learned in practice as if it would be written down for others to benefit from. As the weeks went by, Ilhan would print out pages and bring them to Michel to read and approve. They were taking it note by note and giving it a go.

In about three months time, they had a binder that had started to feel like the weight of a thin book. Ilhan had a friend in town for the weekend who was also a jazz guitarist, and Ilhan took this as an ideal opportunity to test the book.

The friend spent some time working through the book, reading and using their guitar, and all was going pretty well. Ilhan got some good notes on ways to improve the content and make things clearer.

Once the notes were covered, they talked about how different Michel's approach is and how interesting people will likely find it.

"Too bad you have to read this whole thing to really see what's different," Ilhan's friend said, pushing Ilhan sharply down a well of creative possibility.

This was an *incredibly* technical book written for advanced guitarists. It had never even occurred to Ilhan to have a section introducing the method in a simple overview.

Ilhan got to work writing an introduction covering why this approach to jazz guitar was different from the rest out there.

After writing the first draft, Ilhan gave it a read and was struck by how esoteric it all still sounded. Frustrated, and tired of thinking about it, Ilhan leashed their dog and set out on a long walk to do some thinking. The best ideas often came at a beach that was a short 10-minute walk away, so off they went.

It was one of those crystal clear, blue-skies-that-make-you-feel-alive kind of days. But Ilhan was lost in thought.

The technical writer inside was screaming, *Just find the right words, edit it down, it will get there!* At the same time, the creative person, the one who was so drawn to this way of playing guitar in the first place, was slowly adding volume to another melody.

Not even halfway down the beach to their usual fetch spot, Ilhan stopped suddenly, struck with a vision of a color wheel. They were careful in their next thoughts, like walking on cognitive eggshells, trying to not scare off this wild, untamed idea before it could be caught. *There are 12 notes of the guitar, and a color wheel has 12 rays. There are 12 notes of the guitar, and a color wheel has 12 rays.* They thought again, more confident this time.

"There are 12 notes of the guitar, and 12 rays on a color wheel!" they said excitedly out loud, startling themselves and their pup.

As if inhabited by an actual spirit, Ilhan rushed home, trailed by a very confused pup not used to being rushed off the beach so quickly.

Once in the house, materials were quickly assembled. Anything would do. *Aha! There is construction paper and the 12-pack of markers stowed away in the hall closet.*

The wheel came together quickly, then Ilhan added all the notes of the guitar, one per ray. Sure enough, something magical emerged— just like the vision at the beach.

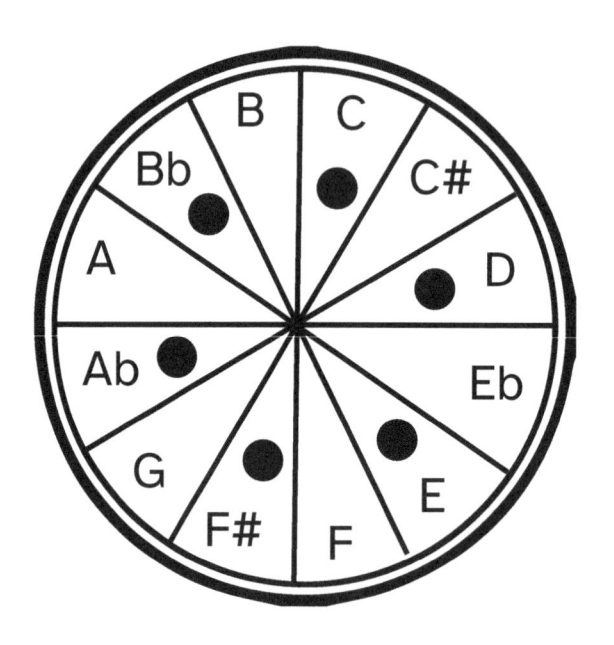

It turned out the notes that aligned to the rays of complementary colors were indeed complementary in Michel's way of teaching jazz chord progressions. Even the tertiary patterns aligned. *Ah, the magic of numbers, patterns, and maths.*

Ilhan was anxious before the next lesson with Michel, eager to see how this color wheel and the introductory content landed. This was after all the only part of the book that Ilhan had not taken direct dictation on.

After their regular lesson, Michel poured the coffee and asked, "So, how is our book coming along?" creating the perfect segue. Ilhan took out the new section and passed it to him.

"After testing the book on my friend last week, I wrote an introduction chapter on their advice. I would love to hear what you think; can I leave this with you? We can discuss it next week after our lesson."

Michel agreed to give it a read, and they said their goodbyes. Ilhan prepared for a long week of wondering how Michel might react, especially to the color wheel.

Around 6 PM that same evening, Ilhan got a phone call from Michel. They had known each other for almost two years now, but they had never actually spoken on the phone.

"Well, you did it," Michel said as soon as it was clear Ilhan was on the line. "You nailed it. I never had thought to compare my teaching to that of other traditions. And the colors, how beautiful. Where did you come up with that idea?"

"At the beach," Ilhan giggled back. "I came up with it at the beach. And I am so glad you like it, Michel. I was nervous sharing it with you, because I know we have worked closely on the book all this time. But I think this part really shows how this system you have created to teach us works. And I am so excited to help you teach even more people."

"Many more people would make it past the first lesson with this introduction. Would you mind if I start to share these with new students as handouts?" Michel inquired shyly.

"It would be my honor, dear teacher. Thank you. Now let's get this book printed and available!" They ended the call shortly thereafter, and Ilhan took a deep, satisfied breath.

For a technical writer there is often a requirement to drop your creative self at the door. But writing this book, specifically this chapter and making that color wheel, had stirred something new inside.

Ilhan knew to expect many more trips to the beach ending abruptly with ideas for visuals to make things they were struggling with in words alone just a bit clearer. And they were ready to bring their fuller creative self to their technical and writerly challenges more often.

What If Ilhan Hadn't Tested the Content with a Friend?

When we left our friend, Ilhan, they were well on their way to publishing the book of their mentor's advanced jazz guitar teaching method. Their beautiful color wheel–inspired diagram had opened their mentor's eyes to how a visual representation could help them reach more people with their complex teachings.

In the story, the critical moment for Ilhan came as they talked with a potential reader of the book, a guitarist friend visiting from out of town. Through sharing the words, Ilhan came to understand something more than words was needed.

Think about how the outcome could have been different had Ilhan not tested the content on that friend. They likely would have never written the overview chapter at all and very surely then never discovered the delight of the guitar note color wheel.

The beauty in Ilhan's story is how the idea for a diagram was actually born from the user research on the content in another form. Our ideas are searching for their final form through our hands. Sometimes we are writing a chapter, get frustrated, take a break, and walk to the beach only to end up catching a wild diagram offering to fix whatever is in the way of us noticing that the sun is shining that day.

Lessons from Ilhan's Story

Inspiration really can come at any time, from anywhere. Sometimes the form a message takes strikes like lightning; other times you have to pour it out like molasses. There is a creative *something* to some diagrammatic moments that is admittedly hard to manufacture. But if we had to set the table or *mise en place* in the hope that inspiration would show up, Ilhan is a good model to learn from. By asking a friend for a read, Ilhan was able to get some needed perspective on where to push their writing next. They also gained a new user, other than themselves, to serve as they went further. This was the soil in which the *idea that would eventually insist on being a diagram* was first planted.

When Ilhan struggled with the writing part, they didn't give in to the frustration or push through, white-knuckled. They gave themselves grace, put the work aside, and took a walk to a place where they found peace in similar moments. Ilhan's is a story of making room for creativity to strike and then wrestling it to the page for others to benefit from. We can take a couple of lessons from Ilhan's experience:

- Always ask for feedback. Especially from potential users. The insights gained outweigh the pain of hearing the truth about our own work, every time. I promise.

- Allow space to wander. If it feels hard, do something else. Take a walk, make tea, phone a friend. Don't stew.

Chapter 5: **Collaboration** | 273

Lee: **Provoking Conversation**

It was cold in Chicago, and Lee had an epic day of wrangling executives ahead. But if you had been sitting next to Lee on the L that morning, you might have mistaken them for a grade school teacher with a roll of fresh craft paper under their arm and a canvas bag overflowing with handouts, markers, stickers, and even some yarn, in case things got really wild.

Lee had been hired to lead a conversation with the executive team of a large global agency. The conversation was about innovation and what the agency could be doing to further invest innovatively.

After reading the brief, Lee was dizzy from all the buzzwords and left thinking, *How many times can one agency use the word innovation wrongly in one deck?*

But Lee had an idea and diagrams ready for the job.

When they arrived in the room, the caterer was thoughtfully putting out pastries and fruit. The coffee had just been delivered and was the exact right temperature of *too hot but oh so caffeinated.*

Lee got to work in setting up the room for the day's event. There were two matrix diagrams that Lee wanted to use that day, both were based on well-known innovation frameworks that they had used and taught in the past. The first was McKinsey's Three Horizons Model.[36] The second was Doblin's Ten Types of Innovation.[37]

Lee knew that the diagrams would be recognizable to this audience and therefore a trustworthy basis for this innovation discussion.

---

[36] See Mehrdad Baghai, Stephen C. Coley, and David White, *The Alchemy of Growth: Kickstarting and Sustaining Growth in Your Company* (London: Texere, 2000).

[37] See Larry Keeley, Ryan Pikkel, Brian Quinn, and Helen Walters, *Ten Types of Innovation: The Discipline of Building Breakthroughs* (Hoboken, NJ: Wiley & Sons, 2013).

Lee used craft paper and Sharpies to create two blank quadrant diagrams on two facing walls in the conference room.

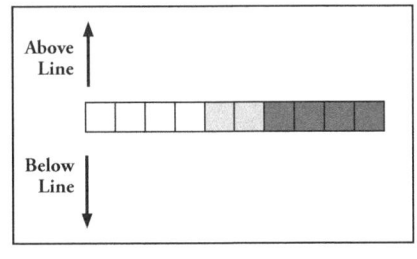

Based on Doblin's Ten Types of Innovation

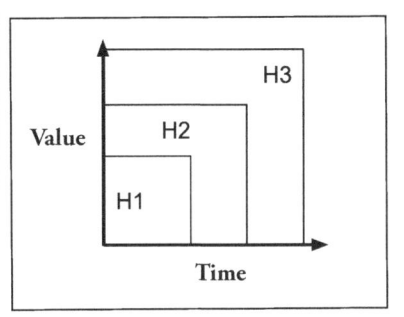

Based on McKinsey's Three Horizons Model

Then they took out two decks of cards on which the 70 initiatives from this agency's "innovation portfolio" were printed in big block letters, one initiative per card.

As the executives filed in, Lee could tell they were expecting a show, but not a tell. Each took a comfortable seat, with or without a pastry, around the conference table, looking at their phone or laptop while occasionally pausing to stare forward at the blank screen, the projector oddly quiet for the boardroom.

It didn't take long for them to see the strange props of the meeting: craft paper and markers, notecards and stickers. Lee greeted each executive as they arrived with some variation of "Don't worry, I won't make you draw." Once everyone had arrived, Lee set up the session and the conversation.

"I asked each of your teams to provide all the initiatives that have been greenlit in your innovation portfolio. They are all printed onto two sets of cards here. We have extra cards in case we missed any." The executives looked curious, and a few looked a bit queasy.

"The conversation we are having today is about how innovative the portfolio is today, so we can get a lay of the land. In this room, we are the judge, and we define what we mean as innovation.

But to help us, I brought two tried-and-true frameworks that are often used to evaluate innovation." Lee then introduced both frameworks to many nodding heads of folks recognizing them from many a conference talk or business class of their past. "We are going to start with the Horizons model. Let's classify our greenlit initiatives into the relevant horizons we think they fall into."

They got into sorting, and, within a few cards, there were quite a lot that weren't actually *innovative* at all. In fact, a lot of the cards were foundational work that needed to be done in order for the agency to ever have a fighting chance at existing 10 years down the line—let alone innovate. These were easy conversations in which empathy was built, and ultimately the team agreed that a new pre-horizon category outside the original framework should be used to capture this innovation-fueling foundational work.

But not all the cards were that easy to move on from. A few were real stinkers, ideas that had gotten bought for the wrong reason and were neither innovative nor foundational to being innovative. If Lee was reading between the lines well, it seemed these initiatives were actually the delighted fantasies of a few creative minds with too much money and power. Rather than call the new emerging category "Delighted Fantasies of the Privileged," Lee thought that perhaps "Pet Projects and Hunches" would be a better vibe. But, by the end, there were far too many cards in that category for any business-minded person to feel comfortable.

After all the cards were sorted into the first framework and everyone got a 45-minute stretch-and-email break, the second framework was up at bat. This went faster, much faster in fact. Not one initiative was customer-experience focused. And only a few were above the line of what customers would actually see or know about at all.

It was a *heartbreakingly* clear picture of a company huffing its own gases, hoping everyone on the outside thought they were being innovative enough to keep surviving. Ouch.

This was the point at which the CFO took off their glasses and started to rub their eyes. Lee knew that a breakthrough was coming; there had been nervous eyes darting between the CFO and CEO for the last 15 minutes, a nonverbal conversation being had about what to do next.

The CEO exhaustingly exclaimed, "We aren't all that innovative after all, huh?! I saw it in the numbers: declining margins, low customer satisfaction, high turnover of our creative teams. … It all makes sense now. But now that I see it on this chart or whatever you call it—well not to be rude, your reports have been great, but this insight pays for the whole engagement."

The rest of the team looked stunned, as if the air had finally been dramatically released from a pressure pot. There was a palpable tension over who would speak next. Lee knew to be quiet.

The CMO quietly but firmly spoke up with the knowing tone of someone speaking on behalf of a scared and quiet room. "In today's environment, the initiatives that are the flashiest and easiest to measure quickly are what gets sold—internally and to our customers. Innovative work has to be willing to take time and also to fail, and to date, long-term thinking and failure haven't been much of an option." The CEO replied, "I can see that; we have some work to do on how we choose what we work on and why. And I see how we are set up to fail at this moment and clearly how we got to this moment. Lee used frameworks we all knew but created this new life for them. I see this as a vision we can all share as we decide what to green light in the future—instead of when there are suddenly 70 things already promised but actually not aligned to our vision."

The conversation that ensued took the rest of the afternoon (as well as many, many months and meetings after) and involved Lee very little. Lee knew it was their job to provide the diagrams and the team's job to take it from there. Lee had other messes to get to.

What If Lee Had Just Told Them They Weren't Innovative Enough?

Lee might have come armed with craft supplies, but the message they actually came to serve that day in Chicago was far from childish. They were there to facilitate a conversation with an executive team about the uncertain future of a multimillion dollar agency.

To accomplish this, Lee leaned on two frameworks the executive team was sure to find trustworthy to lead the team towards a conclusion that Lee alone had come into the room already knowing. Think about how the outcome could have been different had Lee come in to give a presentation of these same two frameworks filled in already with a headline such as:

Your innovations aren't all that innovative.

By setting up the activity and starting from two trusted frameworks, Lee was able to bring the audience to a conclusion together rather than walk into the room and smack them across the face with it.

Diagrams can be great props for getting a group of people, all coming from various points of view, onto the same page, literally.

While it can be tempting to cut to the chase, sometimes bringing people along with us is the more kind and effective way to proceed.

Lessons from **Lee's Story**

Difficult messages don't have to be delivered in ways that make them more difficult. Could Lee have gotten to the difficult message faster had they just whipped out a filled-in set of frameworks showing that the agency wasn't innovative? Sure.

Many of us have been in (or led!) meetings where big bombs like that are dropped, often from someone coming from the outside with trusted frameworks at their side. By taking the extra time to get the audience warmed up to the problem, Lee was able to manufacture that feeling of *slow dawning realization* for the group while using two simple diagrams to catch what they saw together. Lee is such a good model for us in moments when we know the answer will be tough to take all at once and when we need to slow things down to get others on board earlier than the big reveal. We can learn two main lessons from Lee's story.

- Start with a blank diagram. This gives the group the power to control the outcome of the conversation, even if the message is predetermined based on the activity.

- Break the diagram together. In the story, Lee has to break the format of the diagram to better capture the group's decisions. Being flexible allows the group to trust that this is in fact a discovery we are making together, not an amusement park ride designed to feel like we are.

Dani: **Asking Obvious Questions**

For the first two weeks that Dani worked for a local telecommunications company as a writer, the business was still very much a mystery. That changed when Dani was assigned to work on a one-pager to explain the business model to potential customers. Dani was introduced to Kai, the VP of sales, who would be contributing as the subject matter expert.

In their first meeting, Dani could quickly see how well Kai knew the business model. It was artful the way they could break it down easily and explain every part and how it all comes together. But they had spent 90 minutes together, and Dani had to ask a lot of follow-up questions on the basics of the industry and write a lot of notes just to keep up with the complex process and timing of it all. Eventually, they turned to a whiteboard in the conference room to fill it with notes and details that were important for customers to know.

Standing back from the whiteboard after that first session, Dani saw the mess that was ahead. This one-pager was obviously needed. Kai couldn't possibly spend this much time explaining the business offering to each customer every sale. It simply wasn't sustainable or at all scalable. As a new employee, Dani was psyched to get an opportunity to make this much of a mark on the organization so immediately.

With this new knowledge, Dani quickly made a messy spreadsheet of all the notes from the whiteboard and put together a list of follow-up questions for Kai based on this new understanding of the company.

In their whiteboard session, Kai and Dani had drawn a simple timeline to show the key dates that customers needed to keep in mind in making various purchasing and implementation decisions. They had also talked about the importance of making it clear that the cost-savings pitch of their platform was the integration of three different services, provided by three different carriers, into this unique suite of offerings.

They talked about finding ways to add the logos of each service in some way to this piece. Lastly, a three-step process flow was integral to how Kai thought about selling and onboarding new customers. It was elegant but relied on all the other insights about timing and services to really understand in brief.

After a good night's sleep, a vision surfaced early that next morning. Dani imagined this coming together as a visualization rather than as just a written one-pager.

As a writer, Dani's anxiety of making something visual was high, but they also knew they were capable of making the kinds of visuals like the ones on the whiteboard.

While awaiting Kai's response to follow-up questions, Dani opened PowerPoint to start exploring the visual forms that this content might take.

By lunch there was a messy first draft of this visual, and Kai had gotten back with answers to a few questions and agreement on a time the next day to dig back in and take a look at this new "visual direction" Dani had mentioned in the follow-up.

Dani printed out the messy one-pager in preparation for the meeting and wrote questions for Kai right onto it, so it was clear that this was a messy first draft. Kai loved the visual immediately, especially the part where Dani had made a sort of pie chart showing the three brands' logos coming together. They immediately saw how this would be such a valuable visual aid during a sales call.

The main task Dani identified for Kai was to help make all the labels shorter and easier to understand for outsiders new to the space. Dani issued a friendly challenge to get the work started: "For this list of dates and deadlines and this process flow, can we make it so everything is said in fewer than three words per box? That would make this list much easier to scan and understand."

Kai agreed to this in theory, and they got to work. It was like playing tennis. Dani would serve up a label of seven or eight or even 12 (!!) words, and Kai would skillfully return a simpler, more elegant label. Not every serve landed, mind you. Some of the returns were real duds. But there was a bit of laughter when it got tough and even a few inside jokes between them by the end. They knew what they were doing mattered and that while it was hard, it would make a meaningful difference to reaching their intention.

As Kai returned the simpler labels, Dani swapped them out in the one-pager. When they were done with the whole list, the clarity that had just been achieved was obvious.

Kai looked relieved, as if something that had been trapped inside of them before was now out there for all to reference. Dani felt proud—proud to have identified the opportunity to make this assignment impactful in ways that had not been given by the brief and proud of the sense that was being made.

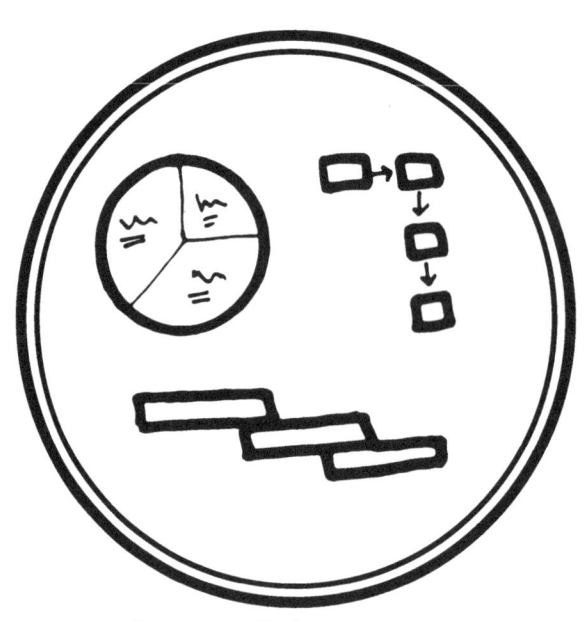

Kai and Dani couldn't wait to show the rest of the company. They talked about the main points that Kai would write into the invitation for the meeting in which they would present this to the rest of the team for more feedback.

Later that week, the meeting time arrived, and everyone filed into the conference room and joined the video call for the big reveal.

282 | STUCK? Diagrams Help.

To kick off the meeting, Kai introduced Dani to the team and talked about how eye-opening this process of working on this one-pager had been, saying proudly, "I didn't know how much was trapped in my head until Dani got it all out and showed me." Dani talked the team through the problem they had identified and the intention that they had delivered on.

"When I first started here, it took me 90 minutes with Kai to even know what we do at this company and how our service delivers value to our customers. With this visual, we wanted to make it so any potential customer can, in just one page, understand who we are, the value we bring, and the service details that matter most to making a decision to work with us. We are open to any and all feedback to improve this first draft, so please do us the kindness of telling us how this looks and feels to you."

They handed print-outs to those in the room and posted a link for those not in the room and gave everyone a few minutes. At the conclusion of the reflection time, the VP of operations piped up timidly to say, "Honestly, I've been here over a year and feel sort of weird admitting this, but until today, I don't know if I even knew how our business really works and how to talk about it with our customers. This visual is so helpful, Dani. Thank you."

Everyone agreed. Most people who worked there didn't seem to understand the real business until seeing this visual. There were minor notes for improvement and some thoughts on making the visual even bigger and better, maybe even paying an outside designer to make it prettier. But for the most part, the diagram's value was settled, and the team was grateful for it.

Six months later, Dani was asked to revise the diagram when a new service was brought into the platform. The pie chart of three logos became four logos, and some federal tax changes had impacted some deadlines that needed to be updated. Kai and team now had a few months of using the one-pager with potential customers and had noticed a change immediately. They spent more time on getting to know the customer and less time explaining the complex landscape in which they were selling.

What If Dani Just Wrote a One-Pager?

Dani is one of several characters in this chapter for whom the diagram-ness of the diagram was a later-stage reveal. In other words, Dani didn't know they were having a diagram at first.

As a writer, Dani had been assigned to write a one-pager for a core product being sold at the company where they were the newest employee.

In the course of talking with Kai, Dani used a whiteboard to doodle simple pictures in an effort to understand different aspects of the business model so they could write about them more clearly. The idea for a visual, as opposed to a written, one-pager was a blurry vision that Dani had to bring to life through some bravery and rudimentary PowerPoint skills.

Think about how the outcome could have been different had Dani just written up the one-pager based on the conversation with Kai. Those simple pictures on the whiteboard did their intended job of better informing Dani so that clearer writing could take place. What if they had died there?

Sometimes we make diagrams for ourselves to understand something. And then sometimes those diagrams call on us to get them better prepared to be shared more widely.

Lessons from **Dani's Story**

If you ever find yourself in a room with an expert (and a talker) like Kai, diagrams can be helpful. Diagrams are a fabulous research tool for organizing our thoughts as we navigate complex territories.

Unlike the one-pager described in the assignment, the visual that Dani made was the project that ended up paying unexpected dividends. By working with Kai to make it visual, they could share the workload of making it clearer. By working on the labels "to better fit into" the diagram, they landed on language their customers (and coworkers) could *actually* understand. By creating a visual presentation of what they offer that traveled well without a Kai to present it, they were able to reach more potential customers with better information. As we think back on Dani's story, the following are the primary lessons to take away:

- Make a straw-diagram to burn for warmth. By making a messy and bloated diagram representing the whiteboard, Dani was able to have a working assignment for Kai in reviewing the one-pager with an eye towards improving it.

- Work on language together. Reworking labels in a diagram with another person can be such a level-up for clarity. Work with an expert if you can. An expert paired with a beginner can yield amazing diagrammatic results.

Chapter 5: **Collaboration** | 285

Cyd: **Changing the Metaphor**

For the first time, Cyd felt their work really mattered to people. As the lead information architect of a charity focused on supporting patients and their families through a chronic illness, Cyd could see easily how their skills organizing information would be helpful to this important cause.

After just a short time on board, Cyd noticed something peculiar. Every meeting, every memo, every investment seemed to be focused on the call center and the print materials produced each year. But Cyd had been doing some digital auditing work and based on the scale of the traffic, there was no way that the phone and print materials were out-delivering the online content in terms of scale.

And the digital team was in dismal shape, not having much attention, investments, or resources. Seemingly a second wave team had been added on as the need for digital increased globally, but the understanding of digital had stayed organizationally stagnant.

Over the years, barnacles had collected on the digital hull. There were 10 microsites across four platforms, all of which needed to be maintained and kept up. The digital team was staffed as though it were just there to keep the lights on. But the team had so much heart and had done their best with what little they had. While each channel had an owner and content that was relatively well maintained, finding the information across this collection of sites was a gauntlet for any user, let alone a user with, or who is supporting someone with, a chronic illness.

If the name of the game was getting information into people's hands quickly, Cyd knew that digital had to be more of a priority than it had been historically. The need for a cultural reckoning about the role and scale of digital was obvious. Now the question was how best to make the case.

Cyd started to poke around at the numbers to see what could be learned about the scale of the various channels from the data sources and relationships that they had currently. They made a messy spreadsheet with metrics they could find, seeing what felt like it could be compared easily without much disagreement from various business owners.

After some time sleuthing and sorting, the "# of users served" emerged as an important metric for all groups. Cyd went about making the calls and writing the emails needed to fill in the number of users served. There was some funny math, like when the print material group reported back that each of their print pieces is expected to have served 1.5 people. While Cyd knew the case for this as *real* data was flimsy for many contexts, in this case it was perfectly acceptable as long as cited clearly.

Cyd's manager Kyle asked for regular updates on this exploration during their one-on-one meetings. On one of these occasions, Cyd brought in a hand-sketched diagram of what looked like a solar system.

"I had this thought in the shower this morning, after spending too much time yesterday trying to make all the spreadsheet chart wizards tell the story with the data I have that I am trying to tell."

Kyle replied, "I'm excited to hear more. Let's dig in."

Cyd pushed the diagram towards Kyle and said, "I've been thinking about how everyone prioritizes the phone and print material production more than digital. And you and I have talked for a while now about needing to change that.

"In this diagram, I am envisioning that we lay out each channel we have our content in as planets that are sized by the only metric we can all seem to agree on: # of users served."

Kyle timidly asked, "Wait, is that huge planet digital? And that small planet print, and the teeny tiny planet that's barely visible, the phone line? Wow. Um, don't take offense to this next question. Are these numbers solid? Like how did you size the planets?"

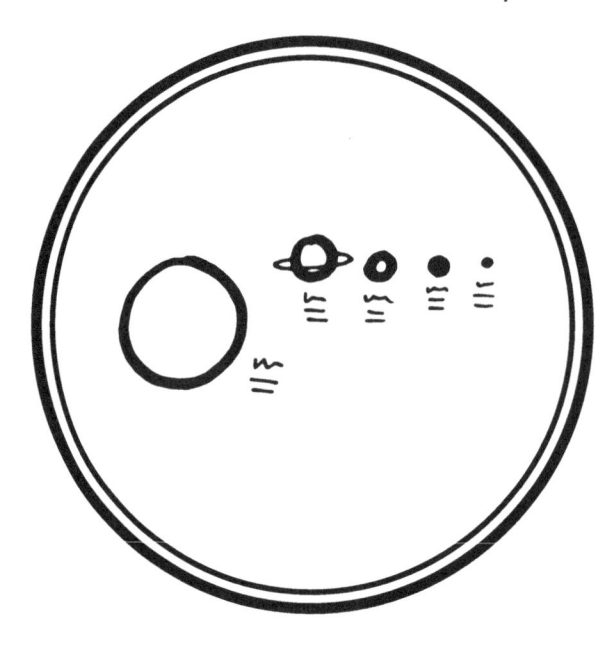

Cyd started, "I tried to make these into a bar chart or pie chart or any chart the wizard would let me make with the data as a table, but it was just another chart. It didn't tell the story that I see with these planets."

Cyd continued planet by planet reassuring Kyle of the numbers and the full, albeit messy, sourcing of them. Kyle sat back at the end and said, "You were right, there is a bigger story than the charts could have shown. This data is not in fact new. But in this planetary metaphor, I can't shake the feeling that we are underinvesting in that poor gigantic planet attempting to support so many people in such need with so little attention or resources. The universe really has changed. That scrappy little digital team accidentally built a rather large civilization that we now need to help them to support! These people showed up on our planet looking for help and all we have to offer them is a smattering of websites stitched together."

It turned out that Kyle was actually the convert that Cyd didn't know they needed.

---

288 | STUCK? Diagrams Help.

Unable to shake the feeling that the planets were literally misaligned, Kyle (with Cyd's help) went on an organizational change rampage, convincing every business owner to shift to a more digital-centric, and customer-centered, publishing and customer support model.

They made the case for massive investment in digital and made all publishing teams cross-channel and digital-first in workflow, investment, and output within the first two years post-planetary alignment.

Together they led the organization to streamline their platforms and their web structures to better support users and make efficient use of their time and resources.

If you could ask Cyd if there was anything they would do differently given the opportunity again (*which, lucky for us, I did*), they would tell you:

> Honestly, no. This diagram took me months to prepare for knowing how to make and then ultimately like five minutes to make. It's not even that well made or a *capital D Diagram*. But it's probably the most valuable thing I've ever made at work. So, no, I wouldn't change a thing. I just hope to have a problem this juicy to work through again at some point in my life. And then hope I can have an idea that simple to bring it all together like this did.
>
> —Cyd (*although that's not their real name*)

What If Cyd Had Let the Data Remain in a Bar Chart?

Gosh, dear reader, this is our last story. And sure enough, we are landing on the one I find to be perhaps overall the most impactful diagram of the whole bunch. Cyd and their planetary diagram representing content channels by number of users served sent shock waves through their manager and spurred organizational change over the long term. Diagrammatic dreams aren't usually this good.

In this story, Cyd had this data but none of the chart wizards could tell the story Cyd wanted to tell with it, so they took it into their own hands, executing on a simple yet powerful visual metaphor. A diagram that took five minutes to make was later described by Cyd as "the most valuable thing I've ever made at work."

Think about how the outcome could have been different had Cyd left the story up to the chart wizards. What if it had just been another bar chart?

In this story, the data needed a cognitive boost and a clear hook to hang on. The data became more powerful as a tool when manipulated into another form than what was expected. As Cyd's manager says in the story, the data was not in fact new, but this planetary metaphor changed the message the data came with. Planets obviously need more resources when more people are there. So why wouldn't that logic apply to serving these users?

Lessons from Cyd's Story

Perhaps the worst lesson you could take from Cyd is this: If you ever find yourself underwhelmed by what the data is presenting, take a shower and all will be revealed as a diagram you can make in five minutes.

The most important part of Cyd's story is not the five minutes it took to make the diagram that changed their universe. It is the five months leading up to that: observing the culture, identifying a problem, stating an intention, gathering the data, and exploring forms that data might best serve to lobby for big change.

Imagine you have been working hard on something for five grueling months and one day in the shower you think, *Huh, what if I drew the content channels as planets, sized by how many users they serve?* If you read that and think, oh great, that data visualization fairy tale could never happen to me, I hope you can instead take these lessons from Cyd:

- Present known data in an unknown way. Cyd could have really blown it if they had shown the bar chart the wizard recommended. It was known data presented in a known way, and it would have gotten a known response.

- Don't hide your ideas until they are polished. It turned out that the mind that needed changing was Kyle's, and all it took was a messy sketch that took five minutes.

How to Diagram with Other People

We have just met eight figments of the imagination, designed to teach you what I have learned about the people part of diagramming. Each was based on at least one real person.

Whether you are arriving at the diagram in the shower like Cyd or on the beach while walking the dog like Ilhan, diagrams can help you to dig deeper with other people.

In each of these stories, there were contextual lessons aplenty, but to make sure those make it to your next diagrammatic dinner party, the following checklist reorganizes those lessons to follow the order of the diagramming process we learned way back in chapter 2.

While *exploring*:

- ❏ Call an audible.
- ❏ Talk to people one-on-one before in a group.
- ❏ Build cohorts of people wanting to work on the diagram.
- ❏ Try starting a group meeting with a blank diagram.

While *modeling*:

- [ ] When words aren't enough, turn to pictures.
- [ ] Allow space to wander.
- [ ] Don't hide your ideas until they are polished.
- [ ] Make a straw-diagram to burn for warmth.
- [ ] Break the diagram together.

While *delivering*:

- [ ] Instead of sticking with the plan, read the room.
- [ ] Use a diagram to shorthand a complex landscape.
- [ ] Always ask for feedback.
- [ ] Work on language together.
- [ ] Present known data in an unknown way.

Diagrams Are Made of People

Ew.

But yes, really.

Diagrams help us to dig deeper with other people. Diagrams are places for thoughts and concepts—even emotions. Diagrams can impact *how* we think about *why* and *what* we think about.

Diagrams come with stories. Stories all wrapped up in people problems. Stories of the circumstances (and people) that prepared diagrams for their arrival. Stories about the diagrammatic decisions that were made (by people) on a diagram's way to existing. Stories about the impacts diagrams were able to have (on people) once they arrived. And most importantly, stories about the people who caught the idea for a diagram and then pinned it down long enough to help someone, even if that someone was themselves.

We can't choose our way out of the people part of diagramming. What if we leaned into it instead? What if we used diagrams to be clearer, kinder, and braver in our lives and work? What if we used diagrams to connect more deeply and get further with others we live and work with?

What if we diagrammed together more and struggled apart less?

A Summer Camp
Goodbye

From misunderstandings of meaning to lightning strikes of creative sensemaking, diagrams sure do run the emotional gamut.

In other words, during our short time together, I feel like we have been through some stuff.

Like summer camp, we have met some new friends whom we might never have met otherwise. Their stories changed us in some way, and we learned a new craft to show off to our friends and family back home.

As we say goodbye, I want to remind you why we started off on this journey together. We had a hunch that there is more to diagramming than what meets the eye, and we were right.

Next time you feel stuck, remember the stability, transparency, understanding, clarity, and kindness that diagramming can provide. I hope you will use the lessons you learned here to make visual representations that are helpful to someone—even if that someone is you.

Thanks for traveling with me this far.

—Abby

i

Resources

This final part of the book was designed for you to return to many times over your life of diagramming. We want you to imagine it as a reference desk at the Diagram Library (*found, of course, at the center of Diagram Town*).

Literature Review & Curated Resources   299
Provides a historical and cultural perspective on where diagramming came from and how it has developed over a few thousand years

Indexed Lexicon   329
Rearranges all the key terms found in bold throughout the book into an alphabetized list with definitions and the needed wayfinding back through the book to find each lesson

Bibliography   340
Lists the resources we used to write this book

Recommended Reading   346
Shines a spotlight on the resources we think you would get alot of practical value out of as you grow in your diagramming practice

Literature Review

Hey, Fellow Nerd.

If you made it this far, your interest about diagrams and their history has been peeked. Rad, welcome.

In the following literature review, Jenny Benevento, a taxonomist and all-around amazing information sleuth, has provided a curated tour through the complexity of researching, writing about, and teaching a concept as large as diagramming.

This book is stronger because of Jenny's work on this subject, and I am one lucky so-and-so to know and work with such an amazing human.

Happy trails.

—Abby

---

[38] To get the academic grape jelly in your practitioner peanut butter.

[39] Mario Schmidt, "The Sankey Diagram in Energy and Material Flow Management: Part II: Methodology and Current Applications," *Journal of Industrial Ecology* 12, no. 2 (2008): 173–185.

The designed world is a diagram.

The practical history and interdisciplinary discourse of diagrams

by Jenny Benevento

While Abby took the practitioner approach to writing this book based on her experience in the field, this literature review intends to give you a connection to the current academic discussion surrounding diagrams.[38]

> **Diagram** (n.)
> A visual representation that helps someone

This book's definition of *diagram* includes endless objects, including helpful doodles in your house that no one else will ever see, so a fully comprehensive review of every diagram or even every type of diagram is its own encyclopedia set. Instead, we're providing a general overview of the current state of academic diagram research (or the lack thereof, in some areas) and how it guided the decisions made in this book.

This book showed you how to diagram for your field, context, intention, or audience.

But what are others writing about diagrams?

Academic authors mostly concentrate on a singular diagram (e.g. Florence Nightingale's Rose Diagram) or a singular type of diagram (e.g. Sankey diagrams) only in their own field (e.g. "The Sankey diagram in energy and material flow management").[39]

The fields that write the most about diagrams tend to be medicine and hard sciences, mathematics, engineering, linguistics, education, philosophy, and psychology.

As psychologists Michael Friendly and Daniel J. Denis put it:

> But there are no accounts that span the entire development of visual thinking and the visual representation of data, and which collate the contributions of disparate disciplines. … practitioners in these fields today tend to be highly specialized, often unaware of related developments in areas outside their domain, much less their history.[40]

Why isn't diagram research interdisciplinary? Because it's hard! A search for "diagram" in research databases can result in irrelevant texts that aren't *about* diagrams but are retrieved because they *contain* diagrams labeled with the word *diagram*.

If you're a practitioner, you likely don't have access to the costly research databases needed to even find others' work. And even as an academic, you're limited by the subscriptions your institution retains, which often just cover only recent research that is digitized. Some important discussions take place in communities of practice, or conferences, and are never recorded or broadcast to anyone outside of the field.

One person's mind map is another's concept map or data structure diagram.

The term for a type of diagram (e.g. flowchart, block diagram, journey map) or even the word *diagram* itself isn't consistent across fields, so even if, for example, a mathematician wanted to see how historians used a certain diagram in their field, it would be very difficult to do so.

Because of this, we've included a list of terms used for diagrams across disciplines in the lexicon section of the book.

---

[40] Friendly and Denis, "Milestones in the History of Thematic Cartography."

Where possible, I'll be using the preferred term used in the field or industry I'm discussing. For example, in the medical field, I'll use *flowchart*, which is synonymous with *flow diagram* and how it is used in this book and other fields.

As a result of this lack of cross-disciplinary awareness, it is common to find similar articles about using a type of diagram (e.g. flowchart) effectively in different fields with no crossover or references between articles or fields.

In medicine, it gets even more siloed as individual specializations each write their own papers on how to use flowcharts to diagnose a disease or condition without reference to whether another specialty has done so before. These papers are buried deep in professional medical journals, but I bet you've been affected by them.

Think about the WebMD quiz you take at 2 AM to diagnose a symptom. That's a flowchart codified and given an interface. However minor your symptom, as the joke goes, that flowchart diagnoses you with cancer (or something similarly horrific). This bad user experience begs the question, Is anyone testing to see if these diagrams help anyone? Academically at least, mostly no.

There are a few exceptions, but they are very specific to their fields. Opthamologists and vision experts conduct studies using diagrams to diagnose visual disabilities. Modern philosophers look at diagrams from ancient mathematics and philosophy to discuss their meaning, language, communication, and epistemology. In education, there are many articles on the effectiveness of diagrams in teaching, but the subjects are mostly school-aged children, and articles on how diagrams might help or hurt specialized populations: the blind, children with neuroatypical learning styles, adults with brain injuries, or people learning a second language. Linguistics has studies about language acquisition in similar groups. The popular conclusion of these articles is to teach better diagram literacy, not to make better diagrams.

None of these fields research diagram effectiveness on a general adult audience. The field of psychology has a few scholars writing about diagrams and their users. Barbara Tversky has many papers on the origin of symbols and how users create and understand diagrams. Michael Friendly is the only scholar I found doing ongoing interdisciplinary research on diagrams and their long historical origin. Many of their papers are recommended below. Their entire canon provides the first steps into understanding the utility of diagrams, their history, and how they help users.

We were expecting to see our own fields represented in this academic literature. We looked at library science and information architecture (IA), information science, knowledge management, and design. These fields evangelize using formal research to create user-friendly experiences, and how do they communicate their user research findings? With diagrams! We use journey maps to make decisions with our colleagues about user experiences, and yet we haven't formally experimented to see if journey maps are helpful to the user! In human-computer interaction (HCI), we see user research for software and interfaces more generally, but not specifically on the efficacy of diagrams. As online tools become more standard and even as education is delivered with online classes and digital whiteboards, we anticipate there will be more research devoted to this area.

We're already seeing the newer field of information design start to produce academic and practitioner work that is very interdisciplinary. Notably, cognitive scientist Alan F. Blackwell has done extensive cross-disciplinary literature reviews in this area.[41]

---

[41] Alan F. Blackwell, "Diagrams about Thoughts about Thoughts about Diagrams," in *Reasoning with Diagrammatic Representations II: Papers from the AAAI Fall Symposium* (Palo Alto, CA: Association for the Advancement of Artificial Intelligence, 1997), 77–84.

[42] TwD98, "Thinking with Diagrams '98," https://web.archive.org/web/19991008092811/http://www.aber.ac.uk:80/~plo/TwD98/.

[43] Peter C.-H. Cheng, Ric K. Lowe, and Mike Scaife, "Cognitive Science Approaches to Understanding Diagrammatic Representations," in *Thinking with Diagrams*, ed. Alan F. Blackwell (Dordrecht: Springer, 2001), 83–84.

Blackwell has also experimented comparing how people understand something with or without a diagram. Still, the research is more focused on the utility of diagrams people draw for themselves and how people think by using diagrams. Cognitive scientists and information designers have written many frameworks for building the best and most useful visualizations and scientifically evaluating them. They've taxonomized and classified the elements of diagrams and developed a language for discussing them in order to create a science out of diagramming.[42] These frameworks are extrapolating cognitive science and psychology's background of understanding about how people learn in general, but they're lacking actual experimenting on diagrams specifically. The preeminent cognitive scientists who work on information design admit as much:

> Claims in the literature that diagrams are better, a priori, than other representations should be treated with caution. One finds in surveys of the research in computer science, psychology and education claims about the benefits of diagrams, and visual representations more generally, that seem to be motivated largely by intuitions and that are only weakly supported by rigorous empirical evaluations or any consistent attempt to derive generalisable theories … without any understanding of what makes external representations effective design will continue to be—as it is now—driven by slogans such as "a picture is worth 10000 words," that "more is more" or that the "sum is greater than the parts" (e.g. Lopuck 1996). Such beliefs are, at best, unsupported as a general claim and often seem to rest on unproven and naive assumptions about the way that external visual representations "produce" internal models (Scaife and Rogers 1996). Current orthodoxies about the intrinsic benefits of visualisation of information, which are grounded on the assumption that it makes the information more accessible, need to be examined far more critically.[43]

Of the studies that have been done, the conclusion is that "a major factor determining a viewer's capacity to make effective use of a diagram is how much that person already knows about the sort of subject matter depicted in the diagram and the specific method of depiction."[44] These articles all recommend duplicating all information in text and diagrams (as we do) and insist that diagram literacy must be taught in order to make diagrams usable. Even those proposing the standards for data visualization literacy don't think we know how well diagrams work: "In addition to laboratory experiments, there is a need to understand how general audiences can construct and interpret data visualizations in real-world settings using so-called 'research in the wild.'"[45] Some experts suggest having "mediators" to explain diagrams intended for specialists (like a hurricane map) to the general public.[46]

If the only studies we've done in multiple fields of academia tell us we can't comprehend diagrams without instruction, should we be using them so widely?

[44] Cheng, Lowe, and Scaife, "Cognitive Science Approaches," 86.

[45] Katy Börner, Andreas Bueckle, and Michael Ginda, "Data Visualization Literacy: Definitions, Conceptual Frameworks, Exercises, and Assessments," *Proceedings of the National Academy of Sciences* 116, no. 6 (2019): 1863.

[46] Alberto Cairo, "If Anything on This Graphic Causes Confusion, Discard the Entire Product," *IEEE Computer Graphics and Applications* 40, no. 2 (2020): 91–97.

[47] Lisa Lozeau and Lucas de Boer, "The Fundamentals of Customer Journey Mapping, and Why Businesses Need It Now," Signavio, last modified December 23, 2021, https://www.signavio.com/post/customer-journey-mapping/#h-the-history-of-journey-mapping; and Jona Moore, Cristina Crespo, Albert Dang, and Emanuele Di Saverio, "How to Deliver Impactful Products to Market," frog, 2021, https://www.frogdesign.com/designmind/how-to-deliver-impactful-products-to-market.

[48] https://miro.com/enterprise/.

[49] "This has enabled the squads to ship new products and features faster and feel more confident in their decisions." Ana Castrillon, "How BT, a 174-Year-Old Company Continues to Push the Telecommunication Industry Forward," *Figma* (blog), July 7, 2020, https://www.figma.com/blog/bt-case-study/; and Tom Kelley, "Build Your Creative Confidence: Customer Journey Map," *IDEO* (blog), March 21, 2019, https://www.ideo.com/blog/build-your-creative-confidence-customer-journey-map.

To misquote Morrissey, academia is not the world, so, what about our fields' practitioners? We read the publications of our colleagues and attended their conference presentations. We found opinions and theories honed after years of experience, just like this book's main text. There wasn't a clear connection to previous academic papers or user research that proved what made diagrams helpful to users, though we recommend you read them anyway (see the recommended reading section).

Consultancies have published business literature and tools for practitioners that test diagrams on users, but this tends to be in service of selling a product. These result in bold claims such as "Organizations that have and use customer journey maps are twice as likely to outperform competitors" or "When a team has access to a design system, they complete their objective 34% faster" with no reference to where the number comes from or what they mean by design system or objectives.[47] Miro claims "46% better ideas in brainstorm" when using their visualization software, with no explanation of how that is calculated.[48] These sites rely on client reviews instead of the actual user research they recommend, many citing they provide clients "more confidence" when making decisions but without proof of better decisions.[49] Most of these claims and statistics are vague and not cited or the study will only be shared when you become a client, which limits how helpful the diagrams or research about them can be. They're positioned as the statistics that will help you convince an executive to buy the services of the consultancy. We can assume some businesses have tested diagrams on their users and do have good evidence but are unlikely to share or publish this to have competitive advantage. Like in academia, these tend to be research on one diagram, not diagrams in general, and the research is behind a paywall, produced only for the elites of the field.

There is one area in which the art and design fields are publishing about diagrams and information visualization: coffee table art books. These tend to be printed in full-color, large format hardcovers and more as "design porn"—more inspiration than research about how diagrams work. One exception is Manuel Lima, who has several books displaying diagrams throughout the ages paired with well-researched historical content. We enjoy these design books as much as the next diagram nerd, but they don't contain much user perspective. Information designer Petra Černe Oven admits,

> Designers today could put their acquired principles in a drawer somewhere and start thinking about things from the user's point of view. For this, however, we need, by and large, an attitude that is different from the one twentieth-century designers adopted.[50]

In case this isn't clear, what I'm saying is:

In most fields and diagrams **neither academics nor practitioners have any scientific or codified evidence that diagrams** *generally* **help users.**

In fact, the few studies we have show users don't understand diagrams well and need to learn diagram literacy to *get* them. And yet we still keep using and selling them!

No one has published the research. It seems like we assume that because diagrams we draw help us, they will logically help others. One major lesson of this book is that diagrams must be user centered to be effective.

---

[50] P. C. Oven, "Introduction: Design as a Response to People's Needs (and Not People's Needs as a Response to Design Results)," in *On Information Design*, ed. P. C. Oven and C. Požar (Ljubljana, Slovenia: Museum of Architecture and Design, 2016), 8.

[51] Andy Hertzfeld, *Revolution in the Valley: The Insanely Great Story of How the Mac Was Made* (Sebastopol, CA: O'Reilly Media, 2011).

[52] Howard Wainer and Michael Friendly, "Visual Revelations: Ancient Visualizations," *CHANCE* 31, no. 2 (2018): 62–64, https://doi.org/10.1080/09332480.2018.1467645; and Barbara Tversky, "Some Ways That Graphics Communicate," in *Working with Words and Images: New Steps in an Old Dance*, ed. Nancy Allen (Westport, CT: Ablex, 2002).

This lack of academic research adds urgency to that lesson. Since no one has done this research into general diagrammatic effectiveness yet, we all need to continually conduct research with our audience while diagramming to make sure our diagrams are effective.

Origin Stories

Abby came to me with questions such as "How do we all know this shape means this?" and "Who was the first person to standardize this line style to mean this?" This was by far the most contentious and time-consuming research challenge around this book. Fields attribute the invention of diagrams and their visual language to the sources they first saw them used in, without understanding that these precedents existed in other fields, even hundreds or thousands of years before computer and printing technology advancements. In some fields, credit was given to the field's standardization bodies, but diagrams were standardized based on what people in the field were already using. Others credit the first who used them in published works, which could date back to Renaissance logicians and Ancient philosophers.

Most knowledge workers first saw common diagram visual language (e.g. diamonds, arrows, hierarchical trees, boxes) in early software. Iconography attribution in these fields can be summarized as "in tech books all roads lead to Apple as the creator of all things good and design oriented." Even that origin is convoluted because it is debated which operating system used them first.[51] But computer science and engineering had used many of these icons for decades in circuitry and entity relationship diagrams. Mathematics (especially descriptive geometry) and philosophical logic standardized some diagram visual language hundreds of years before in meanings we still use today. High-tech statistical graphics and data visualizations rely on principles researchers credit to Ancient Greek philosophy, cave drawings, and First Peoples' texts.[52]

Psychologist Barbara Tversky parallels the graphics used in common diagrams with "lines, blobs, crosses and arrows" used by humans before written language was developed and by non-human primates.[53] "Depictions, maps, and diagrams of actual systems are ancient and universal or nearly universal forms of graphics," Tversky puts it.[54] Though we believe the diagram and its visual language is modern, as Harry S. Truman said, "The only new thing in the world is the history you don't know."[55]

Tracking down the difference between who is widely known for inventing a diagram or visual element or common arrangement versus who *actually* did involves a lot of research and judgment calls that we didn't want to make lightly. We could argue forever (and sometimes it felt like we did!) whether similar *looking* diagrams with a different name (a process chart vs. a flow diagram) are the same diagram. Where we have given credit in this book, it's to the person who was either most cited as the earliest creator or whom we found the most documentation for. Where we do not give credit in this book to a specific person for a certain symbol or diagram, it is because there wasn't one clear creator, even if a certain field credits one creator. In many cases, one person has been credited

---

[53] Quotation from Barbara Tversky, Jeff Zacks, Paul Lee, and Julie Heiser, "Lines, Blobs, Crosses and Arrows: Diagrammatic Communication with Schematic Figures," in *Theory and Application of Diagrams*, ed. Michael Anderson, Peter Cheng, and Volker Haarslev (Berlin: Springer, 2000), 221–230, https://doi.org/:10.1007/3-540-44590-0_21. See also Barbara Tversky, "Spatial Schemas in Depictions," in *Spatial Schemas and Abstract Thought*, ed. Merideth Gattis (Cambridge, MA: MIT Press, 2001).

[54] Tversky, "Some Ways That Graphics Communicate," 59.

[55] As quoted in David McCullough, *Truman* (New York: Simon & Schuster, 1992), 559.

[56] The Gilbreths are the subject of the book *Cheaper by the Dozen* (New York: Thomas Y. Crowell, 1948), about their lives applying efficiency expertise to family life.

[57] Frank B. Gilbreth and Lillian Moller Gilbreth, "Process Charts," in *American Society of Mechanical Engineers* (New York: American Society of Mechanical Engineers, 1921).

[58] Gilbreth and Gilbreth, "Process Charts," 9.

for applying a symbol in a modern field when we have evidence of people using it for this purpose in pre-modern times.

A great example of this fuzzy attribution is the flow diagram, or flowchart, Nassi-Shneiderman diagram, structogram, functional band, functional flowchart, control-flow diagram, process flow diagram, or any one of a dizzying array of other variations people use to mean some specific subset of flow diagram. Depending on what field or subfield, there are increasingly varied and specific kinds of flow diagrams. Despite being used in virtually every field, the flow diagram is most discussed in the fields of business, science, engineering, and medicine. Some writers believe it was created by the ANSI standards developed in the 1960s. Most sources tie the invention of the flow diagram to a speech Frank Gilbreth gave at the American Society of Mechanical Engineers in 1921.

When I looked up the proceedings of that meeting, I found it was credited to not only Frank Gilbreth but also an L. M. Gilbreth. Future digging shows L. M. is Lillian Moller Gilbreth, his wife, a psychologist and industrial engineer who was not a member of the American Society of Mechanical Engineers at the time of publication but outlived and outshadowed her husband in her field.[56] In the paper produced from the talk, the Gilbreths mention that they are only now writing down standards for this type of diagramming (which they call a process chart) that they had been using since 1899.[57] So, already we know that 1921 is the date of its published origin but not its real origin date. The Gilbreths point out that they are not the first people with these ideas:

> While on the subject of range, it is well to call attention to the remarkable attempts of Germany and Holland to provide national standards. ... Although there is much to criticise in these foreign standards, they are highly meritorious, worthy of continuous and careful attention, and a great credit to those who have devised them.[58]

These authors and this date are only its origin in America. While the majority of people credit Frank Gilbreth with this "discovery" individually, scratching the surface shows that diagrams often aren't properly attributed, and when they are, they are usually attributed to the first people to write standards for what was in use in the field. They are extremely field specific and generally only account for the first person in one's field, in one's country. Even in cases where we've found this supposed "first thinker," they're more the "first documenter," and crediting them means not crediting a lot more equally responsible people. Even this quotation regarding the subject shows a winding provenance:

> Stigler's Law of Eponomy [sic] (Stigler 1980)[59] reminds us that standard attributions are often not those of priority. The Law in fact makes a stronger claim: "No scientific discovery is named after its original discoverer." As prima facie evidence, Stigler attributes the origin of this law to Merton.[60]

For a more modern example, as this book alluded to when discussing "stacks," many readers coming from an IA background like Abby probably first saw the visualization of a stack in the 2002 *A Visual Vocabulary for Information Architecture and Interaction Design*" by Jesse James Garrett.

---

[59] Stephen M. Stigler, "Stigler's Law of Eponymy," *Transactions of the New York Academy of Sciences*, series II, 39, no. 1 (1980): 147–157, https://doi.org/10.1111/j.2164-0947.1980.tb02775.x.

[60] Michael Friendly, "Milestones in the History of Data Visualization: A Case Study in Statistical Historiography," in *Classification—the Ubiquitous Challenge*, ed. Claus Weihs and Wolfgang Paul (New York: Springer, 2004), 42, https://doi.org/10.1007/3-540-28084-7_4.

[61] Hertzfeld, *Revolution in the Valley*; and Kate McInnes, "Know Your Icons, Part 1: A Brief History of Computer Icons," Envato Tuts+, July 18, 2010, https://design.tutsplus.com/articles/know-your-icons-part-1-a-brief-history-of-computer-icons--psd-9805; and "Icons: Components," Guidebook, https://guidebookgallery.org/icons/components.

[62] History in the following section is aggregated from the works of Michael Friendly, Daniel J. Denis, and Manuel Lima identified in the list of resources in the "Interdisciplinary Modern History" section.

But we can see examples from early software that also use this icon.[61] Where one person truly invented a diagram alone and documentation points to them alone, we have given credit, but this is generally not the case. In those instances, we have often suggested a work to understand the idea better, rather than its first instance.

A Brief Modern History of Diagrams[62]

A lot of credited "first thinkers" are the first people to document the diagram after a new technology. It's not a coincidence that most diagrams or their components are credited to the beginning of desktop computing, the printing press, or typewriters and copiers becoming the office standard. Having modern typesetting and printing allows us to have records of those diagrams, but it does not mean they did not exist before then. They just weren't standardized, documented, or distributed yet. We have ample evidence of beautifully drawn diagrams before this, but their audience and impact was limited.

We do think of diagrams and their impact as tied to modern technology, and it's for good reason. Whether it's an org chart, assembly instructions, industrial machine process diagram, or a product roadmap, our concept of where diagrams started is inherently tied to their documentation for the Industrial Revolution and, later, their use in computer interfaces. But throughout time, the history and advancement of diagrams are contingent on the technology to create, reproduce, and distribute them.

We know there are ancient origins of diagrams and symbols, and we see beautifully illuminated diagrams in incunabula, but these were limited by time and technology, hard to reproduce, expensive to create, and for a very limited, educated, and wealthy audience. As Friendly and Denis put it:

> Maps, diagrams and graphs have always been (and continue to be) hard to produce, still harder to publish. Initially they were hand drawn, piece-

by-piece. Later they were etched on copper-plate and manually colored. Still later, lithography and photo-etching, and most recently, computer software was used, but graphic-makers have always had to struggle with the limitations of available technology—and still do today.[63]

The invention of the printing press at first provides an impediment to diagrammers, as drawings and typeface aren't easy to typeset together.[64] But eventually the proliferation of printing allows diagrams to be seen by more people. In the 17th century, graphs as we know them were invented. The development in this period revolves around the need for physical measurements, like those in astronomy. As the reliance on statistics increases, the need for visualizations to convey them does too. In the 18th century, this was expanded with new graphical forms: the creation of the line graph, bar chart, and pie chart, all invented by William Playfair.[65] Technology aided these innovations, as Friendly points out:

> Several technological innovations provided necessary nutrients. These facilitated the reproduction of data images (color printing, lithography), while other developments ...

[63] Friendly and Denis, "Milestones in the History of Thematic Cartography," 13.

[64] "1453 Gutenberg Invention of moveable type printing press, and printing of the Mazarin bible (leads to a decline in the use of mixed text and graphics)." Friendly and Denis, "Milestones in the History of Thematic Cartography, Statistical Graphics, and Data Visualization." 2001. http://www.datavis.ca/milestones/.

[65] For the line graph and bar chart, see William Playfair et al., *The Commercial and Political Atlas: Representing, by Means of Stained Copper-Plate Charts, the Exports, Imports, and General Trade of England; the National Debt, and Other Public Accounts ...* (London: Debrett, 1786). For the pie chart, see William Playfair, *The Statistical Breviary: Shewing, on a Principle Entirely New, the Resources of Every State and Kingdom in Europe; Illustrated with Stained Copper-Plate Charts, Representing the Physical Powers of Each Distinct Nation with Ease and Perspicuity* (London: T. Bensley, Bolt Court, Fleet Street, for J. Wallis, 46, Paternoster Row, 1801).

[66] Friendly, "Milestones in the History of Data Visualization," 37.

[67] Friendly, "Milestones in the History of Data Visualization," 39.

[68] Friendly, "Milestones in the History of Data Visualization," 40.

eased the task of creating them. Yet, most of these new graphic forms appeared in publications with limited circulation, unlikely to attract wide attention.[66]

Visualization moves to new academic fields such as geology, medicine, and economics but still in scholarly publications with small circulations. The 19th century is when most data visualizations, symbols, and diagrams we use today are first published. Friendly points to a reason for this:

> Official state statistical offices were established throughout Europe, in recognition of the growing importance of numerical information for social planning, industrialization, commerce, and transportation. Statistical theory, initiated by Gauss and Laplace, and extended to the social realm by Quetelet, provided the means to make sense of large bodies of data.[67]

Industrialization, then, and the need to keep statistics around business and government were driving forces of this uptick in diagrams. Diagrams are no longer solely for scientists but also for much larger business, bureaucratic, and government audiences. They are now being used to simplify information for workers in a variety of fields to track progress and sales. This continues to the extent that visualizations become less important than mathematical specificity:

> There were few graphical innovations, and, by the mid-1930s, the enthusiasm for visualization which characterized the late 1800s had been supplanted by the rise of quantification and formal, often statistical, models in the social sciences. Pictures were—well, just pictures: pretty or evocative, perhaps, but incapable of stating a "fact" to three or more decimals. Or so it seemed to statisticians.[68]

At this point, understanding and innovation take a backseat to precision. We (and many information workers) experience this "either/or ism" in our careers when some people pit big data collected about users against qualitative user experience research, or machine learning artificial intelligence against expert-created metadata. In our experience, both together make the best decisions, and likewise good data and good visualizations together make the best diagrams.

More positively, this period brings diagrams and information graphics to the masses:

> But it is equally fair to view this as a time of necessary dormancy, application, and popularization, rather than one of innovation. In this period statistical graphics became mainstream. It entered textbooks, the curriculum, and standard use in government, commerce and science.[69]

We see diagrams move into business strategy in the 1900s with the Gantt chart (1910–1915) and the flowchart (1921). It's not a coincidence that the Gantt chart and the Model T are contemporaries.

In addition to showing how a business has done in the past, visualizations can help plan a project and set future goals to maximize profit and efficiency. In fact, the previously mentioned Gilbreths brought the efficiency of flowcharts to homemaking and child-rearing: the book *Cheaper by the Dozen* (1948) is an autobiographical novel written by their children.

---

[69] Friendly, "Milestones in the History of Data Visualization," 40.

[70] Gilbreth and Gilbreth, "Process Charts," 10.

---

314 | STUCK? Diagrams Help.

Extolling the virtues of diagrams in the process of industrial efficiency, the Gilbreths noted:

> Particular attention should be called to the fact that the creation of national standards of manufacture, even to the smallest components of the arts and trades, means also the stabilization of employment and business in general, because manufacturers without sufficient orders in their regular lines of business to keep going will find it more profitable, in many instances, to manufacture the national standards and thus to turn their stores inventories into money immediately, rather than let their specially trained and skilled men leave them, with all the disadvantages of a high labor turnover. Here is an endless spiral of benefit, for the more chances there are for a manufacturer to dispose of his inventory for cash and keep his organization together a little longer, even in times of general timidity, the more he will dare be a purchaser of raw material, for the process for such emergencies can be standardized and ready. The result is standardization combined with stabilization of employment, a quick capital turnover and a low labor turnover.[70]

Industrialization and specialization of labor meant much larger projects, with a lot more people, some who would never talk face to face. It required experts in an office to disseminate complex plans to the workers in the factory building and operating machines and equipment. We needed ways to track these projects' progress. Factories meant one worker might need a diagram only to construct one part of a car and not really know how the whole comes together after. The previous period's obsession with statistics became this period's obsession with efficiency and streamlining processes in many fields. Maximum efficiency required an assembly line and hyperspecialization of workers, which required diagrams. These diagrams weren't pretty, but they were for everyone now, democratized and widespread, especially throughout manufacturing.

The "dark ages" of data visualization (as Friendly puts it) came to an end in the 1950s, with the advent of computer data. As the calculating power of computers increased, the graphics available allowed diagrams to drive discovery. In the latter half of the century, data visualization became more advanced. Diagrams can be animated and interactive. No longer are printing methods a limiter, since many people will never print these diagrams, preferring to see computer-created diagrams on a screen. Diagrams become a way to summarize large sets of data no one could possibly wade through.

Diagrams: Now & the Future

There isn't a look back at our progress in the 21st century yet in academic literature, but from the concept maps of knowledge graphs behind the most important technologies running modern life to the rectangular tree maps of the United States federal budget, diagrams are now the human interface to big data. In many cases, we use the astounding computer power we have to find connections we cannot see otherwise, and we make diagrams to make sense of it. Diagrams are now used in everyday life and expected in news reporting.

Raul Niño Zambrano and Yuri Engelhardt in "Diagrams for the Masses" posit that technology has finally democratized diagrams for ordinary people as viewers and creators:

---

[71] Raul Niño Zambrano and Yuri Engelhardt, "Diagrams for the Masses: Raising Public Awareness—from Neurath to Gapminder and Google Earth," in *Diagrammatic Representation and Inference*, ed. Gem Stapleton, John Howse, and John Lee (Berlin: Springer, 2008), 291.

[72] https://popchart.co/products/the-hip-hop-flow-chart.

[73] https://www.thecolorsofmotion.com.

[74] https://xkcd.com/1488/.

[75] https://thisisindexed.com.

> Digital media have enabled "do-it-yourself graphics" and their online peer-to-peer distribution, shifting the role of ordinary people from the passive viewer to the active creator and disseminator of "diagrams for the masses."[71]

This accessibility to data visualization means the diagram is no longer used or created only in formal employment settings but also in our personal lives. One example of this is the diagram as home decor. For example, Pop Chart Labs makes visually pleasing diagrams and charts for wall hangings, such as the concept map "The Magnificent Multitude of Beer" or "Hip-Hop Heads," described as a "hand-drawn, head-spinning chart of lyrical locution, which analyzes via scale and concentric gold rings the lexical freshness of nearly every rapper of repute."[72] The Colors of Motion produces aesthetic abstract prints that depict the average color of every frame of a popular movie of your choice.[73]

When someone produces and then displays a Colors of Motion print in their home or work space, they are helping other people to better understand *them*. The diagram in this case isn't about understanding the movie better, it's about understanding an aesthetic, machine-produced perspective and taste of the person.

Diagrams are now used casually for comedic effect or to convey personal meaning. Webcomics such as *XKCD* frequently use diagrams to teach science and mock programmers, including a flow diagram in which the first decision is "Do you like flowcharts?"[74] People use the phrase "Venn diagram" in casual conversation to talk about their personal lives so much that Jessica Hagy created a comic called *Indexed* in which she draws funny Venn (and other) diagrams about friendship, love, work, and mental health on index cards.[75] On Etsy, you can choose from hundreds of items decorated with the structural formula diagram of the caffeine molecule to profess your love for $C_8H_{10}N_4O_2$ or maybe a medical diagram of the human heart on an I <3 Caffeine tchotchke.

The owners of these diagrams aren't using them for the original purpose, but they do fit the STUCK criteria that this book describes. These diagrams are presented to help an audience *understand* the owner better.

The item allows the owner to communicate and perhaps bond with others over a shared interest in chemistry or coffee. This is reuse of diagrams to convey a new thing—personality, preferences, and/or style.

Finally, some of the most popular and commonly shared diagrams today are about your favorite thing: You. These diagrams are produced in reports that give us a bird's-eye view of our own daily lives. A TripIt map of your travel, your sleep and exercise averages on your Apple Watch, a Swarm visualization of your favorite businesses, Spotify's sharable visualizations of your listening habits, your genetic information and ancestry report at 23andMe—all are diagrams that contain information only about you, allowing you to see the forest for the trees of your own life, sometimes literally with a tree map.

The average person cannot see trends between the random things we listen to or within the sequence of our DNA. The hallmark of the 21st century is the diagram customized for the individual, allowing us to better understand ourselves.

Conclusion

Historically, diagrams were used to illustrate exactness and specificity. More recently, we use them to show us the big picture, partly because we have new and more advanced graphics, partly because diagrams are so omnipresent that they function in our personal lives now too, and partly because we now have such an excess of calculation specificity that it's too difficult and time consuming for us to process *without* diagrams.

As science and technology have democratized and as computers have moved from government and academia into everyone's pocket, diagrams, too, have scaled to be universal yet personal and reused for new meanings. When everyone with a smartphone has more computing power than the supercomputers of yesteryear, the data we create ambiently allow us to make and use more diagrams in our daily lives. As diagrams become not only how we formally describe the world but also how we describe ourselves, we come ever closer to Barbara Tversky's bold statement:

> The designed world is a diagram.[76]

We began with diagrams to understand the magnitude of the universe and humanity, and we now use them to explain ourselves to the world.

---

[76] Barbara Tversky, "Visualizing Thought," in *Handbook of Human Centric Visualization*, ed. Weidong Huang (New York: Springer, 2014), 33, https://doi.org/10.1007/978-1-4614-7485-2_1.

Curated Resources by Theme

A complete list of sources used for this literature review is available at https://pinboard.in/u:jennybento/t:STUCKlitreview.

We additionally curated resources on the following themes:

Interdisciplinary Modern History of Diagrams & Maps	321
Ancient Diagrams	322
Icon & Symbol History	323
Diagrams & Users	324
Beautiful Visualizations & Journalistic Infographics	325
Thinking & Diagrams *(Neurodiversity, Cognitive Science Experimentation)*	326
Frameworks & Standards	327
Information Design	328

Interdisciplinary Modern History of Diagrams & Maps

These works look at the history of diagrams, especially pre–desktop computing, in an interdisciplinary way.

Many of these also contain beautiful reproductions of hand-painted diagrams.

Bender, John B., and Michael Marrinan. *The Culture of Diagram*. Stanford, CA: Stanford University Press, 2010.

Drucker, Johanna. *Graphesis: Visual Forms of Knowledge Production*. Cambridge, MA: Harvard University Press, 2014.

Friendly, Michael. "A Brief History of Data Visualization." In *Handbook of Data Visualization*, edited by Chun-houh Chen, Wolfgang Härdle, and Antony Unwin, 15–56. Berlin: Springer, 2008.

Friendly, Michael. "Milestones in the History of Data Visualization: A Case Study in Statistical Historiography." In *Classification—the Ubiquitous Challenge*, edited by Claus Weihs and Wolfgang Paul, 34–52. Studies in Classification, Data Analysis, and Knowledge Organization. New York: Springer, 2004. https://doi.org/10.1007/3-540-28084-7_4.

Friendly, Michael, and Daniel Denis. "Discussion and comments. Approche graphique en analyse des données. The roots and branches of modern statistical graphics." *Journal de la société française de statistique* 141, no. 4 (2000): 51–60.

Friendly, Michael, and Daniel J. Denis. "Milestones in the History of Thematic Cartography, Statistical Graphics, and Data Visualization." 2001. http://www.datavis.ca/milestones/.

Lima, Manuel. *The Book of Circles: Visualizing Spheres of Knowledge*. New York: Princeton Architectural Press, 2017.

Lima, Manuel. *The Book of Trees: Visualizing Branches of Knowledge*. New York: Princeton Architectural Press, 2014.

Lima, Manuel. *Visual Complexity: Mapping Patterns of Information*. New York: Princeton Architectural Press, 2013.

Ancient Diagrams

These resources look at the interdisciplinary history of diagram design but focus on the ancient roots of symbols and diagrams.

Pettersson, Rune. "Information Design 6: Predecessors & Pioneers." IIID Public Library. Vienna: International Institute for Information Design, 2015. https://www.iiid.net/PublicLibrary/Pettersson-Rune-ID6-Predecessors.pdf.

Tversky, Barbara. "Some Ways That Graphics Communicate." In *Working with Words and Images: New Steps in an Old Dance*, edited by Nancy Allen. Westport, CT: Ablex, 2002.

Tversky, Barbara. "Some Ways That Maps and Diagrams Communicate." In *Spatial Cognition II: Integrating Abstract Theories, Empirical Studies, Formal Methods, and Practical Applications*, 72–79. Lecture Notes in Computer Science. Berlin: Springer, 2000. https://doi.org/10.1007/3-540-45460-8_6.

Tversky, Barbara. "Visualizing Thought." In *Handbook of Human Centric Visualization*, edited by Weidong Huang, 3–40. New York: Springer, 2013. https://doi.org/10.1007/978-1-4614-7485-2_1.

Tversky, Barbara, Jeff Zacks, Paul Lee, and Julie Heiser. "Lines, Blobs, Crosses and Arrows: Diagrammatic Communication with Schematic Figures." In *Theory and Application of Diagrams*, edited by Michael Anderson, Peter Cheng, and Volker Haarslev, 221–230. Lecture Notes in Computer Science. Berlin: Springer, 2000. https://doi.org/10.1007/3-540-44590-0_21.

Wainer, Howard, and Michael Friendly. "Visual Revelations: Ancient Visualizations." *CHANCE* 31, no. 2 (2018): 62–64.

Icon & Symbol History

These resources discuss symbols in printing and computer interfaces.

Dunne, Carey. "The Medieval Roots of the Tree Diagram." Fast Company, January 27, 2015. https://www.fastcompany.com/3041447/the-medieval-roots-of-the-tree-diagram.

Heiser, Julie, and Barbara Tversky. "Arrows in Comprehending and Producing Mechanical Diagrams." *Cognitive Science* 30, no. 3 (2006): 581–592. https://doi.org/10.1207/s15516709cog0000_70.

Hertzfeld, Andy. *Revolution in the Valley: The Insanely Great Story of How the Mac Was Made.* Sebastopol, CA: O'Reilly Media, 2011.

Kurata, Yohei, and Max J. Egenhofer. "Semantics of Simple Arrow Diagrams." In *Reasoning with Mental and External Diagrams: Computational Modeling and Spatial Assistance*, 101–104. Papers from the AAAI Spring Symposium. Palo Alto, CA: Association for the Advancement of Artificial Intelligence, 2005.

Moxon, Paul. "History of the Arrow." American Printing History Association, February 1, 2016. https://printinghistory.org/arrow/.

Neurath, Otto. *International Picture Language: The First Rules OF ISOTYPE.* London: Kegan Paul, 1936.

Diagrams & Users

This research considers users, sometimes in experiments, and how they use diagrams.

It is mostly in the field of psychology and most focuses on how people use diagrams to solve problems.

Candea, Matei. "On Visual Coherence and Visual Excess: Writing, Diagrams, and Anthropological Form." *Social Analysis* 63, no. 4 (2019): 63–88. https://doi.org/10.3167/sa.2019.630404.

Nickerson, Jeffrey V., James E. Corter, Barbara Tversky, Doris Zahner, and Yun Jin Rho. "The Spatial Nature of Thought: Understanding Information Systems Design through Diagrams." *ICIS 2008 Proceedings* (2008). https://aisel.aisnet.org/icis2008/216/.

Pedone, Roberto, John E. Hummel, and Keith J. Holyoak. "The Use of Diagrams in Analogical Problem Solving." *Memory & Cognition* 29, no. 2 (2001): 214–221.

Tversky, Barbara. "Some Ways That Graphics Communicate." In *Working with Words and Images: New Steps in an Old Dance*, edited by Nancy Allen. Westport, CT: Ablex, 2002.

van der Meij, Jan, Marije van Amelsvoort, and Anjo Anjewierden. "How Design Guides Learning from Matrix Diagrams." *Instructional Science* 45, no. 6 (2017): 751–767. http://www.jstor.org/stable/26303068.

Wheeler, Alan E., and Doug Hill. "Diagram-ease." *Science Teacher* 57, no. 5 (1990): 58–63. http://www.jstor.org/stable/24145213.

Beautiful Visualizations & Journalistic Infographics

These works are filled with inspirational examples of infographics and focus on presenting beautiful designs to a general audience.

The authors tend to be journalists and designers.

Cairo, Alberto. *The Functional Art: An Introduction to Information Graphics and Visualization.* Berkeley, CA: New Riders, 2012.

Cairo, Alberto. "If Anything on This Graphic Causes Confusion, Discard the Entire Product." *IEEE Computer Graphics and Applications* 40, no. 2 (2020): 91–97.

Meirelles, Isabel. *Design for Information: An Introduction to the Histories, Theories, and Best Practices behind Effective Information Visualizations.* Beverly, MA: Rockport Publishers, 2013.

Rendgen, Sandra, and Julius Wiedemann. *History of Information Graphics.* Köln, Germany: Taschen, 2019.

Rendgen, Sandra, and Julius Wiedemann. *Information Graphics.* Köln, Germany: Taschen, 2018.

Rendgen, Sandra, and Julius Wiedemann. *Understanding the World: The Atlas of Infographics.* Köln, Germany: Taschen, 2015.

Tufte, Edward R. *The Visual Display of Quantitative Information.* Cheshire, CT: Graphics Press, 2018.

Zambrano, Raul Niño, and Yuri Engelhardt. "Diagrams for the Masses: Raising Public Awareness—from Neurath to Gapminder and Google Earth." In *Diagrammatic Representation and Inference,* edited by Gem Stapleton, John Howse, and John Lee, 282–292. International Conference on Theory and Application of Diagrams. Berlin: Springer, 2008.

Thinking & Diagrams

(Neurodiversity, Cognitive Science Experimentation)

This research attempts to understand how people "think" by using diagrams. It can be philosophical and rely on epistemology and logic, or it can be experimental. The experimenters are usually from the fields of education, cognitive science, psychology, and information design.

Most of these experiments research whether users draw their own diagrams to solve problems, but some pit two diagrams or different designs of the same against each other. The educational research focuses heavily on how children, especially neurodivergent children or those with disabilities, experience diagrams.

Anderson, Michael, Bernd Meyer, and Patrick Olivier, eds. *Diagrammatic Representation and Reasoning*. London: Springer, 2002.

Blackwell, Alan F. "Diagrams about Thoughts about Thoughts about Diagrams." In *Reasoning with Diagrammatic Representations II: Papers from the AAAI Fall Symposium*, 77–84. Palo Alto, CA: Association for the Advancement of Artificial Intelligence, 1997.

Cheng, Peter C.-H., Ric K. Lowe, and Mike Scaife. "Cognitive Science Approaches to Understanding Diagrammatic Representations." In *Thinking with Diagrams*, edited by Alan F. Blackwell, 79–94. Dordrecht: Springer, 2001.

Cohen, Marlene J., and Donna L. Sloan. *Visual Supports for People with Autism: A Guide for Parents and Professionals*. Bethesda, MD: Woodbine House, 2007.

Krämer, Sybille, and Christina Ljungberg, eds. *Thinking with Diagrams: The Semiotic Basis of Human Cognition*. Semiotics, Communication and Cognition, vol. 17. Boston: Walter de Gruyter, 2016.

Frameworks & Standards

Cognitive science and information design have drafted standards and frameworks for discussing diagrams in order to evaluate them scientifically and across disciplines.

They employ the core concepts of linguistics such as morphology and syntax terms to describe types of diagrams and their parts as well as how they function.

Anderson, Michael, Bernd Meyer, and Patrick Olivier, eds. *Diagrammatic Representation and Reasoning*. London: Springer, 2002.

Blackwell, Alan, and Yuri Engelhardt. "A Meta-Taxonomy for Diagram Research." In *Diagrammatic Representation and Reasoning*, edited by Michael Anderson, Bernd Meyer, and Patrick Olivier, 47–64. London: Springer, 2002.

Börner, Katy, Andreas Bueckle, and Michael Ginda. "Data Visualization Literacy: Definitions, Conceptual Frameworks, Exercises, and Assessments." *Proceedings of the National Academy of Sciences* 116, no. 6 (2019): 1857–1864.

Richards, Clive James, ed. *Elements of Diagramming: Design Theories, Analyses and Methods*. Ashgate, 2016.

Richards, Clive. "The Fundamental Design Variables of Diagramming." In *Diagrammatic Representation and Reasoning*, edited by Michael Anderson, Bernd Meyer, and Patrick Olivier, 85–102. London: Springer, 2002.

Information Design

These resources are from an interdisciplinary perspective but tend to be heavy on cognitive science and design.

Černe Oven, Petra, and Cvetka Požar, eds. *On Information Design*. Ljubljana, Slovenia: Museum of Architecture and Design, 2016.

"Diagrammatic Representation and Inference Proceedings of the International Conference on Theory and Application of Diagrams." International Conference on Theory and Application of Diagrams | Springer. Accessed July 28, 2021. https://link.springer.com/conference/diagrams. The IIID maintains a robust public library of documents on its site.

Information Design Journal. John Benjamins Publishing Company, 1979–. https://doi.org/10.1075/idj.

"The International Conference on the Theory and Application of Diagrams." The Theory and Application of Diagrams. Accessed July 28, 2021. http://www.diagrams-conference.org.

International Institute for Information Design (IIID). Accessed July 28, 2021. https://www.iiid.net.

Nickerson, J. V. "The Meaning of Arrows: Diagrams and Other Facets in System Sciences Literature." *Proceedings of the 38th Annual Hawaii International Conference on System Sciences* 4 (2005). https://doi.org/10.1109/hicss.2005.604.

Waller, Rob. "Information Design: How the Disciplines Work Together." Paper presented at Vision Plus Conference, Götzis, Austria, August 1995. Reprinted as Simplification Centre Technical Paper no. 14, March 2011. https://www.academia.edu/3386148/Information_design_how_the_disciplines_work_together.

Indexed Lexicon

The following is an alphabetical list of all the **bold terms** throughout the book. Along with definitions of each, we have indexed the location of the lessons related to each term.

Throughout this book I use a set of five core terms that I also used in *How to Make Sense of Any Mess*. Those core terms are marked with an asterisk(*).

A/B Testing	Two diagrams are shown to members of an audience to see how each is received.	75, 82
Accessible	Able to be accessed and understood by the intended audience.	150–173, 180, 198, 200–201
Affinity	The stated contextual similarities within a group.	105–107, 119
Alignment	The relationship that variable length lines of type have to one another.	162–165, 190–191
Alternative Text/ Alternative Content	Text or other content created when a diagram isn't an accessible form of communication for members of their intended audience.	150–152, 200–201
Ambiguity	The level to which there is the potential for multiple meanings to be perceived.	13, 16, 20–21, 29, 33, 71, 73
Arrangement	How elements relate and form a whole.	43, 46–47, 50, 113–119, 122–123, 127, 147, 156, 214–216
Ascender	The strokes of lowercase letterforms above the x-height (such as in f and t).	188
Association *(or associative)*	When one thing is related to another thing.	123–124, 214–216
Assuming	To take for granted the applicable knowledge of your audience.	87
Audience	Whom you are making the diagram for. What do you know about them, and what do they know about the subject of the diagram?	35, 41, 59, 68–75, 80–81, 86–88, 95, 126, 134–135, 138–141, 150–158, 175, 201

Axis	A line serving as a spatial reference to encode meaning onto the placement of the shapes in a diagram.	125, 130, 176, 263
Baseline	The invisible line on which typographic letters sit.	196–198
Bottom to Top	When a label in a diagram is rotated so the start of the label is below the end.	191–193
Bounded Shape	A shape with a visual demarcation.	110
Bracket	An elbow-like structure that helps make various levels of hierarchy explicit.	111, 116, 123, 127–129, 131, 231
Horizontal Bracket	Brackets that place children in a row under a parent in a hierarchical relationship.	127–129, 131, 231
Vertical Bracket	Brackets that place children in a column under a parent in a hierarchical relationship.	127–129, 131, 231
Bump	A shape created at the intersection of line-crossing.	165, 166
Cap Height	The height of flat capital letters (such as M and T) that is used to determine line height or leading.	188
Card Sort	Members of an audience are provided with a set of cards and asked to organize the cards into groups based on some context around a task or environment.	75, 79, 275–276
Cartography	The study of maps and mapmaking.	147
Centering	Establishing what a diagram will focus on.	43–51, 212–216
Clarity	Freedom from doubt about what something means.	21, 28–29, 33, 73, 211, 295
Cognitive Load	Amount of mental effort that someone has to put in when learning something.	86–87, 137–139, 159–163, 166–167, 200, 201
Cognitive Science	The study of how humans think, organize, and learn.	147, 303–305, 326

330 | STUCK? Diagrams Help.

Collaborative Diagramming	Watching members of your audience make decisions together about how something might be visually represented.	74, 78
Color Coding	Use of color to "mean something."	127, 138, 166, 168, 199–201, 207
Comparative Relationship	Relationship that point out the similarities and differences between things.	130, 170, 234
Complexity	The level of interconnected information involved.	9, 13, 16–17, 20–21, 26–27, 29, 33, 71, 73
Conjoint Retention *See also* Dual Coding	The combination of verbal and non-verbal representations to facilitate increased retention of information.	33
Consideration	One of the five most common intentions of diagrams. Refers to diagrams that show something as it could be.	63
Content Driven	When decisions about what to include, what not to include, and how to frame what is included are driven by audience and intention.	174–185
Context*	The surroundings, circumstances, environments, background, and settings that determine, specify, or clarify the meaning of an event or other occurrence.	43, 48–49, 140–141, 155–156, 187, 194, 197, 199, 201, 203, 207–209
Contrast	Difference that can be perceived.	168–171, 180, 224
Decision Point	A question for the user for which the answer means a difference of path through the diagram.	102–104, 227, 307
Decode	To translate into an understandable form.	139, 199, 201
Delivering	The emotional phase of diagramming when we actually make the visual part of the diagram.	57, 80–83, 93, 133–135, 293
Density	The ratio of blank space to content in a diagram.	179–183
Descender	The strokes of lowercase letterforms below the baseline (such as in p and y).	188

Indexed Lexicon | 331

Diagram	A visual representation that helps someone.	9, 33–51, 59, 72, 143, 207–209, 219, 299, 306, 311, 316
Block Diagram	47, 215–216; *Examples 46, 27, 46, 113, 114, 255*; recipe for, 220–221	
Concept Diagram	46, 47, 215–216, 300; *Examples 110, 113, 118, 124, 126, 160–161, 166, 250*; recipe for, 222–223	
Continuum	48, 49, 215–216; *Examples 168*; recipe for, 224–225	
Flow Diagram	44, 45, 125, 151, 215–216, 309–310, 314; *Examples 12–13, 17, 27, 58, 72, 102, 113, 117, 125, 131, 151, 154, 157, 162*; recipe for, 226–227	
Gantt	44, 45, 215–216, 314; *Examples 218*; recipe for, 228–229	
Hierarchy Diagram	46, 47, 215–216, 250–252; *Examples 22, 107, 113, 116, 127–129, 131, 259*; recipe for, 230–231	
Journey Diagram	44, 45, 215–216, 264; *Examples 57, 66, 89, 96, 120, 263*; recipe for, 232–233	
Quadrant Diagram	48, 49, 130, 215–216, 275; *Examples 94, 130, 275*; recipe for, 234–235	
Schematic Diagram	215–216; *Examples 24, 39, 125, 152, 164, 175, 183, 188, 190–193, 195–196, 202, 270*; recipe for, 236–237	
Sign Diagram	48, 49, 215–216; recipe for, 238–239	
Swim Lane Diagram	44, 45, 215–216; *Examples 197*; recipe for, 240–241	
Venn Diagram	5, 48, 49, 215–216; *Examples 5*; recipe for, 242–243	

Diagramming Tools	Anything that allows free movement to make lines, shapes, and words.	38, 53, 72, 165–167, 228, 302
Diagrammatic Insecurity	The feeling that a diagram is not meant for you as the audience.	140
Diamond	The shape used to represent decision points and variable paths in a diagram.	102–104, 227, 307
Draw & Share	A group individually draws something (a concept, a problem space, a process, etc.) based on a prompt and then shares what they drew.	74, 77
Dual Coding *See also* Conjoint Retention	Making or referencing a visual aid while presenting a concept better supports remembering and deeply grasping information.	33
Edge Direction	The directional rotation of a line label's baseline in relation to the direction of the line being labeled.	196–198
Education	The study of how people learn.	147, 299, 301, 303
Emotional Process	The feelings experienced when diagramming.	56–59, 66–67, 89–90, 96–97
Encode	Use of signals to "mean something."	39, 138–139, 186, 199–201
Equivalent	The multiple labels such as abbreviations, colloquialisms, acronyms, or nicknames for a single object.	105–107
Explanatory Content	Any additional content added to a diagram to provide context or insight.	189
Exploring	The emotional phase of diagramming when we research an audience and set an intention.	56–59, 76–77, 133–134, 216, 292
Forgetting	To omit or neglect without intention.	87
Graphic Design	The art and style of visual communication.	147, 163, 186–198
Grid	A system of guides and rules used to bring order to spatial relationships.	163–165
Headline	The label you give to the diagram as a whole.	175–176, 189

Indexed Lexicon | 333

Hierarchical Relationship	When one thing is a parent to other things.	46–47, 111, 123, 127–129, 214–216, 230–231
Icon	A simplified graphic representation.	202–203, 311
Identification	One of the five most common intentions of diagrams. Refers to diagrams that break down complexity.	63
Image (*or imagery*)	A photographic or illustrative representation.	202–203
Implied Shape	A labeled shape without a visual bounding.	110
Information Architecture	The act of deciding which order the pieces of a whole should be arranged in order to communicate the meaning that is intended to users.	85, 145, 147, 302, 310
Information Design	The study of how to present data effectively to reach an intention.	147, 302–303, 306, 328
Informative Change (*principle of*)	A principle stating when something changes, people will want to interpret the new information introduced.	171
Instance	When things of the same type exist under a higher-level label.	105–107
Instruction	One of the five most common intentions of diagrams. Refers to diagrams that teach a skill or task.	63
Intention	The service you wish the diagram to deliver to the audience. What is the action or change you hope for in making the diagram?	41, 59, 60–67, 81, 91, 138, 141, 150–151, 175, 177
Interaction Mode	The relationship our audience has with our diagrammatic efforts.	93
In-visual Elements	The decisions behind the diagram.	39–41, 58
Key	Information provided within a diagram to define what the visual decisions made in the diagram mean.	40, 59, 136–141, 198
Key Content	The content you put in the key.	139–141, 176, 189, 198
Key Headline	The label you give to the key.	189
Kindness	Generosity and consideration for yourself and others.	30–33, 73, 151, 194, 278, 294–295

Label	A visual and verbal marker you provide for viewers to interpret the diagram.	40, 59, 132–135, 139, 175, 182, 189, 190–198, 201
Label Length	How long a label is allowed to run.	179, 182, 195
Label Orientation (or rotation)	The direction of rotation of a label.	192–198
Leading	Vertical space between baselines of text.	179, 183
Legibility	The measure of how distinguishable individual characters and words are to an audience.	169–170, 179, 181–3, 187–198
Line	An element representing the connection between objects.	40, 50, 59, 99, 112, 122–131, 139, 165–167, 196
Line Label	A label to describe the connections between objects.	124, 179, 189, 191, 192–198
Line Length	How long a line of text can run without breaking.	179, 181–183, 194–195
Line-Crossing (or line-jumping)	When two lines in a diagram pass through one another's trajectory.	165–167
Linguistic Insecurity*	The feeling of anxiety, self-consciousness, or lack of confidence surrounding the use of language in a specific context.	140
Linguistics	The study of language and its structure.	140–141, 147, 299, 301
Manipulation	Changing content to control what can be known by others.	141, 177–178
Marginalia	Notes or commentary included in the diagram.	176, 189, 198
Mechanical Process	The steps we take when diagramming.	56–59, 67
Modeling	The emotional phase of diagramming when we decide on the scope and scale of the diagram.	57, 78–79, 133–134, 293
Neat-and-Tidiness	The level to which needless clutter, inconsistency, and distraction have been removed from the diagram.	159–167
Non-directional Line	A line with a reading order that is not explicit.	118, 123–124

Observational Usability Testing	Members of an audience look at a diagram and describe what they see and how they would use (or not use) it.	75, 80–81, 180
One-Way Line	A line with a reading order that is explicit.	117, 123, 125, 131
Padding	The space that is left between shapes and between the edges of shapes and their labels.	190
People	Whoever is involved in the thing you are diagramming.	26, 30–33, 70–73, 99–101, 106, 134
Places	The contexts, both physical and digital, in the thing you are diagramming.	23, 25, 26, 99–101, 106, 134
Planning	One of the five most common intentions of diagrams. Refers to diagrams that illustrate future actions or goals.	63
Pointer *(or arrow)*	A line associating a label and a shape being labeled.	125
Precision	The level of exactness or specificity at which data is presented.	177–178, 314
Quadrant	The use of lines and shapes to create labeled areas to compare things.	123, 130, 214–216, 234, 274–275
Qualitative Interviewing	One-on-ones with a specific and unique member of an intended audience to ask about the subject you are diagramming.	74, 76
Readability	The measure of how easy or difficult it is to read a diagram based on the design decisions of the maker.	181–183, 186–198
Reading Order	The direction the diagram is intended to be consumed in.	111, 155–158, 191, 193
Reciprocal Relationship	When two or more things give to one another or work together in some form.	123, 126, 131, 222, 238
Reflection	One of the five most common intentions of diagrams. Refers to diagrams that point to a problem.	63
Scale	How big or small and active or passive the space is in which to get the diagram to its audience.	40, 46–47, 59, 92–95, 106, 107, 121, 187, 234
Scope	The boundaries of the content you are representing. What did you decide not to show the audience?	41, 59, 84–91, 99, 142, 180

Semiotics	The study of signs and symbols	147
Sequence	When one thing leads to another thing.	123, 125, 226, 240
Shape	Elements representing objects.	40, 50, 59, 98–121, 168, 190, 307–309
Shape Label	A label used to describe the object.	102–103, 189-191
Similarity *(Gestalt principle of)*	A theory stating when things appear alike, people are more likely to group them together, and when things don't look alike, they can assume the difference means something.	171
Space *See also* Line-crossing	A break in a line allowing for the intersection created when line-crossing.	165
Stability	The level to which information is strong enough to rely on.	21–23, 33, 73, 210, 295
Stack	When two or more shapes overlap in meaningful ways.	102–107, 114–115, 119, 310–311
Collapsed Stack	The visual layering of shapes so that a single label can represent multiple things.	103, 105–107, 114–115, 119, 230, 310
Spread Stack	The visual layering of shapes so that multiple terms are equivalent to one another but differ in label.	103, 105–107, 114–115, 119, 230, 310
Stacked *(or marquis)*	A word or phrase is set with one letter per line.	192–193
Stakeholder* *See also* Audience	Someone with a viable and legitimate interest in the work that you're doing.	70–72
Starting Place	The point on the diagram where you suggest the audience begin.	153–153
Things	The objective or subjective entities that make up the larger entity that you are diagramming.	26, 99–103, 105–109, 134

Indexed Lexicon | 337

Time	The indefinite continued progress of existence and events in the past, present, and future regarded as a whole.	43–45, 67, 141, 155, 176, 208, 214–216
Timescale*	The period of time represented by a diagram.	175–176
Tone	Rhetorical choices of language and/or imagery to enhance an intention.	174–176, 189
Top to Bottom	When a label in a diagram is rotated so the start of the label is above the end.	192–193
Transparency	The level to which information is available.	21, 25, 33, 73, 295
Two-Way Line	Lines with a reading order that supports reading in either direction.	117, 123, 126, 131
Type Size	The scaling of type in a diagram.	179, 181, 198
Type Style	The typeface in a diagram.	169–170, 181, 187–189, 198
Typeface	A font, or a family of fonts, that you choose to use for a diagram.	10, 169, 181, 183, 187–189
Typographic Hierarchy	The visual order that we instill through our typographic choices.	189
Typography	The art and discipline of arranging type on a surface.	110, 147, 182, 187–198
Uncertainty	Lack of confidence in the information provided.	13, 16, 20–21, 25, 33, 71, 73, 252,
Understanding	Insight into and/or comphrehension of information.	21, 26–27, 33, 73, 295
User* *See also* Audience	A person who encounters a message.	10, 70–72, 76–84, 150–152, 166, 169, 194
Visual Elements	What the audience sees as the diagram.	39–41, 58, 137–138
Visual Explanation	The use of graphic props to foster understanding.	147, 150
Visual representation	A concrete or abstract portrayal.	9, 34–35, 39, 50, 55, 90, 143, 174, 311–313
Visually Supported	When visuals are key to the diagram, not an embellishment.	186–205

Volatility	The level to which information is predictable and/or expected.	13, 16, 20–21, 23, 33, 71, 73
VUCA	An acronym standing for *Volatility*, *Uncertainty*, *Complexity*, and *Ambiguity*. This set of situational concerns is based on the leadership theories of Warren Bennis and Burt Nanus as developed in the 1980s by the US Army War College.	20–21, 30–33, 73
x-height	The height of the lowercase x.	188

Index of Exercises, Quizzes & Checklists

Exercise 1: Let's Break Some Eggs	53
Exercise 2: Five Future Intentions	64
Exercise 3: Messy Middle Mad Lib	91
Exercise 4: People, Places & Things	100
Pop Quiz: Stacked Shapes	115
Pop Quiz: Find Four Patterns	131
Checklist: Accessible Diagrams	173
Checklist: Content-Driven Diagrams	185
Checklist: Visually Supported Diagrams	205
Checklist: How to Diagram with Other People	292

Bibliography

ANSI/NISO Z39.19-2005 (R2010). "Guidelines for the Construction, Format, and Management of Monolingual Controlled Vocabularies." National Information Standards Organization, May 13, 2010. http://www.niso.org/publications/ansiniso-z3919-2005-r2010.

Baghai, Mehrdad, Stephen C. Coley, and David White. *The Alchemy of Growth: Kickstarting and Sustaining Growth in Your Company.* London: Texere, 2000.

Blackwell, Alan F. "Diagrams about Thoughts about Thoughts about Diagrams." In *Reasoning with Diagrammatic Representations II: Papers from the AAAI Fall Symposium,* 77–84. Palo Alto, CA: Association for the Advancement of Artificial Intelligence, 1997.

Börner, Katy, Andreas Bueckle, and Michael Ginda. "Data Visualization Literacy: Definitions, Conceptual Frameworks, Exercises, and Assessments." *Proceedings of the National Academy of Sciences* 116, no. 6 (2019): 1857–1864.

Bringhurst, Robert. *The Elements of Typographic Style.* 2nd ed. Vancouver, BC: Hartley & Marks, 1997.

Cairo, Alberto. "If Anything on This Graphic Causes Confusion, Discard the Entire Product." *IEEE Computer Graphics and Applications* 40, no. 2 (2020): 91–97.

Castrillon, Ana. "How BT, a 174-Year-Old Company Continues to Push the Telecommunication Industry Forward." *Figma* (blog), July 7, 2020. https://www.figma.com/blog/bt-case-study/.

Chen, Peter Pin-Shan. "The Entity-Relationship Model—toward a Unified View of Data." *ACM Transactions on Database Systems* 1, no. 1 (March 1976): 9–36. https://doi.org/10.1145/320434.320440.

Cheng, Peter C.-H., Ric K. Lowe, and Mike Scaife. "Cognitive Science Approaches to Understanding Diagrammatic Representations." In *Thinking with Diagrams,* edited by Alan F. Blackwell, 83–84. Dordrecht: Springer, 2001.

Covert, Abby. "Nike Digital Sales Process." Case Studies, September 14, 2020. https://abbycovert.com/ia-case-studies/nike/.

Davidenko, Nicolas, and Alexander Ambard. "Reading Sideways: Effects of Egocentric and Environmental Orientation in a Lexical Decision Task." *Vision Research* 153 (2018): 7–12.

Doyle, Glennon. *Untamed.* New York: Dial Press, 2020.

Finkel, Robert J. "History of the Arrow." American Printing History Association, April 1, 2015. https://printinghistory.org/arrow/.

Friendly, Michael. "Milestones in the History of Data Visualization: A Case Study in Statistical Historiography." In *Classification—the Ubiquitous Challenge*, edited by Claus Weihs and Wolfgang Paul, 34–52. Studies in Classification, Data Analysis, and Knowledge Organization. New York: Springer, 2004. https://doi.org/10.1007/3-540-28084-7_.

Friendly, Michael, and Daniel J. Denis. "Milestones in the History of Thematic Cartography, Statistical Graphics, and Data Visualization." 2001. https://www.datavis.ca/milestones/.

Garrett, Jesse James. "A Visual Vocabulary for Describing Information Architecture and Interaction Design." jjg.net, version 1.1b. Last modified March 6, 2002. http://www.jjg.net/ia/visvocab.

Gibbons, Sarah. "Service Blueprints: Definition." Nielsen Norman Group, August 27, 2017. https://www.nngroup.com/articles/service-blueprints-definition.

Gilbreth, Frank B., and Lillian Moller Gilbreth. "Process Charts." In *American Society of Mechanical Engineers*. New York: American Society of Mechanical Engineers, 1921.

Gilbreth, Frank B., Jr., and Ernestine Gilbreth Carey. *Cheaper by the Dozen.* New York: Thomas Y. Crowell, 1948.

Guidebook. "Icons: Components." https://guidebookgallery.org/icons/components.

Hertzfeld, Andy. *Revolution in the Valley: The Insanely Great Story of How the Mac Was Made.* Sebastopol, CA: O'Reilly Media, 2011.

Huey, Edmund B. "Preliminary Experiments in the Physiology and Psychology of Reading." *American Journal of Psychology* 9, no. 4 (July 1898): 575–586. https://doi.org/10.2307/1412192.

Iliinsky, Noah P. N. "Generation of Complex Diagrams: How to Make Lasagna Instead of Spaghetti." Master's thesis, University of Washington, 2006. https://digital.lib.washington.edu/researchworks/bitstream/handle/1773/3100/iliinsky_complex_diagrams.pdf;sequence=1.

International Organization for Standardization. "ISO 15519-1:2010 (en) Specification for Diagrams for Process Industry—Part 1: General Rules." ISO Online Browsing Platform (OBP). Accessed August 10, 2021. https://www.iso.org/obp/ui/#iso:std:iso:15519:-1:ed-1:v1:en.

Keeley, Larry, Ryan Pikkel, Brian Quinn, and Helen Walters. *Ten Types of Innovation: The Discipline of Building Breakthroughs.* Hoboken, NJ: Wiley & Sons, 2013.

Kelley, Tom. "Build Your Creative Confidence: Customer Journey Map." *IDEO* (blog), March 21, 2019. https://www.ideo.com/blog/build-your-creative-confidence-customer-journey-map.

Kennedy, Chinaro, Ellen Yard, Timothy Dignam, Sharunda Buchanan, Suzanne Condon, Mary Jean Brown, Jaime Raymond et al. "Blood Lead Levels among Children Aged <6 Years—Flint, Michigan, 2013–2016." *Morbidity and Mortality Weekly Report* 65, no. 25 (2016). https://www.cdc.gov/mmwr/volumes/65/wr/pdfs/mm6525e1.pdf.

Kosslyn, Stephen M. *Elements of Graph Design.* New York: Freeman, 1994.

Labov, William. *The Social Stratification of English in New York City.* Washington, DC: Center for Applied Linguistics, 1966.

Lima, Manuel. *The Book of Trees: Visualizing Branches of Knowledge.* New York: Princeton Architectural Press, 2014.

Lozeau, Lisa, and Lucas de Boer. "The Fundamentals of Customer Journey Mapping, and Why Businesses Need It Now." Signavio. Last modified December 23, 2021. https://www.signavio.com/post/customer-journey-mapping/#h-the-history-of-journey-mapping.

McInnes, Kate. "Know Your Icons, Part 1: A Brief History of Computer Icons." Envato Tuts+, July 18, 2010. https://design.tutsplus.com/articles/know-your-icons-part-1-a-brief-history-of-computer-icons--psd-9805.

Miller, George A. "The Magical Number Seven, Plus or Minus Two: Some Limits on Our Capacity for Processing Information." *Psychological Review* 63, no. 2 (1956): 81–97. https://doi.org/10.1037/h0043158.

Moore, Jona, Cristina Crespo, Albert Dang, and Emanuele Di Saverio. "How to Deliver Impactful Products to Market." frog, 2021. https://www.frogdesign.com/designmind/how-to-deliver-impactful-products-to-market.

Moore, Patrick, and Chad Fitz. "Gestalt Theory and Instructional Design." *Journal of Technical Writing and Communication* 23, no. 2 (1993): 137–157.

National Health Service. "Colour Vision Deficiency (Colour Blindness)." Accessed August 10, 2021. https://www.nhs.uk/conditions/colour-vision-deficiency.

Oven, P. C. "Introduction: Design as a Response to People's Needs (and Not People's Needs as a Response to Design Results)." In *On Information Design*, edited by P. C. Oven and C. Požar. Ljubljana, Slovenia: Museum of Architecture and Design, 2016.

Paivio, Allan. *Imagery and Verbal Processes*. New York: Holt, Rinehart and Winston, 1971.

Petroski, Henry. *The Book on the Bookshelf*. New York: Knopf, 1999.

Saffer, Dan. *Designing for Interaction: Creating Innovative Applications and Devices*. Berkeley, CA: New Riders, 2010.

Schmidt, Mario. "The Sankey Diagram in Energy and Material Flow Management: Part II: Methodology and Current Applications." *Journal of Industrial Ecology* 12, no. 2 (2008): 173–185.

Shostack, G. Lynn. "Designing Services That Deliver." *Harvard Business Review*, January 1984. https://hbr.org/1984/01/designing-services-that-deliver.

Spencer, Donna. *Card Sorting: Designing Usable Categories*. Brooklyn, NY: Rosenfeld Media, 2009.

Stigler, Stephen M. "Stigler's Law of Eponymy." *Transactions of the New York Academy of Sciences*, series II, 39, no. 1 (1980): 147–157. https://doi.org/10.1111/j.2164-0947.1980.tb02775.x.

Stinson, Liz. "The First Org Chart Ever Made Is a Masterpiece of Data Design." *Wired*, March 18, 2014. https://www.wired.com/2014/03/stunningly-complex-organization-chart-19th-century.

Sweller, John. "Cognitive Load during Problem Solving: Effects on Learning." *Cognitive Science* 12, no. 2 (April 1988): 257–285. https://doi.org/10.1207/s15516709cog1202_4.

Tversky, Barbara. "Some Ways That Graphics Communicate." In *Working with Words and Images: New Steps in an Old Dance*, edited by Nancy Allen. Westport, CT: Ablex, 2002.

Tversky, Barbara. "Spatial Schemas in Depictions." In *Spatial Schemas and Abstract Thought*, edited by Merideth Gattis. Cambridge, MA: MIT Press, 2001.

Tversky, Barbara. "Visualizing Thought." In *Handbook of Human Centric Visualization*, edited by Weidong Huang. New York: Springer, 2014. https://doi.org/10.1007/978-1-4614-7485-2_1.

Tversky, Barbara, Jeff Zacks, Paul Lee, and Julie Heiser. "Lines, Blobs, Crosses and Arrows: Diagrammatic Communication with Schematic Figures." In *Theory and Application of Diagrams*, edited by Michael Anderson, Peter Cheng, and Volker Haarslev, 221–230. Berlin: Springer, 2000. https://doi.org/:10.1007/3-540-44590-0_21.

TwD98. "Thinking with Diagrams '98." https://web.archive.org/web/19991008092811/http://www.aber.ac.uk:80/~plo/TwD98/.

United States Bureau of the Budget. "Process Charting: Its Use in Procedural Analysis." Washington, DC: US Government Printing Office, 1945.

Venn, John. "On the Diagrammatic and Mechanical Representation of Propositions and Reasonings." *London, Edinburgh, and Dublin Philosophical Magazine and Journal of Science* 10, no. 59 (July 1880): 1–18.

Verou, Lea. "Contrast Ratio." https://contrast-ratio.com.

Wainer, Howard, and Michael Friendly. "Visual Revelations: Ancient Visualizations." *CHANCE* 31, no. 2 (2018): 62–64. https://doi.org/10.1080/09332480.2018.1467645.

W3C. "Understanding Success Criterion 1.4.3: Contrast (Minimum)." www.w3.org/WAI/WCAG21/Understanding/contrast-minimum.html.

Wurman, Richard Saul. *Information Anxiety*. New York: Doubleday, 1989.

Zambrano, Raul Niño, and Yuri Engelhardt. "Diagrams for the Masses: Raising Public Awareness—from Neurath to Gapminder and Google Earth." In *Diagrammatic Representation and Inference*, edited by Gem Stapleton, John Howse, and John Lee. Berlin: Springer, 2008.

Recommended Reading

In order to do the subject of diagramming justice, I had to come at it from a whole lot of angles. To prepare me for this journey, I have spent my career picking up pieces along the way while not quite knowing the quilt it would be woven into later.

The following are the books that changed me as a diagrammer. I highly recommend each of them as you go through your diagrammatic lifetime.

Collaboration and Understanding People

- *Interviewing Users* by Steve Portigal
- *Practical Empathy* by Indi Young
- *Louder than Words* by Benjamin K. Bergen
- *Atlas of the Heart* by Dr. Brené Brown

Visual Literacy & Communication

- *Pencil Me In* by Christina Wodtke
- *The Back of the Napkin* by Dan Roam
- *A Primer of Visual Literacy* by Donis A. Dondis
- *Thoughts on Design* by Paul Rand
- *Judge This* by Chip Kidd
- *Picture This: How Pictures Work* by Molly Bang

Typography

- *Stop Stealing Sheep & Find Out How Type Works* by Erik Spiekermann
- *The Elements of Typographic Style* by Robert Bringhurst
- *Thinking with Type* by Ellen Lupton

(Information) Design & Architecture

- *Designing Information* by Joel Katz
- *Designing Data Visualizations* and *Beautiful Visualization* by Noah Iliinsky and Julie Steele
- *Figure It Out* by Stephen P. Anderson and Karl Fast
- *Knowledge Is Beautiful* by David McCandless
- *Visual Explanations* by Edward Tufte
- *Envisioning Information* by Edward Tufte
- *The Visual Display of Quantitative Information* by Edward Tufte
- *You Are Here: Personal Geographies and Other Maps of the Imagination* by Katharine Harmon
- *Having Words* by Denise Scott Brown
- https://datavis.ca/milestones/: an interactive diagram of diagrammatic history milestones

Color Theory & Meaning

- *Interaction of Color* by Josef Albers
- *The Secret Lives of Color* by Kassia St. Clair
- www.colormatters.com: an easy to digest collection of lessons and resources for beginners of color theory
- www.colorsystem.com: a collection of color theories from antiquity to modern times

Diagram Accessibility

- For guidance on making specific types of diagrams accessible, visit diagramcenter.org.
- For example-based training on when to describe images, visit https://poet.diagramcenter.org/when.html.
- For free and easy tools for checking contrast ratios, visit https://color.adobe.com/create/color-contrast-analyzer.
- For guidance on digital diagram accessibility in accordance with web standards, visit https://www.w3.org/WAI/tutorials/images/complex/.

About the Authors

Abby Covert is an information architect and writer whose first book, *How to Make Sense of Any Mess*, demystified the practice of information architecture and is regarded a must-read for those working in the design and technology industry.

Abby wrote *STUCK? Diagrams Help.* after more than a decade teaching information architecture at business conferences and design schools and noticing that the concept of *diagramming* opened eyes, minds, and hearts no matter the audience or the venue. She hopes that it makes sense.

Abby wrote this book from a tiny studio in the jungle on the Space Coast of Florida where she lives with her husband and son.

Jenny Benevento is a taxonomist, librarian, researcher, and speaker with 20 years of experience creating structured, metadata-based user experiences.

Her clients include Etsy, Sears/Kmart, and the Associated Press. Jenny's work has been reported on in the *Wall Street Journal*, *New York Times*, and *Mad Money*, but most importantly, it's celebrated by people everywhere who want to know whether a dress has pockets or not. She is based mostly on the internet, but physically in Chicago.

Acknowledgments

The number of people who supported me and this book as it was being written is truly staggering. This first list of people helped me to still be a person while I wrote this book. They are my happy place.

> **James Sanford**, who loves me through the hardest parts and keeps showing up to help me to make a life we could never have dreamed of for our family.
>
> **Jamie Sanford**, who reminds me to make time to play.
>
> **Tracey & Jim Sanford**, who put so much of their energy into making sure our family's life is so well loved.
>
> **Andrew Covert**, who taught me "No." is a full sentence.
>
> **Kathy Gator**, who shows me what brave means.
>
> **Jenny Benevento**, who not only stands as my longest running remote-first friendship but also helped me to wrangle this book's facts and wrote a beautiful literature review to help you see how much there is there when it comes to diagrams.
>
> **Dan Klyn**, who reads everything I write and always makes it better. Our friendship has been a core pillar of my life, and I am so thankful for him.
>
> **Carl Collins**, who always shows up for his people. I am lucky to be one of them.
>
> **Kaarin Hoff**, because without her phone calls I would be much, much less ok.

Clair Rock, who helped me make sense of my mess when I needed someone to remind me who I am.

Kathryn Fink, who gave me the tools to do the work and the space and structure to feel my way through this big leap.

Bibiana Nunes, who always asks the best questions and then listens for the real answers.

Allan Chochinov, whose thoughtful feedback got me through some steep hills this time around, as was true with my first book.

Team & Coaches at OTF North Melbourne, who remind me that I am strong AF.

The Boss Ladies, who model for me what it means to live in and by one's own values—even when things *fucking* suck.

Horse Creek Crew, who give me hope for the power of a community. Thank you for being such a lovely part of Jamie's childhood.

The IA Community, where I found a home for the love for the work that I do and a bunch of kind folks who feel the same way.

Contributors & Peer Reviewers: This next list is people who directly contributed diagrammatic expertise and/or stories of diagrammatic realness to the content of this book. If this book feels like people made it, it's because of this group.

Elizabeth Edwards, Holly Schroeder, Noah Iliinsky, Jorge Arango, Debbie Levitt, Elizabeth Hinde, Erin Malone, John Gurley, Julian Gautier, Matt Arnold, Mary Miller, Scott Berkun, Stephen P. Anderson, Rik Williams, Tori Orr, Trent Lutmer

Test Readers & Recipe Testers: You, dear reader, were represented along the way by these kind sensemakers who lent their time and energy to review the content of this book from the reader's perspective as it was developed. This book is 1,000 times better because of their questions and feedback.

Adam Groves, Amanda Costello, Amy Silvers, Andrew Maier, Anna Kruse, Brian Malone, Chris Barnes, Claire Blaustein, David Nicholson, Donna Lay, Dulce Carrillo, Elizabeth Gusnoski, Eloise Marszalek, Fiona Coll, Florence McCambridge, Helena Göransson, Henrik de Gyor, Ian Smile, Jack Holmes, Jacob A. Ratliff, Jacqueline Fouche, James Erwin, Jay Liu, Jessica Beringer, Jessica Lovegood, Jill Armitage, Joe Sokohl, Joey Pearlman, John Jordan, Kati Hoeschen, Kurt Groetsch, Kurt Yalcin, Laura Nash, Lauren Ridenour, Lucas Zambelli, Lynnsey Schneider, Mark Lindner, Mary Beth Baker, Matthew Smith, Pam Drouin, Richard Urban, Sahar Naderi, Sandra Lloyd, Sandra Schweizer, Sarah Lowe, Stéphanie Walter, Stephen Low, Tina Bouallegue, Whitney Lacey, Zuzana Zilkova

Team Citrix: *Michelle Chin, Paul Wagner, Jason McAdoo, Pavithra Olety, Heather Ryan, Mary Fran Thompson, Gary Pilapil, Ian Patrick, Veronica Fuentes, Andres Holguin, Jack McLeod, Devin Soper, Eric Blumberg, Luis Salinas*

Team Etnograph: *Eleonora Corti, Luca De Bortoli, Chiara Grimandi, Paolo Montevecchi*

Special thanks to my past students at Parsons School of Design, Maryland Institute College of Art, the School of Visual Arts, and conferences all over the world who inspired this project. Thank you for asking *such* good questions.

Lastly, I want to acknowledge and honor the Seminole, Mascogo, Kiikaapoi, Peoria, Kaskaskia, Bodwéwadmi, Myaamia, Hoocąk, Očhéthi Šakówin, and Ais peoples on whose stolen land this book was written. A donation has been made to the First Nations Development Institute to mark this book's publication.

Please consider making a donation yourself at https://www.firstnations.org/ and using https://native-land.ca/ to find out whose land you currently reside and/or work on.